Mediaeval Sources in Translation 45

Peter Lombard, The *Sentences*

Book 3: On the Incarnation of the Word

TRANSLATED BY GIULIO SILANO

Peter Lombard's major work, the four books of the *Sentences*, was written in the mid-twelfth century and, as early as the 1160s, the text was glossed and commented on in the schools. There is hardly a theologian of note throughout the rest of the Middle Ages who did not write a commentary on the *Sentences*. Yet in spite of its importance in Western intellectual history and its capacity to excite many generations of students and teachers, the *Sentences* has received little attention in more recent times. Indeed, it has been called "one of the least read of the world's great books."

This volume makes available for the first time in English a full translation of Book 3 of the *Sentences*, which deals with the mystery of the Word made flesh: Christ's incarnation, passion, and death, the consequent restoration of humankind, and the virtues to be practised in imitation of Christ.

Book 3 is divided into forty Distinctions. The first twenty-two are devoted to Christ's incarnation and his redemptive work, with the first fourteen of these focussing on Christ as God and man and the final seven turning to Christ's suffering and its redemptive role. With the question of whether Christ had the virtues of faith, hope, and charity, a transition is made, in Distinction 23, from Christology to a consideration of the virtues; these belong in this Book principally because the Christian is called to live them in imitation of Christ, who embodies all of them perfectly. And so the theological virtues are discussed in Distinctions 23-32 and the cardinal ones in Distinction 33; the gifts of the Holy Spirit, which Peter also considers as virtues, are presented in Distinctions 34 and 35. Distinction 36 concludes the treatment of the virtues with the assertion that they are interconnected by charity. The last four Distinctions outline the Decalogue in the context of the two commandments given by Christ regarding the love of God and neighbour; the Book closes by asserting the superiority of the Gospel over the Law of the Old Testament.

The volume contains an introduction to Book 3, a list of the major chapter headings, and a bibliography.

Saint Michael's College
Mediaeval Translations

Mediaeval Sources in Translation 45

PETER LOMBARD

THE *SENTENCES*

BOOK 3: On the Incarnation of the Word

Translated by

GIULIO SILANO

PONTIFICAL INSTITUTE OF MEDIAEVAL STUDIES

This book has been published with the help of a grant
from the Canadian Federation for the Humanities and Social Sciences,
through the Aid to Scholarly Publications Programme,
using funds provided by the Social Sciences and
Humanities Research Council of Canada.

Library and Archives Canada Cataloguing in Publication

Peter Lombard, Bishop of Paris, ca. 1100-1160
The Sentences / Peter Lombard ; translated by Giulio Silano.

(Mediaeval sources in translation, ISSN 0316-0874 ; 42-43, 45)
(Saint Michael's College mediaeval translations)
Translation of: Sententiae in IV libris distinctae.
Includes bibliographical references and index.
Bk. 1. The mystery of the Trinity – bk. 2. On creation – bk. 3. On the incarnation of the word.
ISBN 978-0-88844-292-5 (bk. 1).– ISBN 978-0-88844-293-2 (bk. 2).
–ISBN 978-0-88844-295-6 (bk. 3)

1. God–Early works to 1800. 2. God–Attributes–Early works to 1800. 3. Trinity–Early works to 1800. 4. Creation–Early works to 1800. 5. Jesus Christ–History of doctrines–Middle Ages, 600-1500. 6. Catholic Church–Doctrines–Early works to 1800. 7. Theology–Early works to 1800. I. Silano, Giulio, 1955– II. Pontifical Institute of Mediaeval Studies III. Title. IV. Series. V. Series.

B765.P33S46 2007 231 C2006-907006-7

Second printing 2010

Pontifical Institute of Mediaeval Studies
59 Queen's Park Crescent East
Toronto, Ontario, Canada M5S 2C4

PRINTED IN CANADA

Contents

Introduction *vii*

Chapter Headings *xli*

Peter Lombard, The *Sentences*

Book 3: On the Incarnation of the Word

Distinction I	*3*	Distinction XXI	*88*
Distinction II	*6*	Distinction XXII	*93*
Distinction III	*9*	Distinction XXIII	*97*
Distinction IV	*14*	Distinction XXIV	*103*
Distinction V	*17*	Distinction XXV	*106*
Distinction VI	*24*	Distinction XXVI	*111*
Distinction VII	*31*	Distinction XXVII	*113*
Distinction VIII	*37*	Distinction XXVIII	*118*
Distinction IX	*39*	Distinction XXIX	*121*
Distinction X	*41*	Distinction XXX	*126*
Distinction XI	*44*	Distinction XXXI	*128*
Distinction XII	*47*	Distinction XXXII	*132*
Distinction XIII	*50*	Distinction XXXIII	*135*
Distinction XIV	*54*	Distinction XXXIV	*136*
Distinction XV	*57*	Distinction XXXV	*144*
Distinction XVI	*66*	Distinction XXXVI	*147*
Distinction XVII	*67*	Distinction XXXVII	*151*
Distinction XVIII	*72*	Distinction XXXVIII	*157*
Distinction XIX	*78*	Distinction XXXIX	*161*
Distinction XX	*84*	Distinction XL	*168*

Bibliography
English translations of works cited in Book 3 *171*

Index of Scriptural and Patristic Authorities *183*

To Francesca

Oh quanto è corto il dire e come fioco
al mio concetto! e questo, a quel ch'i' vidi,
è tanto, che non basta a dicer "poco."
O luce etterna che sola in te sidi,
sola t'intendi, e da te intelletta
e intendente te ami e arridi!
Quella circulazion che sì concetta
pareva in te come lume reflesso,
da li occhi miei alquanto circunspetta,
dentro da sé, del suo colore stesso,
mi parve pinta de la nostra effige:
per che'l mio viso in lei tutto era messo.

(*Paradiso*, 33.121-132)

Introduction

As was discussed in the Introduction to our translation of Book 1 of the work,[1] it is our view that the *Sentences* of Peter Lombard will be more readily intelligible if it is not approached as if its author had known that it was going to become the standard work for the training of theologians for centuries to come. The enormous success, even the monopoly, which the *Sentences* came to enjoy in the professional training of theologians in medieval and early modern universities may lead one to anticipate the date at which theology became a profession and sets up unhelpful comparisons between the *Sentences* and the works of thirteenth-century theologians.

The analogy we have found more attractive to describe Peter's work is the one between it and casebooks meant for the training of experts whose role in the Church and in Christian society was not restricted to the teaching of theology. As a consequence, it seems more useful to consider that, in the *Sentences*, Peter Lombard was introducing his students to a sort of disciplined reflection on the Christian tradition which could lead to, but was not identical with, the later scientific training of theologians. The modern reader who keeps this in mind will avoid sterile repetitions of old doubts about the work's systematic nature or lack thereof; more importantly, such a reader will approach the *Sentences* with a better sense of the fluidity and open-endedness of the academic enterprise in the mid-twelfth century. The distinguishing features of Peter's work may then emerge with greater clarity and joy.

With characteristic and fitting humility, in the first Book of the *Sentences*, Peter Lombard had attempted, as he himself says, to stammer out something of the mysteries of the divine nature. In the second Book, he

[1]That Introduction also contains a sketch of Peter's life and works and a discussion of the structure and purposes of the *Sentences* as a whole, as well as a brief overview of the contents of Book 1. The reader seeking a fuller introduction to Peter Lombard in English will wish to consult the magisterial study by Marcia L. Colish, *Peter Lombard*, 2 vol. (Leiden, New York, Cologne: E.J. Brill 1994). If the occasional disagreement with a few readings of Peter by Colish is noted below, that is no denial of the great value of her study, particularly in setting Peter's teachings in the context of the school debates of his time. A shorter and engaging introduction to Peter's life and thought, which presumes and complements Colish's more substantial work, is Philipp W. Rosemann, *Peter Lombard* (Oxford and New York: Oxford University Press, 2004).

had turned with greater confidence to treat the creation of the world and the fall of humankind.[2] Now, in Book 3, he has as his subject the mystery of the Word made flesh: Christ's incarnation, passion, and death, the consequent restoration of humankind, and the virtues to be practised in imitation of Christ.[3]

Book 3 of the *Sentences* comes to us divided into forty Distinctions. The first twenty-two are devoted to Christ's incarnation and his redemptive work, with the first fourteen of these focussing on Christ as God and man and the final seven turning to Christ's suffering and its redemptive role. With the question of whether Christ had the virtues of faith, hope, and charity, a transition is made, in Distinction 23, from Christology to a consideration of the virtues; these belong in this Book principally because the Christian is called to live them in imitation of Christ, who embodies all of them perfectly. And so the theological virtues are discussed in Distinctions 23-32 and the cardinal ones in Distinction 33; the gifts of the Holy Spirit, which Peter also considers as virtues, are presented in Distinctions 34 and 35. Distinction 36 concludes the treatment of the virtues with the assertion that they are interconnected by charity. The last four Distinctions outline the Decalogue in the context of the two commandments given by Christ regarding the love of God and neighbour; the Book closes with the assertion of the superiority of the Gospel over the Law of the Old Testament.

Christology

Peter begins his introduction to the convolutedly elaborate ancient and contemporary debates about the nature of Christ with the clear and unambiguous affirmation that human beings care about all this because it was through Christ's coming that, in the fullness of time, salvation became available to them in love by their adoption as children of God (dist. 1, before c1).

Throughout the *Sentences*, one of Peter's abiding concerns is to remind his students and readers that, for all the distinction of persons in God, divine life is Trinitarian. Similarly, the work of redemption, even if it is usually—and for good reason—discussed as the work of the Son, is

[2]As was the case in Book 1, the Introduction to Book 2 contains a summary of the Book's contents.

[3]For a brief and lucid description of the structure of Book 3 and a spirited rebuttal of the view that its organization is less than impressive, see Rosemann, *Peter Lombard*, pp. 119-121.

better seen as the work of the Trinity. The interesting manner in which this point is made at the very beginning of Book 3 is by asking why it should have been the Son, rather than the Father or the Holy Spirit, who took on human flesh and form (c1 n1). Three reasons are given. First, since the world was established in the Wisdom which is Christ, it was suitable that the work of reparation should be carried out by that same Wisdom (c1 n2). Second, it was fitting that the Son, who has it from the Father that he is from another from all eternity, should also be sent from another in the incarnation (c1 n2). Third, it was elegantly economic that the one who is Son of God according to divinity from all eternity should become son of man according to humanity in time, and should so retain exclusively the title of son even as he extended to human beings the possibility of their becoming sons by adoption (c1 n4).

These reasons are in no way meant to suggest that the divine omnipotence was bounded and that the Father and the Holy Spirit could not have become incarnate (c2); in discerning and pointing out the suitability of the Son's incarnation, one is simply delighting in the beauty of the divine choice insofar as one is able to glimpse it. There is equal delight in the unambiguous assertion that the Son's incarnation is the work of the entire Trinity, even as it is the Son alone who takes flesh from the Virgin, and the Holy Spirit alone who appears in the form of a dove, and the voice of the Father alone that is heard to proclaim the sonship of the Son (c3 n2).

Against any inclination to safeguard the divinity of Christ at the cost of minimizing his humanity, Peter next insists that the Son took on human nature in its entirety, soul and flesh, and not just some partial form of it. The Son came to share the whole nature of humanity so that he could redeem it whole (dist. 2 c1 n1). Although Christ is absolutely unique by reason of being both perfect God and perfect man, yet the humanity which he took is a fully human nature, soul and flesh, with the accidents and qualities which pertain to both, so that all these may find in him the cure for the ills which had come to afflict them at the fall (c1 nn2-4).

It would not have been suitable for the divine essence to become united to a material body apart from the mediation of the soul (c2). And so, at the very moment of conception, Christ took on soul and body simultaneously; by the work of the Trinity, the Son took on soul and flesh in the Virgin's womb, and so the Word was made flesh (c3).

The insistence on Christ's full humanity might make for the conclusion that his flesh was sinful. But it would have been unsuitable for the Word to take on sinful flesh, and the manner of his conception precluded it. The overshadowing of the Holy Spirit purified the Virgin from all sin and from the urge to sin, even as it prepared the power of begetting the divine Word in her womb without male seed and without concupiscence (dist. 3 c1). And yet the flesh so wonderfully begotten remains fully human (c1 n4). It was in order that she might worthily bear the divine Word that Mary received the wholly singular privilege of being rendered entirely sinless (c2).

But if Christ's flesh was free from sin, how can it be said that he took on flesh in order to free it from sin? Peter resolves this conundrum by introducing a distinction between the burdens which human flesh bears because of the guilt of sin and those which arise from the punishment for sin. Though his flesh was guiltless, Christ willingly took on the punishment for sin. By this voluntary assumption, Christ's flesh bore the likeness of sinful flesh and would suffer and die; this same likeness sufficed for the work of freeing human flesh from sin (c4 n1).

A further occasion to affirm the Trinitarian character of Christ's incarnation is offered by the discussion of why, in Scripture, this work is attributed to the Holy Spirit (dist. 4 c1 n1). A fitting reason for this attribution is that the Spirit is the love and gift of the Father and Son; therefore to call the incarnation a work of the Spirit is to affirm that it is a delightful gift of the loving Trinity (c1 n1). It remains a firm hermeneutical principle that the works which Scripture attributes to one of the divine persons are to be usually understood as being the work of the whole Trinity (c1 n2). In any case, the assertion that Christ is born of the Holy Spirit and of Mary is not to be taken to mean that he is the son of the Spirit in the same way that he is the son of Mary; the mention of the Spirit here denotes the divine grace at work in the joining of humanity and divinity in Christ (c2 nn1-3). Another reason may be that it was through the work of the Spirit that the humanity of Christ was formed from the Virgin's flesh (c2 nn4 and 5).

In the first four Distinctions, Peter has raised relatively peaceful and straightforward questions concerning Christ and his saving work. The tone of his interventions and of his authorities has been principally one of delighted piety before the beautiful benignity of the incarnation. But in Distinction 5 the discussion takes a decidedly technical turn as Peter begins to set out the complex issues which have been raised in the tradition and in the schools regarding the union without confusion of divinity and humanity in Christ. Grammatical and logical problems abound here. In attending to these issues, we will do well to remember Peter's commitment to deepening the piety of his students and encouraging in them an intelligently sensitive and respectful reading of Scripture. It is in aid of such goals that he strives to set forth in a fair and balanced manner the various and frequently heated debates which have been occurring in the schools. Respectful of the lawful freedom of his colleagues and students, Peter presents contending views without always choosing from among them; whenever he believes that the evidence is not compelling on one side or another, he will happily leave his readers to their own preference, now enriched by the survey of possibilities set out in his work.

The first of the technical questions raised asks whether, in describing how the Word of God took flesh, one ought to say that a person took on a person, or a nature a nature, or a person a nature, or a nature a person; furthermore, is it appropriate to say that the divine nature became flesh, as it is to say that God became flesh? (dist. 5 c1 n1). These questions have their historical roots in the memory of the ancient debates about Adoptionism—whether Christ was Son of God by adoption—a position that makes it easy to reject any formulation suggesting that a person is taken on at the incarnation (c1 n2). But the questions retain all their interest because they go to the heart of the Christian's perception of the relationship of the divine and human in Christ, and so also to the heart of the Christian's own relationship with Christ and the divine Trinity. The lovingly delicate glance extended to the constitution of the human Christ brings with it the possibility of an equally delicate attention to the work of the Trinity in each human person.

The easy answer to the questions here raised is that a person took on a nature. Although one cannot say that either a person or a nature took on a person (c1 n2), more challenging is whether a nature took on a nature. In his discussion of this point, Peter stresses that opinions on this have varied among the authorities, and even in one and the same authority (c1 n3). For the view that a nature did not take on a nature, Peter cites a Council of Toledo ruling, which held that "the Son alone took human form in the singularity of his person, not in the unity of the divine nature" (c1 n4). That a nature took on a nature, on the other hand, seems to be held by Augustine, who said: "For that nature, which remains forever begotten of the Father, took our nature free from sin in order to be born of the Virgin" (c1 n5).[4] But an even stronger assertion of nature taking on nature is found in statements by Augustine and Hilary about the Son tak-

[4]Peter professes to be troubled by Augustine's use of 'begotten' here, since he would reserve this term for the Son's person rather than for his nature, which he shares with the other persons of the Trinity (c1 n5).

ing the form of a servant without losing the form of God, with form being taken as the equivalent of nature (c1 nn6 and 7).

Wishing to negotiate safely the minefield which he has just described, Peter confesses his assent to the rightly understood teachings of the orthodox Fathers and Catholic teachers; he then proceeds to express what he regards as their right understanding. He proposes the following careful formulation as the correct synthesis of his authorities:

> And so we say that the person of the Son took on a human nature, and that a divine nature was united to a human nature in the Son, and that he united it to himself or took it, so that he is truly called incarnate (c1 n10).

The statements about the Son alone taking on servile form are to be read to exclude the other divine persons, but not the divine nature (c1 n11). The Council of Toledo's statement can be read in the same sense, as limiting the union of the divine nature and humanity to the hypostasis of the Son (c1 n11). By the use of the term hypostasis here, Peter makes clear his debt to John of Damascus, whom he next cites as the authority who has resolved this issue in the sense just affirmed (c1 n12).

With the qualifications expressed throughout the argument, Peter is now ready to make the bold assertion that "the divine nature became incarnate; and so the same nature is truly said to have taken on a human nature" (c1 n12). This redounds to the dignity of human nature, since it is obviously a great thing to say that it was taken by the divine nature. The qualifications, on the other hand, make clear that this assumption of human nature does not occur at the expense of the unchangeable perfection of the divine nature. This latter concern helps to explain Peter's refusal, in the absence of scriptural warrant, to say that the divine nature 'became flesh' in the Son, or that the same nature was made man (c2).

In the incarnation, the divine Word assumed human nature, consisting of body and soul, but not a person. There was no pre-existent human Jesus that was taken on by the Son. In Jesus, God and man, human soul and human flesh became one, and then became one with the divine Word (c3 n1). Those who hold otherwise do so on the basis of Boethius' definition of person as "a rational substance of an individual nature" (c3 n2). Peter holds that this definition may adequately describe a human soul or an angel, but not a human person composed of body and soul, and so it is not applicable to the union of divinity and humanity in Christ (c3 n2). As for those scriptural phrases which seem to speak of the Word taking on a person, Peter defines magisterially that they are to be read as referring to the nature of a man and not to the person (c3 nn3 and 4). The conclusion, then, is that in Christ there is one person, the divine person of the Son, who has assumed full humanity by taking a human body and a human soul. Peter is most firm in the counterintuitive view that to deny the existence of a human person in Christ is not at all inconsistent with the affirmation that he is fully human.

The concern that the incarnation not be understood in such a way as to posit change in God, even as the full humanity of Christ is strenuously defended, will continue to exercise Peter for a considerable space.[5] The next form which this concern takes is to raise the difficult question of how one is to read expressions like 'God was made man,' and 'the Son of God was made son of man,' and whether they indicate that God is made anything which he was not before (dist. 6 c1). In discussing this question, Peter begins to outline the three principal theories regarding the union of divinity and humanity in Christ, or hypostatic union. These three are usually named the *assumptus homo*, subsistence, and *habitus* theories of the hypostatic union.[6] The differences among these theories can be subtle, for all Peter's view that their proponents differ deeply (c1 n2).

The ancient framers of the *assumptus homo* theory had had as their main concern the countering of Adoptionism, so at the heart of their view is the denial that the divine Word takes on ('adopts') a pre-existent man. In the incarnation, soul and flesh become united to constitute a man, "[a]nd that man began to be God, not indeed by the nature of God, but by the person of the Word; and God began to be that man. They also grant that that man was assumed by the Word and united to the Word, and yet that he was the Word" (c2 n1). In this view, the expression 'God was made man' is used to denote that, in the incarnation, God began to be "some substance subsisting from a rational soul and human flesh. ... And yet not by the passage of [one] nature into [another] nature" (c2 n1). But the proponents of this theory fail to profess that Christ was composed of two natures, divine and human (c2 n1). In all they say and in all they fail to say, they can claim the support of authorities, and particularly of Augustine (c2 nn2-9).

[5]Rosemann, *Peter Lombard*, p. 127, posits the issue in terms of whether God, in becoming man, became other than himself, and he notes that "[t]he Lombard attempts to answer this question by means of the single most extended treatment of a particular point in the entire *Book of Sentences*."

[6]For a useful introduction to these theories and Peter's attitude to them, see Colish, *Peter Lombard*, 1.400-417, 424-427, and 427-438 on the virulent debates to which Peter's treatment was to give rise. A shorter introduction to the same issues is found in Rosemann, *Peter Lombard*, pp. 110-119, 127-133.

The subsistence theory is presented as largely agreeing with the first one, with the modification that it describes Christ as "not composed only of a rational soul and flesh, but also of a divine and human nature, that is, of three substances: divinity, flesh, and soul" (c3 n1). By the incarnation, divinity and humanity combine so that a simple divine person is made into a person composed of divinity, body, and soul, who now subsists in two natures (c3 n1). This theory, too, is bolstered by venerable authorities (c3 nn2-6).

The third theory seems to differ radically from the other two since it begins with the denial that the incarnation results in a composite person; in this view, human soul and flesh are worn as a garment by the Word of God "in order to appear suitably to the eyes of mortals" (c4 n1). The proponents of this theory see it as a way to avoid positing quaternity in God, which seems to them to follow from the other theories (c4 n2). For all its apparent radicalness, this theory also does not lack for support in the authorities (cc5 and 6). In particular, an extended Augustinian consideration of the various possible meanings of 'habit' is set forth in order to conclude that the meaning of habit as a garment that conforms to its wearer is the most suitable one to denote what happens at the incarnation (c5, esp. nn3 and 4).

Distinction 6 has served to set out the three theories of the hypostatic union and the authorities which support each of them; Distinction 7 discusses some of the difficulties inherent to the first two in particular. The first theory is open to the objection that it seems to posit change in God by the introduction of a substance which was not always God (c1 n2). The objections made to the second theory are less blunt, but all seem to be concerned with the composition of the person of Christ and the possible confusions which can arise from the way in which its proponents describe that composition (c1 nn4-15).[7]

Peter's discussion of the hypostatic union ends with the firm assertion that, throughout the discussion, he has asserted no position of his own, and will not do so now. He regards the question as open and encourages the reader to consult "other, perhaps better considered and argued, treatments" (c3 n3). But the concerns which have animated his presentation are reiterated in the concluding authority, which stresses once more that, in the incarnation, divinity is not changed and humanity retains its integ-

[7]So gentle and thorough is Peter's discussion of the subsistence theory that some commentators have concluded that he preferred it over the others; see Rosemann, *Peter Lombard*, p. 130.

rity "because a transformation or changeableness makes for a diminution of nature and the abolition of substance" (c3 n3).

In Distinction 8, Peter briefly disposes of two subsidiary questions concerning the relationship of divinity and humanity in Christ. The first question addresses the propriety of referring to the divine nature as being born of the Virgin; on balance, Peter would not use the expression (c1). On the other hand, he does not have the same difficulty with saying that God was born twice, according to divinity and according to humanity (c2).

Distinction 9 is concerned with the degree of worship which is to be extended to Christ's humanity, a subject on which Peter's views appear to have undergone evolution.[8] From earlier debates in Christian history, Peter and his contemporaries inherit a distinction between a degree of adoration due to God alone (*latria*) and the sort of veneration which may be extended to any creature whom God has sanctified *(dulia*). It seemed to some that to adore Christ's humanity by *latria* was idolatry (c1 n1). Some of the holders of this view preserved the special reverence due to Christ by distinguishing two kinds of *dulia*, one of which stood between ordinary *dulia* and *latria* and was extended to Christ's humanity alone, which "is to be venerated and loved above all other creatures" (c1 n2). A third view held that *latria* could be extended to Christ's humanity without fear of idolatry because it was adored for the sake of the Word with whom it was united (c1 n3). Peter had come to share this view under the influence of John of Damascus' particularly beautiful formulation of the attitude, which he next reports (c1 n4). The formulation strongly intends to engender piety, without risking confusion of natures and without simply subsuming Christ's humanity into his divinity—all criteria which we have seen Peter apply to these questions with great coherence.

In Distinction 10, he broaches a question which is highly provocative in form: whether Christ, according to his humanity, can be said to be a person, or even anything (c1 n1). This question would be said to raise the prospect of Christological nihilism and was to engender much discussion in subsequent years, even giving rise to the possibility of condemning the *Sentences* because of it.[9] But the points being made in the Distinction are relatively straightforward and peaceful, given what has already been considered and settled in the earlier Distinctions concerning the hypostatic union.

[8]Colish, *Peter Lombard*, 1.428.
[9]Ibid., 1.427-438; Rosemann, *Peter Lombard*, pp. 131-133.

Some of Peter's contemporaries had come to the conclusion that Christ, according to his being a man, was not anything. They reached this conclusion as follows: as a man, Christ is either a person, or a substance, or something else. It is only plausible that he be a person, since he is not something else and, if a substance, then a rational one, which is also a person. But if he is a person also as a man, then one is led to assert quaternity in God as a result of the incarnation. To avoid such an unsuitable conclusion, it seems safer to say that, according to his being a man, Christ is not a person or anything (c1 nn2 and 3).

Peter appears to have some sympathy with the concerns which underlie this dramatic proposition. And yet he remains convinced that the difficulty is largely due to the inadequate definition of person as rational substance (c1 n4).[10] If one is not confined by such a definition, then it is still possible to avoid saying that Christ, according to his being a man, is not anything. Indeed, one can affirm that, "even now the soul of Christ is a rational substance, and yet not a person because it does not speak by itself,[11] and, indeed, is joined to another thing. But that description of person is not given for those three persons [of the Trinity]" (c1 n4). And so it remains possible, as well as necessary, according to Peter, to assert unchanging divinity and whole humanity in Christ, even while firmly denying that there are two persons in him. Corollaries of this position assert that Christ is not to be called an adoptive son according to his being a man (c2), but he may with some qualifications be said to have been predestined according to both his divinity and humanity (c3).

With the most difficult questions out of the way, Peter settles a series of further questions about Christ with greater briskness and assurance. The first of these concerns whether Christ is to be called made, created, or a creature (dist. 11 c1 n1). If there were no risk of impiety, these words could be freely used of Christ's humanity. But experience shows that the careless use of such language does great harm because it ends up misapplying what is true of Christ's humanity to his divinity. Such was the case with the Arians of old (c2). It is better, then, to be aware of the unsuitability of calling Christ a creature (c1 nn2 and 3), before one grants grudgingly that one may properly if carefully call Christ a creature ac-

[10] Rosemann, *Peter Lombard*, pp. 132-133, reports evidence that Peter, in his oral teaching, may have been more emphatic in expressing the dangers of referring to Christ as being anything according to his being a man.

[11] The phrase "does not speak by itself" is a translation of *per se sonans*, the traditional etymology of the Latin word *persona*.

cording to his humanity (c2). With similar care, one will not say that Christ, or the Son of God, began to be, though this may be said of his human nature (dist. 12 c1). Once more, we discern here Peter's commitment to safeguard the truth of both Christ's divinity and his humanity.

Divine sovereignty is so perfect that the Word of God was under no necessity to take up the particular man Jesus, or even someone from Adam's stock (c2 n1). Although the question strikes Peter as affected, he is willing to grant that God could have taken human form as a woman, but he more suitably chose to take male form and be born of woman so that the liberation of humankind should manifest itself in both sexes, in the Son and in his Virgin Mother (c4).[12]

Interjected among these topics is also the question of whether the man Christ was able to sin, which is the same as asking whether he was able not to be God (c3 n1). The answer to this requires a distinction. If Christ's human nature had existed without being united to the divine Word, then it would have been able to sin; in union with the same Word, it is unable to sin (c3 n2). And it is frivolous to suggest that this inability to sin is a limitation of free choice; this is no truer for Christ than for the angels, who "are so confirmed by grace that they cannot sin. And so how much more [free choice did] that man [have] to whom the Spirit was given without measure?" (c3 n3).

But if Christ, even in his humanity, has received the fullness of the Spirit, can he be said to have made progress in wisdom and grace, as the Gospel seems to affirm? (dist. 13 c1 nn1-4). In this question, too, we see Peter's concern with preserving the plausibility of the assertion that Christ was wholly human, even as it is impossible to say that God's wisdom and grace can increase. And so the determination of the question is that, from his conception, Christ was as full of wisdom and grace as it is possible for a human being to be, but there was progress in the manifestation of these gifts to others and for their benefit. Furthermore, as is usual with human nature, he made progress in age from infancy to youth and his gifts became more and more manifest in the course of this progress (c1 n5). As for an authority which seems to hold that Christ made progress in his human understanding, it is to be read in the light of the fact that, although Christ was endowed with a twofold wisdom, the one divine

[12]Colish, *Peter Lombard*, 1.438, has Peter 'note' that God's incarnation in male form "made sense since, given the morés of His time and place, Christ's mission was facilitated by His incarnation in masculine form." We have failed to find any mention or support of this view in Peter's text.

and the other human, these are not two different wisdoms. It follows that it is safer to say that there was progress in the manifestation of Christ's understanding to others, but not in the understanding itself, which was forever perfect (c1 nn6-9).[13]

But is this wisdom of Christ's equal to God's, and does it know all the things that God knows? (dist. 14 c1 n2). To those who object that a creature, such as Christ's soul, can never be equated to the Creator (c1 n2), Peter answers that, in its union with the divine Word, Christ's soul "knows all things which God knows, but cannot do all the things that God can do" (c1 n3). And yet the creature is not equated to the Creator, even in knowledge, because Christ's soul does not know things as clearly or as worthily and perfectly as God does (c1 n3). The discrepancy in power between God and Christ's soul implies also that the latter does not have the power to do everything which it knows how to do (c1 n6).

Christ's Redemptive Role

Distinction 15 introduces the consideration of Christ's deeds for human salvation. The first of these is Christ's assumption of human defects, that is, of the flesh's capacity to suffer and die. To show that he took a true body, he took the body's defects, such as hunger and thirst; to show that he had a true soul, he took sadness, fear, pain, and similar things (dist. 15 c1 n1). But this distinction between defects of the body and of the soul should not be taken too far because even the defects of the body are sensed by the soul using the body as an instrument (c1 n2).

The distinction which is more crucial is that between defects that flow from punishment and those that flow from the guilt of sin. Christ took only the former, and only those among them "which it was suitable for him as man to assume and which did not derogate from his dignity" (c1 n3). In so doing there was a wondrous exchange, "[f]or he took the ancientness [of our nature] in order to infuse his newness in us. He took a single ancientness, that is, the one of punishment, in order to destroy our twofold one, that is, of punishment and fault" (c1 n3).

[13]There are illuminating reflections on this matter in Rosemann, *Peter Lombard*, pp. 134-135. Less enlightening are the censorious remarks of Colish, *Peter Lombard*, 1.442-443. Colish regards the Lombard as incoherent in his description of Christ's psychology; although committed to a spirited assertion of the fruitful importance of Christ's humanity, Peter is said to end up unwilling to allow Christ "a fully human psychology of knowledge" (p. 443). This conviction of the inadequacy of Peter's view of Christ's psychology will become a fixed, repetitious, and unhelpful theme in Colish's discussion of Peter's presentation of the virtues.

Chief among the flaws of human nature which Christ did not take are ignorance and the related difficulty of our weakened will to will and do what is good (c1 nn4 and 5). He did not take these defects because they would have been unsuitable for him and unprofitable for us. The general rule regarding the defects which Christ took is that "he took them either to demonstrate his true humanity: such as fear and sadness; or to fulfil the work for which he had come: such as the capacity to suffer and die; or to raise our hope from our despair of immortality: such as death" (c1 n7).

In other human beings, the defects which Christ took are present as a consequence of sin; in Christ, who was conceived and born without sin, and who preserved his sinlessness throughout his life, the taking of these flaws flowed entirely from compassion (c1 n8). But he took them truly, and his fear and suffering were real; those opinions ought to be rejected which argue that "Christ bore a likeness and semblance of suffering and pain, but did not at all endure pain or suffering [itself]" (c1 n9).[14]

Some authorities, and scriptural ones in particular, seem to differ on the reality of Christ's suffering, and of his fear and sadness especially. The apparent contradiction is resolved by the application of a distinction between 'passion' and 'propassion' (c2 n1). These terms are defined using the examples of fear and suffering: in us, their experience can be such "that the mind's understanding is not as a consequence removed from righteousness or the contemplation of God, and then it is propassion. But at times it is removed or troubled, and then it is passion" (c2 n2). In Christ, who is subject to these defects by his own free compassion and not by the necessity of sin, true fear and sadness are present only according to propassion and in no way affect his righteousness or contemplation of God (c2 nn3 and 4).

A particularly troublesome authority on these matters is Hilary of Poitiers, who, in a number of statements, appears to claim that the blows and wounds inflicted on Christ in the course of his passion did not cause suffering, and that fear did not trouble him (c3 nn1-4). But there is no real conflict between Hilary's statements and what Peter has just been saying since the former can be read in harmony with the distinction between pro-

[14]A brief discussion follows, at nn10-12, of authorities attesting to the reality of Christ's suffering, whereas n13 disposes of authorities that seem to attest the contrary.

passion and passion to mean that in Christ there was no necessity to suffer and no necessity to fear (c3 n5).[15]

But the necessity to suffer and die is not a defect tied to sin, since it is integral to our bodies. Was a similar necessity also in Christ's body? Moreover, before sin, even the necessity of suffering was not tied to death; was Christ bound only by the capacity for death, or by the necessity for it and its concomitant suffering? If the latter, then he cannot be said to have taken these defects by compassion (dist. 16 c1 n1). But Christ took these defects like the others willingly, and not by the necessity of his condition, since he was immune from sin (c1 n2). Indeed, it may be said that Christ took something from each of the four states of humankind. From the state of men before sin, he took immunity from sin; from the state after sin and before grace, he took the punishment for sin; from the state of grace, he took the fullness of grace; from the state of glory to come, "he took the inability to sin and the perfect contemplation of God" (c2).

In Distinction 17, Peter tackles the complex question of the coexistence of several wills in Christ, and does so under the guise of asking whether every prayer or will of Christ was fulfilled. The specific prayer at the heart of this question is the fruitfully troublesome one by which Christ asks: "Father, if it is possible, let this cup pass from me. But not my will, but yours, be done" (Mt. 26, 39; dist. 17 c1). This prayer is taken to be evidence of two wills in Christ, one divine and the other human. The human will is refractory before the prospect of suffering and death, but it immediately conforms to the divine will by asking that the Father's will be done. Moreover, in Christ's human will, as in any man's, a distinction can be made between its sensual disposition, by which he wished not to die, and its rational disposition, by which he willed to do the Father's will even unto death (c2 n1). Nor does the Gospel text reveal a struggle between Christ's flesh and his spirit; such a struggle would betray the existence of concupiscence, which has no place in the sinless Christ. The prayer is best seen then as being offered for our sake by God's will so that we should be convinced of the truth of Christ's humanity (c2 n2). Furthermore, the prayer is exemplary for us, his members, in that it teaches us how we are to meet our own tribulations; we may pray for their removal, but we must also strive to conform our will to God's (c2 n9).

[15]Whatever one may think of Peter's reading of Hilary's texts, it is difficult to see how one could say, with Colish, *Peter Lombard*, 1.444, that "Peter feels impelled to reject flat out the claim of Hilary of Poitiers that Christ was incapable of suffering."

In Distinction 18, Peter begins his treatment of Christ's saving passion with the question of what Christ merited by his suffering and death. Some say that Christ merited nothing for himself, but only for the members of his body, which is the Church (c1 n1), for whom "he merited redemption from the devil, from sin, from punishment, and the opening of the kingdom" (c1 n2). Despite this view to the contrary, Peter holds that the man Christ merited for himself the glory of impassibility of soul and immortality of body (c1 nn2-5). And yet it was not by his suffering and death that Christ merited these rewards; from the very moment of his conception, and then at all other points of his perfect earthly life, Christ already merited all that he received in glory because of his perfectly obedient adherence to the will of the Father in all that he did (c2 nn1 and 2). Nor ought one ever to say that his soul was better and more blessed after his death than it had been before; the most one can say is that perhaps it is now more blessed because of immunity from all misery (c2 n3).

Another benefit, if such it may be called, accruing to Christ by his passion was the exaltation of his name above all other names, that is, that he should be known as God. By this benefit, that which the Son of God has by nature from all eternity is extended to the man Jesus through grace (c3 n1). By means of the cross, that which the Son of God already had was given by grace to the obedient servant (c3 n2). And yet even this may be doubted, namely that the suffering of Christ merited for him this benefit; it is perhaps better to say that he had this benefit also from the moment of his conception, but that his suffering and death merited the manifesting of his name and power (c3 nn3 and 4). Christ's suffering and death were not required for his acquisition of the three benefits, however. Since God's power is unbounded, Christ could have taken immediately the glorious body which became his at the resurrection; but having chosen to come as a passible man, he could not come to glory without merit (c4 n1). And yet the merit of his virtues would have been sufficient, so that "through his passion he merited nothing for himself which he had not already merited earlier through his virtues" (c4 n2).

If Peter has belaboured the point of how unnecessary Christ's sufferings were for his own sake, it is so that the reader should be all the more appreciative of Christ's compassionate condescension. For now the question can be asked and the answer given in the following beautiful terms:

> To what end, then, did he will to suffer and die, if his virtues were sufficient for him to merit those things? For your sake, not for his own. How for my sake? So that his passion and death should be model and cause to

> you: the model of virtue and humility, the cause of glory and liberty, the model of being obedient to God even unto death, and the cause of your liberation and blessedness (c5 n1).

By the conditions which God had decreed for himself, Christ's practice of the virtues, then, was sufficient for his own rewards, but did not merit for us "entrance to paradise, and redemption from sin, punishment, and the devil" (c5 n1). It was in order to confer these benefits on us, to bring us redemption and adoption as children of glory, that Christ "was made the victim offered for our liberation" (c5 n1).

At the fall, it had been God's mysterious decree that man be banned from paradise and contemplation of God, "unless so much humility should be found in one man which might suffice for all who follow him, just as in the first man was found such pride as to harm all who followed him" (c5 n2). Although there had been righteous men before Jesus who strove to practice humility, their virtue was barely sufficient for themselves. The fulfillment of all justice occurred in Christ alone, who "was a sufficient and a perfect victim; he was much more humbled in tasting the bitterness of death, than Adam had become proud in his guilty pleasure through his eating of the forbidden tree" (c5 n2). Christ's humble death met all the requirements of God's decree and the gates of heaven's kingdom were opened to all who follow him (c5 n2).

These are wonderfully ineffable matters, but Peter can still judiciously conclude his glorious presentation with the gloriously restrained observation: "See, we have seen to some extent how entry to the kingdom was readied for us by Christ's death" (c5 n3).

After setting out the benefits for humankind of Christ's redemptive work so movingly and elegantly, Peter proceeds to outline the mechanics, as it were, of this greatest of works. How does Christ redeem? By justifying sinful men, that is, releasing them from their sins, which are the devil's bonds (dist. 19 c1 n1). This brief allusion to the devil's former power over men is quickly overtaken by the more extended consideration of the great change which Christ's redemption can work in man's ability to love. In Christ's death, God's charity is revealed so strikingly that "we are moved to, and kindled with, love of God, who has done so much for us; in this way, we are justified, that is, we are released from our sins, and so we are made just. Indeed, Christ's death justifies us, as by it charity is kindled in our hearts" (c1 n2). By the awesome example of Christ's love, a conversion of heart can take place which covers up sins and justifies the sinner.

It is in the light of this conversion that the crucified Christ can become the sign of faith to which the sinner can look in the continuing struggle with the devil. Temptation does not end after the incarnation, or even after the redemption, but now man can look to Christ on the cross and find in him freedom from sin and the power to overcome the tempter; if he has accepted Christ into his heart, the one tempted will find that seduction will not follow temptation (c1 n3).

In order to vanquish the devil in this way, it was just that a man overcome, as it had been a man who had submitted to the devil in the beginning. But for a man to overcome, he had to be immune from sin, and this could only be with God in him. "And so the Son of God took on passible human form, in which he tasted even death," in order to redeem humankind from slavery to the devil, "that is, from sin (for sin is slavery to the devil), and from punishment" (c2).

The punishment from which Christ frees men by his death is first the eternal one, which was owed for the first sin, and then the temporal one, which he will abolish entirely by the granting of immortality when death itself shall be destroyed (c3). In human souls, this liberation is already partially achieved; man is still subject to the fault of sin, but is no longer dominated by it (c3). And by Christ's bearing of our sins, the temporal punishment due for sin is abolished in baptism; for sin committed after baptism, Christ's merits offer once again relief from such punishment by the sacrament of penance (c4). Furthermore, the redeeming effects of Christ's sacrifice extend even to the just who lived before his coming (c4).

With this, Peter is ready to make the humble claim that now "it has been partially explained how and what Christ, by his death, merited and accomplished for us" (c4). Next follows a brief discussion of whether the title of redeemer ought to be reserved for Christ alone. The issue arises because Scripture refers also to the Father and the Holy Spirit as redeemer. Peter holds that Father and Holy Spirit are termed redeemer "only by reference to the use of power, not as an example of humility and obedience" (c5). In the Son, there were both power and obedience, and so "the Son is properly called redeemer because he both fulfilled in himself those things by which we are justified, and worked the same justification by the power of the Godhead with the Father and the Holy Spirit" (c5). In this brief discussion of a seemingly very technical issue, Peter manages to have his students reflect on the Trinitarian dimension even of what seems most singularly the Son's work. Moreover, the affirmation of the human contribution is not neglected since the Son "is more frequently called redeemer according to his humanity, because according to it and in it he took up and fulfilled those sacraments which are the cause of our redemption" (c5).

The title of mediator is also said to be exclusive to Christ because he alone is placed between God and men in order to reconcile the latter to God (c6 n1). But this is not to be understood in the sense that Christ had to placate God and induce him to love men. This would have been entirely unnecessary because God has never ceased to love humankind from before the creation of the world. It is men that Christ comes to change so that they may cease to make themselves enemies of God by sin (c6 nn2 and 3). And it is according to his humanity that he is mediator (c7).

It was possible for God to work our salvation in any manner that he found pleasing, but none could have been more fitting for human misery than the one which God chose (dist. 20 c1). None other would have been a more effective cure for human despair of immortality and none better able to convert the mind of man than to see the Son of God enter into fellowship with us and bear the evils that afflict us (c2 n1). It was also the case that, in so doing, he overcame the devil by justice, not by power (c2 n2). Aside from the fittingness of vanquishing the devil by the righteousness which he hates most, this means of redemption was an example to men that they ought to love justice more than power (c3 n1).

Peter next asks to whom responsibility should be assigned for Christ's crucifixion; the Father, the Son, Judas, and the Jews are all responsible for the event, but in different ways and for different reasons (c5 n1). The Son handed himself over freely; the Father (indeed, the whole Trinity) willed that he should be handed over and suffer; Judas betrayed him, and the Jews instigated his death. Although there was only one act of handing over, it was a good act on the part of Christ and the Father because their will was good; the will of Judas and the Jews was evil, and so the same act was evil on their part (c5 n2). This reflection on causation and responsibility ends with the suggestion that the act of the Jews, although evil, may be considered a good thing because Christ's passion, which is a good thing, derived from it (c6).

After completing his consideration of the fittingness and the effects of Christ's suffering and death, Peter next turns to the question of what happened to Christ's soul in the time between his death and his resurrection. First, he asks whether, at death, Christ's soul and flesh were separated from the divine Word (dist. 21 c1 n1). This question, which springs naturally enough from attention to the events of Christ's salvific passion and connects to the issue of the liberation of the just who had lived before

Christ's coming, also recalls the earlier discussion of the hypostatic union. One's perception of the manner of union between divinity and humanity in Christ would tend to dictate how one presents the state of that union during the time in which Christ's body lies in the tomb.

The first view which Peter sets out holds that Christ's flesh, while in the tomb, was separated from both Christ's soul and the divine Word; since the Word and Christ were united through Christ's soul, the separation of the soul from the body (without which there would have been no true death) of necessity involved separation from the Word (c1 n2). That this was the case seems to be supported by an assertion of Ambrose that the Godhead had abandoned Christ at his death (c1 n3). Peter rejects this opinion, if it requires holding that the Godhead abandoned Christ at some point before his death. He thinks that Ambrose's text can only be construed in the sense that God abandoned Christ in some way that did not involve the dissolution of the union between God and man in him. Indeed, some form of abandonment was necessary, if Christ was to die, since God is life. The solution: "The Godhead severed itself because it took away its protection, but did not dissolve the union; it separated itself outwardly so that it was not there to defend him, but was not absent inwardly in regard to the union" (c1 n4).

Peter next sets out the view of those who hold that, at death, the Godhead withdrew from Christ's flesh, otherwise it would not make sense to say, as Athanasius had done, that, at the resurrection, the whole man, whom the Son of God had taken, rose again from the dead (c1 n5). Peter criticizes this reasoning because it seems as applicable to Christ's soul as to his flesh (c1 nn6 and 7). Peter's own view remains that the soul became severed from the body by divine power, but that there was no separation of the Word of God from either Christ's body or his soul (c1 n8). And it is wrong to say that even Christ's flesh was abandoned in the tomb (c1 n9). And yet it remains proper to say that God suffered and died, for it cannot be said that God did not suffer whatever Christ's flesh suffered; in the same way, you cannot be said to have suffered no injury if your clothing is torn, even though you cannot be reduced to your clothing. In this sense, although the Word is able neither to die, nor to suffer, it can be said that God suffers whatever is suffered by the flesh united to the Word (c2). In summary, "it may rightly be said that God died and did not die, that the Son of God suffered and did not suffer, that the third person suffered and did not suffer, that the Word was crucified and was not crucified. According to the one nature he suffered, and according to the other he was unable to suffer" (c2 n5). The wonders of the hypostatic union!

A question that gives rise to a certain impatience in Peter is that of whether Christ was a man while he was in the tomb (dist. 22 c1 n1). Those who hold that he was not assert that a dead man is not a man. If he was still a man, then he was neither mortal, since already dead, nor immortal, since not yet risen (c1 n2). Peter calls for the simple assertion that "although he was a dead man, yet God was man in death" (c1 n3). Anything else is a philosophical quibble, against which he invokes Ambrose's dismissal: "Put aside your arguments, where faith is required. Let dialectic be silent, even in her own schools. We believe fishermen, not dialecticians" (c1 n3).

If Peter becomes indignant at what he regards as quibbles, it is perhaps due to his view that the unity of divinity and humanity in Christ is too crucial a truth to be subject to classroom games and the vain display of cleverness. Right piety and human beatitude hang in the balance, and so one should not be reckless with the matter, even in regard to merely subsidiary questions. And so, he takes up with great earnestness a related subsidiary question of his own having to do with the ubiquity of Christ in death (c2 n1). Since Peter has repeatedly asserted that the union of Christ with the Word continues even while the body rests in the tomb, and given that the Godhead is everywhere, then Christ is ubiquitous even as he lies in the tomb (c2 n1). Although ubiquity can be ascribed to Christ's divinity, it ought not to be said that his humanity was ubiquitous. But his humanity consisted of soul and body, both of which were in union with the divine Wisdom, and the body remained in the tomb while the soul descended to hell, and yet Wisdom remained united with both (c2 nn2-4). Nor ought one to hold that parts of Christ are present in each of these places or everywhere; it is always the whole Christ who is present "at the same time in hell, in heaven, and everywhere" (c3 n1). But although he is whole everywhere, he is not wholly everywhere, for he is present everywhere as God, but not as man (c3 n2).

The Virtues

Peter's presentation of the crucifixion as the ultimate call to conversion of heart has already served to alert his readers to the extent to which all Christ's work serves to engage human freedom in the direction of love. The exemplary character of Christ's life and death means that anyone moved to respond to Christ's call to love will find in that life and in that death the ways and means by which to attempt such a response. To aid in the framing of a loving response, Peter proceeds immediately from his consideration of Christ's passion to the enucleation of Christ's practice of the virtues. With his gaze fixed upon Christ's virtues, the Christian will be better able to strive to imitate his exemplar.

The treatise on the virtues begins with the question of whether Christ can rightly be said to have had the fullness of grace, unless he had faith and hope as he had charity (dist. 23 c1 n1). The resolution of this question will require a definition of its terms, and so it becomes the occasion to initiate a discussion of the three theological virtues of faith, hope, and charity.

Faith is defined as the virtue by which unseen things pertaining to religion are believed (c2). The term may also denote that which is believed and that through which belief in other things occurs (c3 n1). Faith is only a virtue if it is accompanied by love because there can be no virtue without charity, the mother of all virtues (c3 n2). If faith is accompanied by love, then it is the unchangeable foundation upon which our salvation rests because it allows Christ to live in the hearts of those who practice it (c3 n3). But if faith is unaccompanied by love, even the devil can be said to have faith (c3 n4).

In relation to God, faith cannot be reduced to asserting that he exists and speaks the truth; evil men and devils can believe in this sense, without benefit to themselves or to others. True belief in God consists in loving by believing, in seeking union with him in his Church through faith. This is the faith that justifies sinners and enables them to produce works of love (c4 n1). In demons and bad Christians, faith has not acquired the form which charity alone can give to it; and yet even this larvated faith can be called a gift of God (c4 n2). It may be that this is the very faith that becomes formed as a virtue, if a bad Christian turns toward God in charity (c5).

Faith is said to be one with regard to its content because all Catholic faithful believe the same thing (c6 nn1 and 2). Faith in the sense of that through which belief occurs is also one, but by reason of likeness and not identity (c6 n3). Properly speaking, faith can concern only unseen things; visible things are the object of knowledge (c7 n1). Faith itself, while invisible to others, is visible intellectually to the one who has it (c7 n4).[16] It provides conviction and proof "that there are some things which do not appear, since faith only concerns things that do not appear" (c7 n4).

Reflecting further on the scriptural text which is at the heart of his definition of faith (Hebr. 11, 1), Peter notes that the unseen things which

[16]Colish, *Peter Lombard*, 1.498, misreads the text here, attributing to Peter the view that what is known by faith is known intellectually.

are the object of faith are also called the things to be hoped for; these things, which begin to be in the Christian by faith, are those that he hopes will ultimately be in him through experience in glory (c8 n1). And although one might complain that this manner of putting things risks confusing faith and hope, the risk is perhaps worth running, if it points out the necessary unity of faith, hope, and love; faith cannot exist without hope and is useless without love (c8 n2). But it remains the case that faith needs to precede hope, for "nothing can be hoped for which is not believed" (c8 n3).

It is because of this precedence of faith that it alone is "called the foundation of all virtues and good works" (c9 n1). But it does not enjoy priority over, and so is not called the foundation of, charity, which is the Holy Spirit and the cause of all the virtues, and which excels all gifts (c9 n2).

There are instances in Scripture in which the term faith is used with reference to things seen (dist. 24 c1 n1). Although this usage is common enough ('I believe my own eyes!'), yet this is not the most appropriate use of the term. This apparent digression may be intended to convey that faith, by looking for things unseen, sees more deeply and more important realities than what one's eyes perceive. Both the Apostle Peter and a Jewish bystander witnessed the suffering of Christ, and both could believe what their eyes perceived, but Peter alone knew by faith that it was God who suffered (c2 n1). The perception that Christ was suffering gained no merit; faith that God was suffering gained merit (c2 n2).

But if faith concerns only things unseen, does it deal only with unknown things of which we are ignorant? (c3 n1). The question in this form confuses exterior and interior perception; it also treats faith as if it were a bodily sense. Faith is best regarded as an ability of the heart to perceive a resonance between something of which it is not wholly ignorant and a proposal which is set before it by hearing in an interior way (c3 n2). This knowledge of the heart is not limited by what one is able to understand by natural reason; indeed, there are things which one will not understand, unless one has first believed them (c3 n3). Even in the case of things whose understanding precedes faith, "they are better understood through faith, by which hearts are cleansed, because unless God is loved through faith, the heart is not cleansed to know him" (c3 n4).

Peter turns next to the question of what degree of faith is sufficient for salvation before the coming of Christ and after (dist. 25 c1 n1). The minimal faith required for salvation appears to be belief that God exists and that he rewards those who hope in him (c1 n1). But a number of authorities seem to hold that no one, even before Christ's coming, is saved without faith in the mediator; after Christ's incarnation, faith in what is contained in the Creeds is required (c1 n2). But the just men of old could be, and were, saved by their faith in the mediator who was to come (c1 nn3-5).[17] Even simple persons among the Jews, who did not have the privilege of the sort of revelation that was made to Abraham and Moses, could assent simply to those revelations and gain salvation (c2). The same happens now in the Church, where the simple may not be able to explain the content of the Creed which they firmly believe, and yet their humble faith suffices (c2 n2).

To conclude his discussion of faith, Peter reiterates that, for all the usefulness of analysing the virtues distinctly, they operate conjointly and are, in some fundamental sense, equal in this life, because, as Gregory says, "[f]or so long as we are in this life, we find that in us faith, hope, charity, and work are equal to each other because we love as much as we believe, and insofar as we love we are certain of our hope" (c5 n1). And if charity is sometimes termed greater, it is because it shall remain after the others become unnecessary (c5 n1). And yet charity cannot come to anyone without faith and hope, while these can exist, if to no good effect, without charity (c5 n2).

In comparison with the extended discussion of faith, hope gets short shrift. It is defined as "the virtue by which spiritual and eternal goods are hoped for, that is, they are awaited with trust" (dist. 26 c1). Eternal blessedness is the great object of hope, which looks to it in expectation because of merits and God's grace; such a hope will not exist without charity (c1). Like faith, hope has invisible things as its object (c2). But whereas faith is concerned with things which are good and bad, present, past, and future, and how these touch on anyone, so long as they are concerned with religion, hope looks only to those good future things which touch on the one who hopes (c3).

Peter strives next to answer the question with which he began his discussion of the virtues, namely whether faith and hope were in Christ. The short answer is that, although Christ believed and hoped, he did not have

[17]Colish, *Peter Lombard*, 2.498-499, seems wildly misleading in representing the Lombard as saying that Israel's faith before the coming of Christ "since it knew nothing of Christ, was not sufficient to save them."

the virtues of faith and hope because they were unnecessary to him (c4).[18] In Christ, as in the saints in heaven, faith and hope appear to be forms of knowledge rather than virtues. On the other hand, the ancients who awaited Christ in hell can be said to have had the virtues of faith and hope because they believed and hoped, but, until Christ's passion, the direct knowledge of God was not available to them (c5).

Peter's extended discussion of charity begins with the movingly pious and touching assertion of the degree to which charity was most perfectly embodied and exemplified in Christ:

> Although Christ did not have faith and hope, yet as a man he had such love than which there can be no greater; it was due to his most excellent charity that he gave his life for his friends and for his enemies. He also had in his heart that charity which he showed to us by deed, so that by the form of his showing he might instruct us in love (dist. 27 c1).

This beautifully simple and loving bow toward Christ's love serves also to evoke in the reader the appropriate attitude for the consideration of this most sublime of topics.

Peter defines charity as "the love by which God is loved for his own sake, and our neighbour is loved for the sake of God or in God" (c2 n1). He then reports Christ's summation of the Law in the two commandments to love God and neighbour (c2 n2). In glossing these commandments, he asks whether God and neighbour are loved by one love or by two distinct ones. The answer is that there is only one love, and it is the Holy Spirit (c3). In this manner, the Christian life is presented as participation in the very life of the Trinity.[19]

Christ gave two commandments to love by the one love because of its two objects, namely God and neighbour. And of the two commandments, the first is greater and the second lesser (c4 n2). As to the manner of loving, God is to be loved for his own sake with the whole heart, the neighbour is to be loved in the same way in which one is to love oneself, that is, "in goodness and for the sake of God" (c5 n1). Anyone who fails to love himself for the sake of God can be said to hate himself (c5 n2). Alternatively, it can be said that one is to love one's neighbour as Christ

[18]Colish, *Peter Lombard*, 2.499-500, is thoroughly puzzling on this issue. Without any evidence whatsoever, she imputes to Peter a desire to argue that Christ had the virtues of faith and hope. Her discussion of this issue seems thoroughly misguided.

[19]Colish, *Peter Lombard*, 2.501, contends that Peter "seeks to avoid a participatory or immanental view of the mission of the Holy Spirit."

loves, namely so that one's neighbour and oneself may "become children [of God] and have life" (c5 n3). As for the love of God, one may also say that he is to be loved with one's whole intellect, will, and memory, so that one brings one's whole self to God (c5 n4).

Daunting as Christ's two commandments are, man is called to attempt to keep them in this life in the awareness that they cannot be fulfilled here. So long as concupiscence remains in man's heart, his love will remain partial and imperfect; it follows that charity will find its perfection in heaven, where charity alone shall remain and be fulfilled (c6 n1). And yet, though unattainable, these commandments serve the purpose of setting out the goal of the whole Christian life (c6 n2).

Distinction 28 concerns the command to love our neighbour and shows how the term 'neighbour' extends to ourselves and our bodies. All manner of things are commanded to be loved by the two commandments, including God, ourselves, our neighbour, and our bodies; the second and fourth of these did not need to be specifically commanded, in part because they are contained within love of neighbour (dist. 28 c1). The definition of neighbour moves on to the question of whether our love ought to extend to the angels (c2). Because the term 'neighbour' includes even enemies, to whom there is an obligation to show mercy, and since, in turn, those who show mercy to us are also our neighbours, angels and Christ according to his humanity fall within the definition (c3).

Since our love can and must have so many objects, the question arises of how our loves are to be ordered (dist. 29 c1 n1). Right order requires that not everything be loved and that not all objects of our love be loved equally. A man is not to be loved insofar as he is a sinner, but he is to be loved for God's sake insofar as he is a man. God is to be loved for his own sake and more than one's own self. A neighbour is to be loved more than our own body, since he is capable of enjoying God with us (c1 n2).

Our neighbours can be loved with equal affection, but with unequal manifestation of respect. More of the latter is to be shown to those who have been placed close to us and who, in some measure, share our destiny (c2 n2). Fellow Christians, for example, are to be loved by a special love (c2 n2). Several authorities support the view that we are to love with a graduated affection "God before all, ourselves second, parents third, then children and siblings, then members of our household, and finally enemies" (c2 n6). This hierarchy may be subject to revision, if any of its members prove to be evil (c2 n10).

It may serve to avoid discouragement to be reminded that charity has degrees within its own development, "for there is a beginning charity, a progressing one, a perfect one, and a most perfect one" (c3 n1). The perfection of charity consists in laying down one's life for one's friends, and also for one's enemies in order to make them friends (c3 n2).

The next question asks whether it is better or more meritorious to love one's friends or one's enemies (dist. 30 c1 n1). An answer to this troubling question may, in particular cases, require the weighing of degrees of difficulty and fervour (c1 n1). But Augustine holds that loving an enemy is a rarely fulfilled achievement; despite the frequently repeated promise in the Lord's prayer to forgive one's debtors, most petitioners achieve only the ability to extend forgiveness to those enemies who seek it. This is the very minimum which is required by the command to love one's neighbour (c1 n2).

Fittingly, reflection on the enduring character of charity begins to conclude Peter's discussion of this subject. The reflection hinges on Paul's assertion that "charity shall never fall away" (1 Cor. 13, 8). Does this mean that, once one has charity, one can never lose it, and that one not predestined for salvation can never have it? (dist. 31 c1 n1). After setting out authorities appearing to hold that charity, once had, can never be lost (c1 nn2-5), Peter argues that, in any case, the authorities say nothing about those to be damned never having charity (c1 n6). Furthermore, reason and other authorities make it evident that some people are good for a time and then fall away (c1 n7). The verse from Paul refers not to charity as it appears or disappears in a particular person, but to the fact that "it shall exist here and in the future; but faith and hope shall be made void, as will knowledge" (c1 n8). The authorities may also be read to refer to perfect charity, which once had is not lost, whereas lesser degrees of it can be acquired and lost (c1 n9). Even in its less than perfect state, charity "does not allow the one who has it to sin criminally" (c1 n10).

Since the discussion of the virtues began with the question of whether Christ had them, Peter now asks whether Christ, in his love, observed the right order and loved everyone like his own self. If he did and willed salvation for all, how is it that not all are saved? (c3 n1). But to frame the question in this way is to presume that Christ had charity as those do who are not yet in the fatherland. Christ's charity however was always perfect, as of one who was already in heaven, where only those are loved whom God has predestined for salvation. It follows that "Christ loved the elect alone like himself and desired their salvation" (c3 n2).

After discussing so fully the love which human beings are to practice, Peter turns briefly to the question of the love by which God loves us, noting that it "is nothing else than the love by which we love him. For God's love is the divine *usia*, and it is by the same love that Father, Son, and Holy Spirit love each other and us" (dist. 32 c1 n1). Since it is the divine substance itself, this love is unchangeable and eternal. And yet it is unequal. Although this love extends to all that he has made, he loves only what is good in his creatures, and so "he loves rational creatures more; and of these, he loves more those that are members of his only-begotten, and much more the only-begotten himself" (c1 n2). This difference in the degree to which God loves even the elect does not indicate mutability in the divine will, but the variety of goods which he has willed to confer on the variety of his members from all eternity (c2).

This difference of degree in divine love is more safely understood, if one remembers that God's love can be considered in two ways: according to essence and efficacy. Variety is only relevant to efficacy, that is, to the greater or lesser good that God prepared for each one (c3 n1). As for the reprobates, one ought not to say simply that God loved them from all eternity; it is safe to say that God "loved them insofar as they were to be his work, that is, he loved what and of what kind he was going to make them" (c5).

Closing his reflections on charity with this charming image of the divine craftsman who loves his craft, Peter briefly outlines the four cardinal virtues of justice, fortitude, prudence, and temperance (dist. 33 c1 n1). His presentation of these virtues is entirely consistent with that of the theological virtues. He has chosen not to distract his students with irrelevant philosophical considerations, placing these virtues, too, squarely within the Christian pursuit of the imitation of Christ.[20]

A brief definition of these virtues as they apply in this life is taken from Augustine: "Justice consists in helping the wretched, prudence in guarding against treacheries, fortitude in bearing troubles, temperance in controlling evil pleasures" (c1 n2). These virtues allow one to live well in this life and to come to eternal life (c1 n3). Moreover, they were present in their perfection in Christ, who exercised them primarily as they will be in eternity (c2). It follows that these virtues can be practised in imitation of Christ.

As is already implicit in what has been said of Christ's practice of them, these virtues shall probably not cease in eternity, but they will have a different use (c3 n1). Justice will certainly survive and be made perfect

[20]See Colish, *Peter Lombard*, 2.504-505, on the alternative schemes of presentation by Peter's contemporaries that made more use of philosophical approaches in discussing these virtues.

in that it will acknowledge the beauty of the divine nature and become fully subject to it (c3 n2). As for the other three, it may be that they will also continue, but with other functions, since the ills which they counter in this life have no place in heaven, and so "there it will pertain to prudence to prefer or equate no other good to God; and to fortitude to adhere to him with the greatest steadfastness; and to temperance to take pleasure in no harmful defect" (c3 n3). In effect, this formulation seems to be little more than a charming confirmation that love alone will last.

There is authority for including the seven gifts of the Holy Spirit among the virtues, and so Peter next turns to these (dist. 34 c1). That they are virtues is attested by Ambrose, who notes that they exist also in the angels, and so will not cease in eternity (c2 n1). But they are better thought of as sanctifications of the Holy Spirit, that is, the various ways in which the Holy Spirit sanctifies the minds of the faithful (c2 nn1 and 2). That these gifts were in Christ is attested by Isaias (11, 2-3), who is taken to describe Christ as endowed with the spirit of wisdom, understanding, counsel, fortitude, knowledge, piety, and the fear of the Lord (c2 n2).

The inclusion of the fear of the Lord among the gifts seems problematic. There is good authority for the view that there shall be no fear in heaven, so how can this gift and the others be said to continue in eternity? (c3 nn2 and 3). The answer lies in the changed use of these virtues, too, in heaven. In this life, filial fear is a combination of fear of separation and reverence; in eternity, there is no fear of separation, "but only reverence, which is love mixed with submission" (c3 n4).

But since the issue of fear has been raised, Peter proceeds to a fuller treatment of the subject, perhaps because of its intimate connection to love in human experience. Fear is distinguished into worldly, human, servile, initial, and chaste or filial or friendly. By worldly or human fear, we fear the loss of worldly goods or the dangers of the flesh, and this fear leads to sin. By servile fear, we refrain from sin out of fear of hell; although insufficient, this fear is good and leads to an elementary practice of justice. Initial fear succeeds to the servile one when love begins to be the motive for doing the good. By chaste or friendly fear, we begin to fear separation from the Bridegroom: this is the fear that makes perfect and will endure for eternity (c4 n1).

The question remains as to whether fear and love can coexist. The answer appears to be that they can, so long as the fear is chaste, because such fear is entirely concerned with the Beloved and the possibility of the loss of his presence, so that "you embrace him and you long to enjoy him" (c5 n3).

Like the other gifts of the Holy Spirit, fear was also in Christ, but according to the use which it has in heaven, since "Christ did not fear to be separated from, or to offend, God, but he revered him before all things" (c8 n2). As for the fear of suffering which Christ seemed to express before his passion, it does not fall among the fears listed above and "may be called natural or human, which exists in all men, by which death makes one shiver and pain engenders fear" (c9 n2). In effect, this fear is only proof that Christ is perfectly human.

Among the other gifts of the Holy Spirit, Peter chooses to focus exclusively on the distinction and connection of wisdom, knowledge, and understanding, asking first how wisdom and knowledge differ (dist. 35 c1 n1). Consideration of a variety of Augustinian statements leads to the conclusion that wisdom is concerned with divine things and knowledge with human ones (c1 nn2-6). Understanding occupies a middle place between wisdom and knowledge, since it is concerned not only with eternal things, but also with the appearance of invisible and spiritual things in time. Wisdom contemplates the Creator alone; understanding looks also to the creature. But it is wisdom that engenders delight (c2 n1). An alternative summary of the relationship of these three gifts is to say that "knowledge is effective for the right administration of temporal things and for good relations among the wicked; understanding for enquiry about the Creator and invisible creatures; but wisdom for the contemplation of, and delectation in, eternal truth alone" (c2 n2).

Peter concludes his discussion of these gifts with the caveat that the gifts of understanding and knowledge are not to be confused with their natural counterparts that go under the same names. The latter are all from God by the benefit of creation, but these gifts come from the Holy Spirit and are given to the faithful for righteousness so that they may reform and assist their natural faculties (c3 n1). And as for the gift of wisdom, it is of God, but it is not the same wisdom by which God is wise (c3 n2).

The completion of the work of distinguishing the various virtues evokes next the question of whether they may be possessed separately (dist. 36 c1 n1). The answer appears to be that they cannot because all the virtues are the fruit of charity, and whoever has all the charities cannot but have all the virtues. They will grow in him as charity does (c1 nn1 and 2), and they will be equal in him in the mind, but not in exterior acts (c2).

The Ten Commandments

The reaffirmation of the primacy of charity leads next to the question of how the whole Law may be said to hang from it; this in turn serves as a transition to the treatment of the ten commandments (c3 n1). If the whole Law and the Prophets hang from the commandment of love, why are many ceremonial precepts of the Old Testament no longer observed? They are not observed because they were not given for the sake of justification, which is the fruit of charity, "but as a prefiguring of what was to come, and they were imposed as a burden; once truth came shining out, they ceased as if a shadow" (c3 n1). The spiritual understanding of the ceremonial precepts continues to be valid, and the same is true of the moral commandments. But all that is of enduring value in all these precepts issues from and is summarized in the ten commandments, which in turn can all be referred to the two commandments of love, so that they can only be fulfilled in love and must have love as their end (c3 n1). If time should be lacking to read the Bible or sermons, it more than suffices to preserve charity, from which all the commandments depend, "because it is the perfection and end of them all" (c3 n2).

That the ten commandments are contained within Christ's two commandments to love God and neighbour is shown by their distribution on their two tablets: "the three which are on the first tablet pertain to God, namely to the knowledge and love of the Trinity; the seven which are on the second tablet pertain to the love of neighbour" (dist. 37 c1 n1).

The first commandment forbids the worship of other gods and the making of graven things or likenesses (c1 n2). The second forbids the taking of God's name in vain. The allegorical content of this commandment is that Christ be held to be equal to the Father (c2 n3). The third commandment commands the sanctification of the Sabbath. Allegorically, the command is "that you hope for rest—here from vices and in the future in contemplation of God—from the Holy Spirit, that is, from God's charity and gift" (c2 n4). This brief outline of the first three commandments concludes with a reaffirmation of their Trinitarian character because "the first, which is about the worship of the one God, pertains to the Father, in whom is unity or authority; the second to the Son, in whom is equality; the third to the Holy Spirit, in whom is the fellowship of both" (c3 n2).

The other seven commandments, of the second tablet, pertain to love of neighbour (c4 n1). The first of these refers to the father according to the flesh, commanding the honouring of one's father and mother. This honour consists in reverence and the provision of necessities (c4 n2). The second commandment forbids killing—literally, only homicide is forbidden by it; spiritually and in light of an evangelical emendation, even the will to kill is forbidden by it (c4 n3). Mention of this emendation provides the occasion to reflect that even the letter of the Gospel expresses a spiritual understanding for a spiritual people, whereas the letter of the old Law expresses a carnal understanding for a carnal people, and so was in need of correction (c4 n4).

The third commandment of the second tablet forbids adultery, by which is now understood any use of the sexual organs outside of marriage (c4 n5). The fourth forbids theft and sacrilege, and every form of rapine and usury (c5 nn1-3). But the commandment would not have forbidden the pillaging of the Egyptians in which the children of Israel engaged before their exodus; they took the goods of the Egyptians at the command of God, the giver of the Law, and so committed no sin (c5 n4).

The fifth commandment forbids the bearing of false witness and is taken to include a general prohibition on lying and perjury (c6 n1), subjects on which Peter will engage in a detailed analysis because "the question regarding lying is a great one, and cannot be explained hurriedly" (c6 n2). Three different kinds of lies can be distinguished: to help someone, for amusement, or for malice. The first two are slight faults, especially in those who are not perfect; the third kind is awful for all (dist. 38 c1 n1). Examples of lying to protect someone are those of the Hebrew midwives in Exodus, who lied in order to save the lives of children, and of Raab, who lied to help the Hebrew spies. Both of these committed a sin, but it was venial and forgiven because of the good that followed. But this form of reasoning is risky and should not be extended to other sins, otherwise detestable evils may follow (c1 n3).

A more detailed classification of lies is offered from Augustine's *On Lying*, in which eight types of lies are distinguished. The first and most serious, which all ought to avoid, is lying in the teaching of religion. The second is a lie that hurts someone without aiding anyone. The third aids someone, but hurts another person. The fourth is lying for its own sake. The fifth is a flattering lie. All these ought to be avoided. The sixth is a lie to thieves looking for someone else's money. The seventh is a lie to avoid betraying a man to someone who wishes to kill him. The eighth is a lie to preserve someone from sexual sin. The list arranges the variety of lies in decreasing gravity of sin, but even the last will be avoided by anyone who wishes to avoid self-deception (c2).

After such a comprehensive survey of lies, the time seems ripe for a definition, again borrowed from Augustine: "A lie is a false signification of speech with the intention of deceiving" (c3). A lie, then, requires objective falsehood and subjective intention to deceive by uttering the falsehood. From the perspective of the liar, on the other hand, the objective element is not required; it is sufficient that he intend to deceive, even if what he believes to be a lie is, in fact, true (c4 n1). A classic example of this sort of discrepancy is the one of the Jew who says that Christ is God, not believing it in his heart; he is a liar who utters the truth (c4 n2).

Every lie is a sin, but it matters much whether one lies to help or to do harm, and whether one misleads another as to an earthly or a heavenly matter (c5 n1). And every lie is wrong not only because a man ought to say what is in his soul, but also because lying corrupts and does violence to language, which is meant for human sociability and communication (c5 n2). And so a lie is a sin, even if it helps or does no other harm (c5 nn3 and 4). But not every lie seems to be forbidden by the commandment and the amusing lie has not been discussed (c5 n5).

Since lying gives rise to error, it is worth noting that not every error is equally dangerous. To engender or cultivate error with regard to the obtaining of the kingdom of God is the most serious offence; other errors can be trifling sins (c6 n1). But ignorance and error are not to be confused, even if the one often gives rise to the other, and ignorance is not always a bad thing (c6 n2).

Finally, Peter cites the case of Jacob, who passed himself off to his blind father as Esau, his older brother. On the authority of Augustine, Jacob is excused because he carried out the fraud in obedience to his mother, who had commanded him to do so on the counsel of the Holy Spirit (c6 n3). Aside from providing a key in which to read an important scriptural story, this consideration of Jacob's case has the effect of reminding the reader about the risks of rushing to judgement without knowing all the circumstances of a case.

Perjury is a lie made under oath (dist. 39 c1). It is a debated question whether one who swears to a lie unwittingly is guilty of perjury (c2). The better view seems to be that perjury is incurred in such a case because the person was careless in affirming under oath something of whose truth he had not made certain (c3 nn1 and 2).

Is it evil to swear oaths at all? Not if they are necessary to achieve some good, such as to assert one's innocence, to make peace, or to persuade others of something which is good for them (c4 n1). But the Lord forbids the swearing of unnecessary oaths (c4 nn3 and 4).

If one has to swear an oath, is it preferable to swear by creatures or by the Creator? In the Old Testament, weak people were allowed to swear by the Creator, lest they extend undue honour to the creature, but those firm in faith were allowed to swear even by creatures; in the Gospel, Christ forbade swearing by a creature (c5). Certainly, to swear by God is more binding (c6). And the effect of swearing by God is to call God as a witness (c6), and sometimes has the effect of binding over some goods or persons before God as a pledge of the truth of what is being sworn (c7 nn3 and 4). Although a Christian may not swear by false gods, he may rely on the good oath of another who does so (c9 n1).

Not every oath is to be kept. An oath sworn against faith or charity, if it would make for a bad outcome, is to be changed, not fulfilled (c9 n1). Impious oaths may be rescinded, since they bind one to sin (c9 n2). Even merely careless oaths ought not to be kept, if keeping them will make for a worse outcome; perjury should be incurred to avoid a greater crime (c9 n3). One who swears carelessly commits a grave sin, but the observance of an oath that turns out to be unjust would add a second grave sin, and this ought to be avoided (c9 n4).

Artfulness in swearing is also not to be practised. If clever wording is used to say one thing and mean another, the oath is to be interpreted in the sense in which it is understood by the one who receives it (c11). Finally, one should not compel another to swear an oath, if he knows that the other will lie; to do this is akin to murder (c12).

Returning to his outline of the commandments, Peter lists the last two on the second tablet, which forbid desire for a neighbour's wife and coveting a neighbour's goods. These prohibitions might have been taken as included under the earlier prohibitions against adultery and theft, but they are listed separately to brand as evil not only the deed, but also the desire (dist. 40 c1 n1). This brief reflection nicely closes the discussion of all that has gone before concerning the virtues with a reminder that, in the practice of virtue and the avoidance of vice, the person's inner disposition is always as relevant as the outward action.

This long reflection on the Law evokes for Peter a final pondering on its relationship to the Gospel. He has no hesitation in concurring in the judgement that even the Decalogue, which he has just expounded, can be termed the letter that kills because its prohibition of sin has the effect of increasing concupiscence and transgression, in the absence of grace, "which grace is not as abundant in the Law as it is in the Gospel." (c2).

The Gospel is superior to the Law because it promises heavenly things rather than earthly ones. And the sacraments of the Gospel confer grace, while those of the Law only signified it. The moral commandments of the Law remain in the Gospel, but more fully (c3 n1). This rather cool evaluation of the Law sets the stage for the next Book of the *Sentences*, concerned principally with the grace-bearing sacraments of the new dispensation, which can take the sting away from the literalness of the Law. To close his third Book, Peter yields to the poetic temptation to affirm once more the primacy of charity, here with regard to the commandments:

> You have heard the ten chords of the lute which have been imposed on both sexes; they are to be plucked with charity, so that the wild beasts of the vices may be killed (c3 n2).

* * *

The third book of the *Sentences*, for a variety of reasons (at some of which Dante hints in the dedication), has been the most congenial in which to become immersed, and so it is perhaps the hardest to let go. Without Jean Hoff's unfailingly gracious encouragement to release it, in a version which owes to her more than I can properly acknowledge, I might still be holding it firmly in my grasp. I renew my thanks to the Frati Editori di Quaracchi, for the "placet" to translate the *Sentences* from Fr. Brady's edition. Professor Joseph W. Goering, of St. Michael's College and the University of Toronto, has continued in his role of benevolent censor: he says all the right things about the importance of the project (as his *socii* in the classroom purportedly attest) and gently ensures that, however glacially, the thing moves on. Fred Unwalla, as ever, is to be thanked for the glorious colour scheme.

This third book of the *Sentences* is dedicated to Francesca, third of my children. Like her brothers, Francesca has not shown any marked inclination to commune with the Lombard, but the topics of the book are ones with which she has been wrestling in a variety of interesting contexts of her own. With my jaundiced eye, I cannot but think that, in this, she is an indirect beneficiary of Peter's work, so it is a special pleasure to present her with this sign of my paternal affection.

Giulio Silano
St. Michael's College, Toronto
Exaltation of the Holy Cross, 2008

Chapter Headings

HERE BEGIN THE CHAPTERS OF THE THIRD BOOK

[DISTINCTION I]
Ch. 1 Why the Son took on flesh, and not the Father or the Holy Spirit.
2 Whether the Father or the Holy Spirit could have become incarnate.
3 Whether the Son, who alone took on flesh, did something that the Father or the Holy Spirit did not do.

[DISTINCTION II]
Ch. 1 (4) Why he took the whole human nature, and what is understood by the term nature.
2 (5) On the union of Word and flesh through the soul.
3 (6) That the Word took on flesh and soul at the same time, nor was the flesh conceived before it was taken on.

[DISTINCTION III]
Ch. 1 (7) On the flesh that was taken, what it was like before.
2 (8) That no one here is without sin, apart from the Virgin.
3 (9) Why Christ did not pay tithes in Abraham, as Levi did.
4 (10) For what reason Christ's flesh is said not to have been sinful, but like sinful flesh.

[DISTINCTION IV]
Ch. 1 (11) Why the incarnation is attributed to the Holy Spirit, even though it is the work of the whole Trinity.
2 (12) For what reason Christ is said to have been conceived and born of the Holy Spirit.
3 (13) Why the Apostle says that Christ was made, but we profess that he was born.

[DISTINCTION V]
Ch. 1 (14) Whether a person or nature took on a person or nature, and whether God's nature became incarnate.
2 (15) Whether the divine nature ought to be said to have been made flesh.

3 (16) Why [the Word] did not take the person of a man, even though it took a man; but some strive to prove the contrary.

[DISTINCTION VI]

Ch. 1 (17) On the meaning of these expressions: God is man, God was made man, etc. He sets out three opinions.

2 (18) The first is the opinion of those who say that, in the incarnation, some man was constituted from soul and flesh, and that man was made God, and God was made that man; and he sets out the authorities on the strength of which they say this.

3 (19) The second is the opinion of those who say that that man was constituted of three substances or two natures, and they profess this to be one person: only one simple person before the incarnation, and a composite one at the incarnation; and he sets out the authorities by which these defend themselves.

4 (20) The third is the opinion of those who not only deny [the existence of] a person composed of natures, but also disavow that there was any man or any substance there composed of soul and flesh. They say that these two things, namely soul and flesh, were united to the Word, not so that any substance or person was composed from those two things, but so that God might be clothed with those two as with clothing in order to appear to the eyes of mortals. These understand the order of the incarnation according to habit.

5 (21) Then he sets forth the authorities by which this opinion is strengthened.

6 (22) Four kinds of habit are distinguished.

[DISTINCTION VII]

Ch. 1 (23) Next, he sets out the reasons that seem to go against each of those opinions.

2 (24) In what sense Christ is called predestined.

3 (25) That he is not to be called the Lord's man.

[DISTINCTION VIII]

Ch. 1 (26) Whether the divine nature ought to be said to be born of the Virgin.

2 (27) On the twofold birth of Christ, who was born twice.

[DISTINCTION IX]

Ch. 1 (28) On the adoration to be shown to Christ's humanity.

[DISTINCTION X]
Ch. 1 (29) Whether Christ, according to his being a man, is a person or anything.
2 (30) Whether Christ is an adoptive son according to his being man.
3 (31) Whether the person or the nature was predestined.

[DISTINCTION XI]
Ch. 1 (32) Whether Christ is a creature or was made.
2 (33) On the perfidy and punishment of Arius.

[DISTINCTION XII]
Ch. 1 (34) Whether that man always was.
2 (35) Whether God could have taken some other form or from other than the stock of Adam.
3 (36) If it would have been possible for that man to sin or not be God.
4 (37) If God could have taken human form in the female sex.

[DISTINCTION XIII]
Ch. 1 (38) Concerning Christ's wisdom and grace as a man, and whether he could have made progress in them.

[DISTINCTION XIV]
Ch. 1 (39) Whether the soul of Christ had wisdom equal to God's and whether it knows all things that God knows.
2 (40) Why God did not give to that soul the power over, as well as the knowledge of, all things.

[DISTINCTION XV]
Ch. 1 (41) Of man's defects which Christ took on.
2 (42) On the propassion and passion of fear or sadness.
3 (43) On some rather obscure chapters of Hilary which appear to remove the sufferings of the passion from Christ's flesh.
4 (44) On Christ's sorrow and its cause according to the same.

[DISTINCTION XVI]
Ch. 1 (45) Whether in Christ there was the necessity to suffer and die, which is a general defect.
2 (46) Of the states of man, and what Christ took from each of them.

[DISTINCTION XVII]
Ch. 1 (47) Whether every prayer or will of Christ was fulfilled.
2 (48) On the wills of Christ according to his two natures.

3 (49) On some chapters of Ambrose and Hilary where Christ's doubt and fear are discussed.

[DISTINCTION XVIII]
Ch. 1 (50) Whether Christ merited for himself and for us, and what for himself, what for us.
2 (51) That Christ merited for himself the same things from his conception as through his passion.
3 (52) Concerning that text: He gave to him the name which is above all other names.
4 (53) Whether Christ could have had those things without any merit which he obtained by his merit.
5 (54) On the cause of the passion and death of Christ.

[DISTINCTION XIX]
Ch. 1 (55) How, by his death, Christ redeemed us from the devil and sin.
2 (56) Why God man and dead.
3 (57) How Christ redeemed us from punishment.
4 (58) How he bore our punishment.
5 (59) Whether Christ alone is to be called redeemer, as he alone is to be called mediator.
6 (60) On the [title] mediator.
7 (61) According to which nature is he mediator.

[DISTINCTION XX]
Ch. 1 (62) That he could have freed us in some other manner.
2 (63) Why rather in this manner.
3 (64) By what righteousness was the devil overcome.
4 (65) On the litigation among God, man, and the devil.
5 (66) On the handing over of Christ done by Judas, God, and the Jews.
6 (67) Whether Christ's passion is the work of God or of the Jews.

[DISTINCTION XXI]
Ch. 1 (68) Whether at Christ's death the soul or flesh was separated from the Word.
2 (69) For what reason Christ is said to have died or suffered.

[DISTINCTION XXII]
Ch. 1 (70) Whether Christ was a man in death.
2 (71) Whether in death Christ is a man wherever he is.
3 (72) That the whole Christ is everywhere, yet not wholly, just as he is whole man or God, yet not wholly.

4 (73) Whether those things which are said of God or of the Son of God can be said of that man or of the son of man.

[DISTINCTION XXIII]

Ch. 1 (74) Whether Christ had faith and hope, as he had charity.
2 (75) What is faith.
3 (76) In how many ways the term faith is used.
4 (77) What it is to believe God, or in a God, or in God.
5 (78) Of that formless quality of mind which is in the evil Christian.
6 (79) In what sense faith is said to be one.
7 (80) That faith properly concerns things which are not seen, and yet it is itself seen by the one in whom it is.
8 (81) Description of faith.
9 (82) Why faith alone is called the foundation.

[DISTINCTION XXIV]

Ch. 1 (83) How that text: 'When it comes to pass, you may believe' is to be understood.
2 (84) Whether Peter had faith in the passion when he saw that man suffer.
3 (85) Whether some things are known which are believed.

[DISTINCTION XXV]

Ch. 1 (86) On the faith of the ancients.
2 (87) On the faith of the simple.
3 (88) What it was sufficient to believe before [Christ's] coming.
4 (89) On the faith of Cornelius.
5 (90) On the equality of faith, hope, charity, and work.

[DISTINCTION XXVI]

Ch. 1 (91) On hope, what it is.
2 (92) With what is hope concerned.
3 (93) In what hope and faith differ.
4 (94) Whether faith or hope was in Christ.
5 (95) Whether the just in hell had faith and hope.

[DISTINCTION XXVII]

Ch. 1 (96) On the charity toward God and neighbour which is in Christ and in us.
2 (97) What is charity.
3 (98) Whether God and neighbour are loved by the same love.
4 (99) Why there are said to be two commandments of charity.
5 (100) On the manner of loving.

6 (101) On the fulfillment of that commandment: You shall love the Lord your God with your whole heart.
7 (102) That the one mandate is contained in the other.
8 (103) What things are to be loved in charity.

[DISTINCTION XXVIII]
Ch. 1 (104) Whether we are commanded to love all of our neighbour and our whole selves.
2 (105) That the love of angels is included in the love of neighbour.
3 (106) What is our neighbour.
4 (107) In what ways the term neighbour is used.

[DISTINCTION XXIX]
Ch. 1 (108) On the order of loving: what [comes] before, what after.
2 (109) Whether all men are to be loved equally.
3 (110) On the degrees of charity.

[DISTINCTION XXX]
Ch. 1 (111) Whether it is better to love enemies than friends.

[DISTINCTION XXXI]
Ch. 1 (112) Whether charity, once had, may be lost.
2 (113) Why faith, hope, and knowledge are said to be made void, and not charity, even though it too is only in part.
3 (114) Whether Christ observed the same order of charity as we do.

[DISTINCTION XXXII]
Ch. 1 (115) On God's charity.
2 (116) How God is said to love this one more and that one less.
3 (117) That God's love is to be regarded in two ways.
4 (118) Whether one is loved more or less by God at one time than at another.
5 (119) Whether God loved the reprobate from all eternity.

[DISTINCTION XXXIII]
Ch. 1 (120) On the four principal virtues.
2 (121) Whether these virtues were in Christ and are in the angels.
3 (122) On their uses.

[DISTINCTION XXXIV]
Ch. 1 (123) On the seven gifts of the Holy Spirit.
2 (124) Whether they are virtues and whether they are in the angels.
3 (125) Whether they were in Christ.

4 (126) On the distinction of fears.
5 (127) On chaste, servile, and initial fear.
6 (128) How chaste and servile fear differ.
7 (129) That servile and initial fear are called the beginning of wisdom, but differently.
8 (130) How chaste fear remains forever.
9 (131) Whether the fear of pain, which was in Christ, was servile or initial.

[DISTINCTION XXXV]
Ch. 1 (132) How wisdom and knowledge differ.
2 (133) In what wisdom differs from understanding.
3 (134) Whether the understanding and knowledge which are numbered among the gifts [of the Holy Spirit] are the ones which man has naturally.

[DISTINCTION XXXVI]
Ch. 1 (135) On the connection of the virtues which are not separated.
2 (136) Whether all the virtues are equally present in anyone in whom they are.
3 (137) How the whole Law hangs from charity.

[DISTINCTION XXXVII]
Ch. 1 (138) On the ten commandments: how they are contained in the two [commandments of charity].
2 (139) How an idol is said to be nothing in the world.
3 (140) Why remission of sins is properly said to be done in the Holy Spirit.
4 (141) On the spiritual and carnal senses of the Law.
5 (142) On theft.
6 (143) On lying.

[DISTINCTION XXXVIII]
Ch. 1 (144) On the threefold kind of lying.
2 (145) On the eight kinds of lying.
3 (146) What is lying.
4 (147) What is it to lie.
5 (148) That every lie is a sin, whether it is of help or not, and why.
6 (149) In what is it dangerous to err, in what not.

[DISTINCTION XXXIX]
Ch. 1 (150) On perjury.

2 (151) Whether there can be a perjury which is not a lie.
3 (152) On the triple manner of perjury.
4 (153) Whether it is an evil to swear oaths.
5 (154) On the oath which is sworn by creatures.
6 (155) Which oath is more binding, whether the one done 'by God,' or 'by creatures,' or 'by the Gospel.'
7 (156) What it means to say: By God.
8 (157) Concerning those who swear by false gods.
9 (158) That an oath or promise made against God is not to be kept.
10 (159) Whether he is a perjurer, who does not do what he has incautiously sworn.
11 (160) Concerning those who swear with verbal artfulness.
12 (161) Concerning him who compels another to swear.

[DISTINCTION XL]
Ch. 1 (162) Why the Law is said to restrain the hand, but not the spirit.
2 (163) What is the letter that kills.
3 (164) On the difference between the Law and the Gospel.

The *Sentences*, Book 3

On the Incarnation of the Word

Here Begins the Third Book

On the Incarnation of the Word

Let us now readily attend, with the whole consideration of our mind, to understanding and treating those things which pertain to the mystery of the Word made flesh, so that, with God revealing, we may be able to utter some little thing on these ineffable matters.

THE CONTENTS OF THIS VOLUME ARE PRESENTED IN A SUMMARY WAY. —In the first book, through the unassailable witness of the saints, we said something on the inexplicable mystery of the most high Trinity. Then, in the second book, observing the certain rules of authority, we indicated the order of the creation of things and the fall of man. Now, the order of reason requires that, in the third and fourth books, we discuss the restoration of man accomplished through the grace of the mediator of God and men,[1] and the sacraments of human redemption, by which man's bruises are bound up[2] and the wounds of sins are cured. In this way, the Samaritan may come to the one who is wounded,[3] the physician to the one who is sick,[4] grace to the one who is miserable.

Distinction I

And so, as the Apostle says: *When the fullness of time came, God sent his Son, made of a woman, made under the Law, so as to redeem those who were under the Law, that we might receive adoption as sons of God.*[1] Now, the time of fullness is called the time of grace, which took its beginnings from the coming of the Saviour. This is *the time of mercy*[2] and *the year of benignity*,[3] in which *grace and truth was made through Jesus*

[1]Cf. 1 Tim. 2, 5; Gal. 3, 20.
[2]Cf. Ps. 146, 3.
[3]Cf. Lk. 10, 33-34.
[4]Cf. Mt. 9, 12.

[1]Gal. 4, 4-5.
[2]Ps. 101, 14.
[3]Ps. 64, 12.

Christ:[4] *grace*, because through charity is fulfilled what was commanded in the Law; *truth*, because by Christ's advent is exhibited and achieved the promise of human redemption made of old. And so the sending of the Son is the incarnation itself.[5] For he was sent so that he appeared visible to the world in the form of a man, about which we have already spoken sufficiently.[6]

Chapter 1

1. WHY THE SON TOOK ON FLESH, AND NOT THE FATHER OR THE HOLY SPIRIT. But it is to be diligently noted why the Son took on flesh, and not the Father or the Holy Spirit: for the Son alone took on human form.

2. FIRST REASON. Which God's wisdom did by an entirely suitable order and high counsel, so that God, who had established the world in his wisdom, according to the text: *You made all things in wisdom, Lord,*[1] should in the same wisdom restore *the things which are in the heavens and those which are on earth.*[2] This wisdom is the woman of the Gospel who *lights the lamp* and finds *the tenth coin* which had been lost,[3] namely the Wisdom of the Father, which lit the lamp of human weakness with the light of its divinity and restored man, who was lost, marked with the name and image of the king.

3. SECOND REASON. And so also the Son was sent, and not the Father, because it was more fitting that the one be sent who is from another, than the one who is from no one; and the Son is from the Father, but the Father is not from anyone else.—AUGUSTINE. For as Augustine says, in the book *On the Trinity*: "He has no one from whom to be. ... Therefore, just as the Father begot and the Son was begotten, so also suitably the Father sent, the Son was sent. ... For the Word of God is aptly sent by him whose Word he is; he is sent by him of whom he was born; what was begotten is sent; but the Father, who sent, is from no one."[4] And so the Father is not sent lest, if he be sent, he be thought to be from another.

4. THIRD REASON. And so the Son, who is from the Father alone, was sent first; then also the Holy Spirit, who is from the Father and the Son; but the Son alone was sent in the flesh, not the Holy Spirit, just as not the Father. And this was done so that he who was Son of God in divinity should become son of man in humanity. Neither the Father nor the Holy

[4]Jn. 1, 17.
[5]Augustine, *In Ioannem*, tr. 40 n6; *De Trinitate*, bk 2 c5 n8.
[6]Bk 1 dist. 15, esp. in cc2 and 4.

[1]Ps. 103, 24.
[2]Cf. Eph. 1, 10.
[3]Cf. Lk. 15, 8-9.
[4]Augustine, *De Trinitate*, bk 4 c20 nn28-29.

Spirit was clothed with flesh lest one be the Son in divinity, another in humanity, and lest the same [person] be father and son, if God the Father were born of man.—*On Ecclesiastical Dogmas*. Hence in *On Ecclesiastical Dogmas*: "Neither the Father took on flesh, nor the Holy Spirit, but the Son alone, so that he who was Son of God in divinity should become son of man in humanity, lest the name of son pass to another, who would not be son by birth. And so the Son of God was made son of man, born according to the truth of nature Son of God from God, and according to the truth of nature son of man from man. In this way, the truth of the begotten would have the name of son, not by adoption, nor by title, but by being born in each birth, and the one Son would be true God and true man. Therefore we do not affirm two Christs, nor two sons, but the one Son who is God and man, whom we on that account call the only-begotten, abiding in two substances, according to the conferral of the truth of nature on him, with the natures being neither confused nor mixed, as the Timotheans[5] would have it, but united in partnership."[6] See, you have why the Son took on flesh, and not the Father or the Holy Spirit.

Chapter 2

WHETHER THE FATHER OR THE HOLY SPIRIT COULD HAVE BECOME INCARNATE OR COULD DO SO NOW. But if it is asked whether the Father or the Holy Spirit could have become incarnate, or could even do so now, it may be answered affirmatively: that the Father or the Holy Spirit could formerly and can now take on flesh and become man. For just as the Son was made man, so the Father or the Holy Spirit could and can be.

Chapter 3

1. WHETHER THE SON, WHO ALONE TOOK ON FLESH, DID SOMETHING THAT THE FATHER OR THE HOLY SPIRIT DID NOT DO. But perhaps some will say: Since the works of the Trinity are undivided,[1] if the Son took on flesh, so did the Father and the Holy Spirit, because, if the Son took on flesh, but the Father or the Holy Spirit did not, then the Father or the Holy Spirit does not do all that the Son does; but Father, and Son, and the Spirit of both "work all things together, equally, and in accord."[2]

2. RESPONSE. To which we say that the Son does nothing without the Father and the Holy Spirit, but the operation of these three is one, undivided, and in no way dissimilar, and yet the Son took on flesh, and not the

[5]Followers of Timothy, Monophysite archbishop of Alexandria.
[6]Gennadius, *Liber seu diffinitio ecclesiasticorum dogmatum*, c2.

[1]Augustine, *Enchiridion*, c38.
[2]Augustine, *De Trinitate*, bk 13 c11 n15.

Father or the Holy Spirit. Nevertheless it was the Trinity which worked this taking on of flesh, as Augustine says in the book *On Faith to Peter*: "We were reconciled *through* the Son alone according to the flesh, but not *to* the Son alone according to divinity. For the Trinity reconciled us to itself by that same Trinity making the Word alone flesh."[3] And so the Trinity worked the taking on of flesh, but on the Word, not on the Father or the Holy Spirit. For if the Father had worked the taking on of flesh on himself, and the Son on himself, or the Father on the Son, and the Son on the Father, then the work of both would be divided and would no longer be the same.—AUGUSTINE, IN BOOK 1 OF *ON THE TRINITY*. But just as the unity of substance of the three is inseparable and undivided, as Augustine says in the book *On the Trinity*, so also is their operation: "and yet Catholic authors did not teach that this same Trinity was born of the Virgin, and was crucified and buried, but only the Son; nor that the same Trinity descended over Jesus in the form of a dove, but only the Holy Spirit;[4] nor that the same Trinity said from heaven: *You are my Son*,[5] but only the Father's voice was addressed to the Son. And yet Father, Son, and Holy Spirit, as they are inseparable, so they also work inseparably. This is my faith because it is the Catholic faith."[6]—And so, although the Son alone took on flesh, yet he worked that same incarnation with the Father and the Holy Spirit.

DISTINCTION II

Chapter 1 (4)

1. WHY HE TOOK THE WHOLE HUMAN NATURE, AND WHAT IS UNDERSTOOD BY THE TERM HUMANITY OR HUMAN NATURE. And because the whole human nature was corrupted in man by sin, he took it whole, that is, soul and flesh, so that he might sanctify and make it whole.—JEROME. Jerome teaches clearly that by the term human nature or humanity are to be understood soul and flesh; in the *Exposition of the Catholic Faith*, he says: "We confess that the one person of the Son is in Christ in such a way as to say that there are two perfect and whole substances, that is, of the divinity and of the humanity, [the latter of] which is comprised of the soul and the body."[1] See, he openly shows that soul and body are understood by the term humanity, and the Son of God is understood to have taken

[3]Rather, Fulgentius, *De fide ad Petrum*, c2 n23.
[4]Cf. Lk. 3, 22.
[5]Lk. 3, 22.
[6]Augustine, *De Trinitate*, bk 13 c4 n7.

[1]That is, Pelagius, *Libellus fidei ad Innocentium Papam*, n4.

on these two when we read that he took on human form, or humanity, or human nature.

2. HE TOUCHES UPON THE ERROR OF SOME WHO UNDERSTAND HUMANITY IMPROPERLY. And so they are in error who contend that, whenever Christ's humanity is recalled, it is not the substance that is understood by the term humanity, but some property by which he is called a man.—JOHN OF DAMASCUS. For John of Damascus says: "It is truly to be understood that the terms divinity and humanity are representative of the substances, namely of the natures."[2]

3. For with regard to Christ nature is not taken in the same way as it is when we say that the nature of all men is one. The same John clearly shows this, ascribing a different reason for using this word when human nature is said to be in Christ, and when the nature of all men is said to be one. For he says: "When we say that the nature of men is one, it is to be understood that we say this without considering the relationship of soul and body. For it is impossible to say that" the Lord's "body and soul, when mutually compared, are of one nature. But because there are many human persons, and they all take the same kind of nature—for all are composed of body and soul, and all share the nature of the soul and possess the substance of the body—we call the common form of the several and different persons one nature, namely of every person having two natures and completely existing in two natures, namely of soul and body. In the Lord Jesus Christ, however, it is not a matter of accepting a common form. For another such was never made, nor is made now, nor ever will be made. But Christ, constituted from divinity and humanity, in his divinity and humanity, is both perfect God and perfect man."[3]

4. And so God took on the whole human nature, that is, soul and flesh, and the properties and accidents of both; he did not take flesh without soul, nor soul without reason, as the heretics would have it,[4] but flesh and soul with the senses pertaining to them.—Hence John of Damascus says: "The Word of God took on all things which he had planted in our nature, namely body and intellectual soul, and their properties. For he in his wholeness took on me in my wholeness so that he should graciously grant salvation to all of me. For whatever is not capable of being taken on is incurable."[5]

[2]John of Damascus, *De fide orthodoxa*, bk 3 c4.
[3]Ibid., bk 3 c3.
[4]Cf. Gennadius, *Liber seu diffinitio ecclesiasticorum dogmatum*, c2.
[5]John of Damascus, *De fide orthodoxa*, bk 3 c6.

Chapter 2 (5)

1. ON THE UNION OF WORD AND FLESH THROUGH THE SOUL. And so the Son of God took on flesh and soul, but the flesh through the soul.—JOHN OF DAMASCUS: "The Word of God was united to the flesh by means of the intellect."[1] For the divine essence is of such great fineness and simplicity that it would not have been suitable for it to become united to a body formed from the mud of the earth, other than by means of the rational essence.

2. And that union was so inexplicable that even John [the Baptist], who had been sanctified *from the womb*,[2] confessed that he was not worthy *to untie the strap of* Jesus' *shoe*,[3] because he was not sufficient to investigate and explain to others the manner of that union.

3. AUGUSTINE, *ON THE CHRISTIAN COMBAT*: "And so do not listen to those who say that the Son of God did not take on true humanity, nor was born of a woman, but that he showed false flesh and a fake image of a body to on-lookers."[4] They fall into this error because they fear what cannot happen, namely that the truth and substance of God be polluted by human flesh. "And yet they preach that our visible sun spreads its rays over all manner of offal, but keeps them clean and pure. Therefore, if pure things which are visible can be touched by visible things which are unclean and not share their pollution, how much more did the unchangeable and invisible Truth, receiving a soul through the spirit and a body through the soul, take on the whole man without contamination to itself and free him from all infirmities?"[5]—See, he says here that God's wisdom took on a soul through the spirit and a body through the soul. For the spirit, namely the higher part of the soul,[6] is closer to God by a greater likeness than the soul, namely the same thing in its lower part, and the soul is closer than the body; and so, not unsuitably, the soul is said to be taken on through the spirit, and the body through the soul.

Chapter 3 (6)

1. THAT THE WORD TOOK ON FLESH AND SOUL AT THE SAME TIME, NOR WAS THE FLESH CONCEIVED BEFORE IT WAS TAKEN ON. But if it is asked whether the Word took on flesh and soul at the same time, or the soul before the flesh, or the flesh before the soul, and whether that flesh was

[1]John of Damascus, *De fide orthodoxa*, bk 3 c3.
[2]Cf. Lk. 1, 15.
[3]Cf. Mk. 1, 17.
[4]Augustine, *De agone christiano*, c18 n20.
[5]Ibid.
[6]See above, Bk 2 dist. 24 cc4-5.

first conceived in the Virgin's womb and afterwards taken on, we say most truly and without any ambiguity that, from the moment that God took on human form, he took on the whole man, and joined to himself soul and flesh together; nor was the flesh first conceived and then taken on, but it was conceived as it was taken and taken as it was conceived.

2. AUGUSTINE. Hence Augustine, in the book *On Faith to Peter*: "Hold most firmly, and do not at all doubt, that Christ's flesh was not conceived without divinity in the Virgin's womb before it was taken by the Word, but that God the Word himself was conceived by taking on his own flesh, and that the flesh itself was conceived by the incarnation of the Word."[1]—The same [Augustine] in the book *On the Trinity*: "He would not be mediator of God and men, unless the same were God, the same man, one and true in both."[2] "The whole Trinity, whose will and operation is one, made the servile[3] form which was taken by the Son alone."[4] "But it was not the case that the flesh was first taken in the Virgin's womb and divinity came into the flesh afterwards. Instead, as soon as the Word came into the womb, preserving the truth of its own nature, *it was made flesh*[5] and was perfect man, that is, he was born in the truth of the flesh and the soul."[6]—GREGORY. Concerning this, Gregory too, in the *Moralia*, says: "At the angel's annunciation and the coming of the Spirit, as soon as the Word was in the womb, the Word was flesh within the womb."[7]

DISTINCTION III

Chapter 1 (7)

1. ON THE FLESH WHICH THE WORD TOOK, WHAT IT WAS LIKE BEFORE AND WHEN IT WAS TAKEN. Concerning the Word's flesh, it is also asked whether, before it was conceived, it was in bondage to sin, and whether it was so when it was taken by the Word.—It can surely be said and is necessary to believe, according to the agreement of the testimony of the saints, that "it was first subject to sin,"[1] like the rest of the Virgin's flesh, but it was so cleansed by the work of the Holy Spirit that, immune from all contagion of sin, it might be united to the Word; the punishment alone remained, but by the taker's will and not by necessity.

[1]Fulgentius, *De fide ad Petrum*, c18 n59.
[2]Rather, Leo I, *Epistola 35*, c3.
[3]Cf. Phil. 2, 7.
[4]Cf. Augustine, *De Trinitate*, bk 2 c5 n9.
[5]Cf. Jn. 1, 14.
[6]Gregory, *Epistola 67*.
[7]Gregory, *Moralia*, bk 18 c52 n85.

[1]Cf. Augustine, *De peccatorum meritis seu de baptismo parvulorum*, bk 2 c24.

2. THAT NOT ONLY THAT FLESH, BUT ALSO THE HOLY VIRGIN, WAS CLEANSED FROM ALL CONTAGION OF SIN BY THE HOLY SPIRIT. The Holy Spirit, by descending upon her, entirely purified Mary too from sin and also freed her from the urge to sin, either by entirely removing the urge itself, as some would have it, or by so weakening and reducing it that she afterwards had no further occasion to sin.

3. The Spirit also prepared in the Virgin the power of begetting without the seed of a man. For this is what the words of the Gospel teach, when the angel speaks to the Virgin, saying: *The Holy Spirit will come upon you, and the power of the Most High will overshadow you, and the holy thing that will be born from you shall be called the Son of God.*[2] The holy Virgin responds to him: *Behold the handmaiden of the Lord; let it be done to me according to your word.*[3]—JOHN OF DAMASCUS. John, in expounding this, says: "And so, after the assent of the holy Virgin, the Holy Spirit descended upon her, according to the word of the Lord which the angel had spoken, purified her and prepared both the power to receive and the power to beget the Word of the divinity. And then the Wisdom and Power of the most high God[4] existing in itself, that is, the Son of God, *homousios* or consubstantial with the Father, overshadowed her, like a divine seed. From the most holy and most pure blood of the same Virgin, he did not procreate, but created through the Holy Spirit, and joined to himself, flesh of our ancient mixture,[5] animated with a rational and intellective soul. Therefore he is at once flesh, at once flesh of God: at once flesh animated with a rational and intellective soul, at once flesh of the Word of God animated with a rational and intellective soul."[6]

4. From these words, what we said earlier[7] is made very clear, namely that the flesh of the Word was conceived and taken at the same time, and that the same flesh, indeed the whole Virgin, with the coming of the Holy Spirit, was made chaste from all shame of sin.—AUGUSTINE, *ON FAITH TO PETER*: And on her was conferred the power "to beget in a new manner, so that" the conception of God and man should be completed in the womb of the Virgin "without joining with a man, without lust of the conceiver."[8] "For that flesh, which God deigned to unite to himself from the Virgin, was conceived without vice and born without sin. And yet do not believe

[2]Lk. 1, 35.
[3]Lk. 1, 38.
[4]Cf. 1 Cor. 1, 24.
[5]Cf. 1 Cor. 5, 7.
[6]John of Damascus, *De fide orthodoxa*, bk 3 c2.
[7]In dist. 2 c3.
[8]Fulgentius, *De fide ad Petrum*, c2 n17.

this flesh to be of a celestial, or airy, or of some other nature, but of the same nature as the flesh of all men."[9]

Chapter 2 (8)

HE CONFIRMS BY AUTHORITY THAT FROM THAT TIME THE VIRGIN WAS IMMUNE FROM SIN. And Augustine, in the book *On Nature and Grace*, clearly shows that the holy Virgin from that time was immune from all sin, saying: "With the exception of the holy Virgin Mary, concerning whom I wish to exclude all question when discussing sin for the honour due to the Lord (for from that time forth we know that more grace was given to her to conquer sin completely because she deserved to conceive and bear the one who most certainly was without sin); therefore, with the exception of this Virgin, if all the saints, both men and women, could be gathered together, and they were asked whether they had any sin, what would they answer, other than what John said: *If we say that we are without sin, we deceive ourselves*?"[1,2]—AUGUSTINE, *ON FAITH TO PETER*: "That Virgin was visited and filled by a singular grace so that she might bear as fruit of her womb the one whom the universe has as its Lord from the beginning";[3] "so that what was born from the offspring of the first man might derive only the origin of kind, not also of crime."[4]

Chapter 3 (9)

1. WHY CHRIST DID NOT PAY TITHES IN ABRAHAM, AS LEVI DID, EVEN THOUGH THE FLESH WHICH HE TOOK WAS IN BONDAGE TO SIN IN ABRAHAM. But since that flesh, whose singular excellence words are not adequate to explain, before it was united to the Word, would have been in bondage to sin in Mary and in the others from whom it was derived by propagation, it may not unworthily appear that it would have been subject to sin in Abraham, whose entire flesh was subject to sin. And so it usual to ask why Levi, but not Christ, paid tithes in Abraham,[1] since each of them was in Abraham's loins according to material reason when Abraham was tithed, that is, gave tithes to Melchisedech.[2]

2. IN WHAT SENSE LEVI IS SAID TO BE TITHED IN ABRAHAM. For the Apostle says that Levi was tithed in Abraham as if in respect to a material

[9]Fulgentius, *De fide ad Petrum*, c2 n15.

[1]1 Jn. 1, 8.
[2]Augustine, *De natura et gratia*, c36 n42.
[3]Fulgentius, *De fide ad Petrum*, c2 n17.
[4]Augustine, *De Trinitate*, bk 13 c18 n23.

[1]Cf. Hebr. 7, 9-10.
[2]Cf. Gen. 14, 18-20.

cause because, just as Abraham is shown by that tithing to be less than Melchisedech, to whom he personally pays tithe, so too was the Levitical order, which was in Abraham according to seminal reason and descended from him through the concupiscence of the flesh. But Christ was not tithed because, although he was there [in the loins of Abraham] according to the flesh, yet he did not descend from there according to the common law, namely through the lust of the flesh; just as also in Adam *all sinned*,[3] but not Christ.—AUGUSTINE: LEVI WAS THERE IN SOME MANNER BY WHICH CHRIST WAS NOT. Hence Augustine, in *On Genesis*: "Just as those who were in his loins sinned when Adam sinned, so also those who were in his loins were tithed when Abraham paid tithes. But this does not follow in the case of Christ, even though he was in the loins of Adam and Abraham, because he did not descend from them by the concupiscence of the flesh."[4] "And so, although Levi and Christ were in Abraham's loins according to the flesh when he was tithed, they were not equally tithed on that account, because Christ was there in some manner by which Levi was not."[5] "Indeed, Levi was there according to that seminal reason by which he would come into his mother through sexual intercourse; Christ's flesh was not there according to this reason, even though Mary's flesh was there according to it."[6] "Levi was tithed in Abraham who was in Abraham's loins as Abraham had been in his own father's, that is, who was born from his father Abraham as Abraham had been born of his own father, namely through the law of the flesh and invisible concupiscence."[7]

Chapter 4 (10)

1. FOR WHAT REASON CHRIST'S FLESH IS SAID IN SCRIPTURE NOT TO HAVE BEEN SINFUL, BUT LIKE SINFUL FLESH: WHERE IT IS REVEALED WHY THE FLESH WAS NOT IN BONDAGE TO SIN IN THE CASE OF CHRIST. And so Christ is rightly said to have taken on 'the first-fruits of our mass,'[1] because he did not take the flesh of sin, but the likeness of sinful flesh. For as the Apostle says, *God sent his Son in the likeness of sinful flesh.*[2] For the Word took flesh like that of a sinner as to punishment, but not as to fault, and so it was not sinful.—AUGUSTINE, ON THE WORDS OF THE APOSTLE: "But all other flesh of men is sinful: only his is not sinful flesh because his Mother conceived him through grace, and not through concupiscence. And yet it has *the likeness of sinful flesh* through its ability to

[3]Cf. Rom. 5, 12.
[4]Ordinary gloss, on Heb. 7, 10.
[5]Cf. Augustine, *De Genesi ad litteram*, bk 10 c19 n34.
[6]Ibid., c20 n35.
[7]Ibid., c20 n36.

[1]John of Damascus, *De fide orthodoxa*, bk 3 c2.
[2]Rom. 8, 3.

suffer and die, because it suffered hunger, thirst, and suchlike."[3] "And so, although his flesh is the same as ours, yet it was not made in the womb in the same way as ours. For it was sanctified in the womb and was born without sin, and also he did not ever sin in it. And so it is similar to our flesh as to punishment, but not as to the quality of sin,"[4] because (ORIGEN:) "it did not at all have the same pollution as flesh which is conceived from the movement of concupiscence,"[5] "nor was it born from carnal pleasure."[6]—HE SETS OUT THREE CAUSES. *And so he came to a spotless body,*[7] which had been conceived apart from the concupiscence of lust; nor did he have in himself that vice which is the cause of sin in others; nor did he sin in it. And so it is truly said that the flesh of the Word was not in bondage to sin in the case of Christ.

2. SOMETHING APPEARS TO BE IN CONTRADICTION WITH THAT SENTENCE IN WHICH IT WAS SAID THAT THE FLESH OF CHRIST WAS NOT CONCEIVED BEFORE IT WAS TAKEN. But what Augustine says, in *On John*, appears to go against that sentence in which we said above[8] that the flesh of the Word was not conceived before it was taken. We there read: *Destroy this temple and in three days I will raise it up again. Then the Jews said: This temple was built in forty-six years, and you will raise it up again in three days?*[9] Augustine says: "This number is suitable for the perfecting of the Lord's body because, as the natural philosophers say, the form of the human body is completed in as many days."[10]

3. By reason of these words, some have presumed to say that the form of the Lord's body, like other bodies, was completed and differentiated according to the shapes of the different parts in that many days, and the Word of God immediately united to himself flesh and soul. And it is in this way, they say, that that number is suitable for the perfecting of the Lord's body.

4. But there is another reason for that statement, from which a sound understanding of it flows. For Augustine did not say it because, as soon as that flesh was sanctified by the work of the Holy Spirit and separated from the rest, it was united to the Word of God with the soul, so that he was perfect and true God and perfect and true man; but because the differentiation of the parts of the Lord's body, at the very moment of conception and union of God and man, was so delicate and small that it could

[3]Augustine, *Sermo 152*, n8.
[4]Ambrosiaster, *In Epistolas s. Pauli*, Rom. 8, 3.
[5]Origen, *In Epistolam ad Romanos* 8, 3.
[6]Augustine, *De diversis quaestionibus 83*, q66 n6.
[7]Origen, *In Epistolam ad Romanos* 8, 3; cf. Wis. 8, 20.
[8]Dist. 2 c3 n1.
[9]Jn. 2, 19-20.
[10]Cf. Augustine, *De Trinitate*, bk 4 c5 n9.

scarcely be subjected to human gaze; but in those days which Augustine recalls, it had become complete and observable.

5. HOW HE WHO WAS EVERYWHERE WAS IN THE VIRGIN.—JOHN OF DAMASCUS. And so, as John says: "The Word was made flesh, and did not abandon its own incorporeality; and it was entirely made flesh, and it was entirely uncircumscribed. In respect to its body, it is made less and contracts; in respect to its divinity, it is uncircumscribed, the flesh not being coextensive with the uncircumscribed divinity."[11] "And so he was in all things and over all things, and he existed in the womb of his holy Mother; but he was in her by the act of the incarnation."[12]

DISTINCTION IV

Chapter 1 (11)

1. WHY IN SCRIPTURE THE INCARNATION, WHICH IS THE WORK OF THE TRINITY, IS MORE OFTEN ATTRIBUTED TO THE HOLY SPIRIT, AND [CHRIST] IS EVEN SAID TO HAVE BEEN CONCEIVED AND BORN OF THE HOLY SPIRIT. But since the incarnation of the Word, as was discussed above,[1] is truly the operation of Father, Son, and Holy Spirit, it seems to us worthy of investigation why in Scripture this work is more often attributed to the Holy Spirit, and Christ is said to have been conceived and born of the Holy Spirit.—For the work of the incarnation is more often attributed to the Holy Spirit not because he did it alone, without the Father and the Son, but because the Holy Spirit is the charity and gift of Father and Son: it was in God's ineffable charity that God's *Word was made flesh*,[2] and it was by God's inestimable gift that the Son of God joined to himself *the form of a servant*.[3] And so the frequent mention of the Holy Spirit does not exclude the Father or the Son from that work; it is rather the case that, by the naming of the one, the three are understood, as often happens with reference to other works.

2. AUGUSTINE: THE STATING OF THE QUESTION. Hence Augustine, raising a question with regard to this, determines it in the following way in the *Enchiridion*, saying: "That creature which the Virgin conceived and bore, although it pertained to the person of the Son alone, was nevertheless the work of the whole Trinity. Since this is so, and the works of the Trinity are not severable, why is the Holy Spirit alone named in making

[11]John of Damascus, *De fide orthodoxa*, bk 3 c7.
[12]Ibid.

[1]Dist. 1 c3 n2.
[2]Cf. Jn. 1, 14.
[3]Cf. Phil. 2, 7.

them?"—SOLUTION. "Or is it that, when one of the three is named with reference to any work, the Trinity is understood to work everything? This is truly the case, and it can be taught by examples."[4] You have heard the question being stated and its exposition.

Chapter 2 (12)

IN WHAT SENSE CHRIST IS SAID TO HAVE BEEN CONCEIVED AND BORN OF THE HOLY SPIRIT.—AUGUSTINE, IN THE *ENCHIRIDION*. "But we must not dwell on this too long. For the other question urges us: how Christ is said to have been 'born of the Holy Spirit,' since he is not in any way the son of the Holy Spirit. ... Are we then to say that the Holy Spirit is the father of Christ the man, so that God the Father would have begotten the Word, and the Holy Spirit would have begotten the man? And that, from these two substances, there was one Christ, on the one hand, Son of God the Father according to his being Word, and, on the other hand, son of the Holy Spirit according to his being man, because the Holy Spirit, as it were his father, had begotten him from the Virgin Mother? Who shall dare to say this, since it is so absurd that believers' ears are not able to bear it? And so, ... since we profess that Christ was born of the Holy Spirit from the Virgin Mary, it is difficult to explain how he is not the son of the Holy Spirit, but is the son of the Virgin, even though he was born of the one and the other. Undoubtedly, he was not born from him as from a father, but he was from her as from a mother."[1]

2. THAT WHATEVER IS BORN OF SOME THING IS NOT NECESSARILY CALLED ITS SON. "But it is not to be granted that whatever is born of some thing is necessarily to be called the son of that thing. I pass over the fact that a son is born of a man otherwise than a hair, a louse, a worm in the stomach is, and none of these is a son. I pass over this because it is unsuitable to compare them to the great matter under consideration; but, surely, no one would rightly call those who are born *from water and the Holy Spirit*[2] the sons of water, but they are called sons of God the Father and of Mother Church. In the same way, Christ was born of the Holy Spirit, and yet he is not the son of the Holy Spirit. (NOR ARE ALL THOSE WHO ARE CALLED SOMEONE'S SONS NECESSARILY BORN OF HIM.) Conversely, it does not necessarily follow that all who are called someone's sons are also to be said to be born of him, like those who are adopted.

[4]Augustine, *Enchiridion*, c38.

[1]Augustine, *Enchiridion*, c38.
[2]Cf. Jn. 3, 5.

Some are even called *sons of hell*,[3] not because they are born from it, but because they are prepared for it."[4]

3. "And so, one thing may be born of another, and yet not so as to be its son; on the other hand, everyone who is called a son is not born of the one whose son he is called: it is clear that this manner in which Christ is born, of Mary as son and of the Holy Spirit not as son, indicates to us the grace of God. By this grace, a man, without any preceding merits, at the very beginning of his human existence, was joined to the Word of God into such unity of person that the same was the Son of God who was son of man, and the son of man who was Son of God; and that, in the taking up of human nature, that grace became in some way natural to that man and by it he was not able to commit any sin. This grace is signified by the Holy Spirit because he is specifically God in such a way as to be also *Gift of God*."[5,6]—"And so, through the fact that Christ's nativity is said to be of the Holy Spirit, what else is shown than that grace itself,"[7] by which man, "in a wonderful and ineffable manner, is joined with the Word of God"[8] and formed and corporeally filled with divine grace.[9]

4. ANOTHER REASON WHY HE IS SAID TO BE BORN OF THE HOLY SPIRIT. —AUGUSTINE, IN THE *ENCHIRIDION*. Christ can also be said to have been born of the Holy Spirit in respect to his humanity "because he made him: for as the Apostle says,[10] insofar as he was man, he was also made."[11]—JEROME IN THE *EXPOSITION OF THE CATHOLIC FAITH*. And so he is said to have been conceived and born of the Holy Spirit not because the Holy Spirit stood "in the place of the seed"[12] to the Virgin: for what was born did not take seed from the substance of the Holy Spirit; but because, by the grace of God and the operation of the Holy Spirit, what was united to the Word was taken from the flesh of the Virgin.

5. AMBROSE. Also, in the Gospel, according to this understanding, we read of Mary that *she was found to be with child of the Holy Spirit*.[13] Indicating the reason for this statement, Ambrose, in *On the Holy Spirit*, book 2, says: "What is from something is either from its substance or from its power. From substance, like the Son who proceeds from the Father, and the Holy Spirit who proceeds from the Father and the Son;

[3]Cf. Mt. 23, 15.
[4]Augustine, *Enchiridion*, c39.
[5]Cf. Acts 8, 20.
[6]Augustine, *Enchiridion*, c40.
[7]Ibid., c37.
[8]Ibid., c41.
[9]Cf. Col. 2, 9.
[10]Rom. 1, 3.
[11]Augustine, *Enchiridion*, c38.
[12]Pelagius, *Libellus fidei ad Innocentium Papam*, n4.
[13]Mt. 1, 18.

from power, as all things are from God. And so how was Mary with child from the Holy Spirit? If as from substance, then was the Spirit changed into flesh and bones? Certainly not. But if the Virgin conceived as from the Spirit's operation and power, who would deny that the Holy Spirit is the author of the Lord's incarnation?"[14]

Chapter 3 (13)

1. WHY THE APOSTLE SAYS THAT CHRIST WAS MADE, BUT WE PROFESS THAT HE WAS BORN.—AMBROSE. But it can be asked: "Since we profess that the Saviour was born, why does the Apostle say that he was *made from the seed of David,*[1] and in another place, *made from a woman,*[2] even though to be made is one thing, and to be born another? The Apostle must have signified something else by his statement.—The Apostle says *made*, and not *born,* because the Lord's flesh was formed and given bodily shape in the Virgin's womb not by human seed, but by the working and power of the Holy Spirit. For it is one thing to beget by the mixture of seed and the coagulation of blood; it is another to procreate not by commixture, but by power."[3] Men can beget human children, but they cannot make them. —That is why the Apostle said *made*, not *born*, namely so that his birth, which occurred without the seed of a man, should not be held to be like ours, which is done by the commixture of seeds.

2. WHY FROM THE SEED OF DAVID. AUGUSTINE, IN THE BOOK *ON THE TRINITY*. And so, when the Apostle said *made*, he added *from the seed of David*, because "although no seed of man intervened in the Virgin's conceiving, yet, because Christ was formed from that flesh which had descended from seed, it is rightly said that he was made [from the seed]."[4]

DISTINCTION V

Chapter 1 (14)

1. WHETHER A PERSON OR NATURE TOOK ON A PERSON OR NATURE, AND WHETHER GOD'S NATURE BECAME FLESH. Moreover, since it is clear from the foregoing that the Word of God took at once flesh and soul into the unity of its person, it is necessary to inquire which of these is more to be granted: namely that a person took on a person, or a nature a nature, or a

[14]Ambrose, *De Spiritu sancto*, c5 nn42-43.

[1]Cf. Rom. 1, 3.
[2]Cf. Gal. 4, 4.
[3]Ambrosiaster, *Quaestiones ex Novo Testamento*, q44.
[4]Cf. Syagrius, *Sermo 238.*

person a nature, or a nature a person; and whether it is as suitable to say that divine nature became flesh, as it is truly said that God became incarnate and the Word became incarnate.—This inquiry or approach to the question, according to the testimonies of the sacred authorities, is partially implicit and difficult, but partially explicit and manifest.

2. ON THE PART OF THE QUESTION WHICH IS CLEAR. For it is certain, and true without ambiguity, that it was not a nature that took on a person, nor a person a person, but a person a nature.—This is proved by the testimonies of the saints here appended and is concluded from the evidence. For Augustine says, in the book *On Faith to Peter*: "The only-begotten God, in his conception, took the truth of the flesh from the Virgin; in his birth, he preserved the integrity of virginity in his Mother."[1] And a little later: "The same God took human nature into the unity of person, who, humbling himself through mercy, filled the womb of the undefiled Virgin from whom he would be born. And so the same God took into his person *the form of a servant*,[2] that is, the nature of a servant."[3] Also: "For God the Word did not take the person of a man, but the nature of a man."[4] Also: "The only-begotten Son of God, in order to cleanse the flesh and soul of man, became man by taking on flesh and a rational soul."[5]—By these and many other authorities, it is clearly shown that it was not a nature that took on a person, nor a person a person, but a person a nature.

3. ON THE DIFFICULT PART OF THE QUESTION. But as to the fourth article of the question, namely whether a nature took on a nature, the question is troublesome even among the learned, because even those who were famously authoritative and more learned than the rest in the sacred Page appear to disagree much with regard to this. Indeed, they seem to disagree not just with each other, but also with themselves, as the following chapters teach.

4. HERE HE SETS FORTH THOSE [ARGUMENTS] WHICH APPEAR TO INDICATE THAT A NATURE DID NOT TAKE ON A NATURE.—ON THE COUNCIL OF TOLEDO VIII. For we read that at the Council of Toledo VIII the following was handed down: "*The Word* alone *was made flesh and dwelled among us*.[6] And although the entire Trinity worked the making of the man who was taken, because the works of the Trinity are not severable, yet the Son alone took human form in the singularity of his person, not in the unity of the divine nature, that is, that which is proper to the Son

[1]Fulgentius, *De fide ad Petrum*, c2 n17.
[2]Cf. Phil. 2, 7.
[3]Fulgentius, *De fide ad Petrum*, c2 n28.
[4]Ibid., c17 n58.
[5]Ibid., c2 n17.
[6]Cf. Jn. 1, 14.

alone, not that which is common to the Trinity."[7]—Also, at the Council of Toledo XI: "We believe God the Father and the Son and the Holy Spirit to be of one substance; yet we do not say that the Virgin Mary gave birth to the unity of this Trinity, but only to the Son, who alone took on our nature into the unity of his person. In the same way too, the entire Trinity is to be believed to have worked the incarnation of the Son of God; but the Son alone took the form of a servant into the singularity of his person."[8]—By these words, it appears to be indicated that only a person took on a nature, not a nature a nature. For if what is common to the Trinity did not take human form, then the divine nature, which is common to the three persons, did not do so.

5. HERE HE SETS OUT THOSE [ARGUMENTS] BY WHICH IT IS PROVED THAT A NATURE TOOK ON A NATURE. What Augustine says in the book *On Faith to Peter*, appears to go against what was said above; he states: "The divinity of Christ is not alien to the Father's nature, since *in the beginning was the Word*;[9] nor is his humanity alien to his Mother's nature, since *the Word was made flesh.*[10] For that nature, which remains forever begotten of the Father, took our nature free from sin in order to be born of the Virgin."[11]—By this authority, it appears to be handed down that the divine nature took on a human one. Where we can be strongly troubled is by his saying it to be eternally 'begotten' of the Father; unless perhaps he here uses nature in the sense of person. Otherwise, if we said that the nature which is common to the three persons was 'begotten,' we will contradict what we discussed in the treatise on the Trinity,[12] where we said that a person begot a person, and not a nature a nature, because, if a nature begot a nature, since the nature of the Trinity is one and the same, the same thing would have begotten itself; which Augustine denies to be possible.[13]

6. But elsewhere we find sure evidence by which it is shown that a nature took on a nature. For Augustine says, in *On the Trinity*, book 1: "The Son was made even less than his own self in *taking the form of a servant.*[14] For he did not take *the form of a servant* so as to lose *the form of God*, in which he was equal to the Father: since, in both the form of a servant and the form of God, he is the same only-begotten Son of the Father because the form of God took the form of a servant."[15] But if the form of God took the form of a servant, without doubt a nature took on a

[7]Rather, Toledo VI, c1.
[8]Creed of Toledo XI.
[9]Cf. Jn. 1, 1.
[10]Jn. 1, 14.
[11]Fulgentius, *De fide ad Petrum*, c2 n14.
[12]Bk 1 dist. 5 c1.
[13]Augustine, *De Trinitate*, bk 1 c1 n1.
[14]Cf. Phil. 2, 6-7.
[15]Augustine, *De Trinitate*, bk 1 c7 n14.

nature.—WHAT IS UNDERSTOOD BY THE TERM FORM. For by the term 'form' nature is understood, as Augustine clearly teaches in the book *On Faith to Peter*, saying: "When you hear of Christ that *he was in the form of God*,[16] it is necessary that you acknowledge and hold most firmly that, in that term 'form,' the fullness of nature is to be understood. And so he was in the form of God because he was forever in the nature of God the Father, of whom he was born."[17]

7. HILARY. Hilary too, in *On the Trinity*, book 12, says: "To be in *the form of God* means nothing else than to remain in the nature of God."[18]—You have learned that the meaning of 'form' is nature, and you have heard that the form of God took the form of a servant: and so it follows that divine nature took on human nature.—JEROME. Jerome too, in the *Explanation of the Faith*, clearly indicates the same, saying: "The Son of God suffered not putatively, but truly; he suffered in accordance with that which was capable of suffering, that is, not according to the substance which took, but according to the substance which was taken."[19] From which it is apparent that the divine substance took on the human one.

8. AUGUSTINE, *ON FAITH TO PETER*. But the words of Augustine set out above, if they are examined with diligence, appear to indicate that the Word alone was made flesh and it alone took on a human nature, and that the divine nature took the same human nature. For he says: "The Trinity reconciled us to itself through the fact that the Trinity itself made the Word alone flesh. In this the truth of divine and human nature remains so unchangeable that, just as the divinity which it has from the Father is forever true, so also is forever true and unchangeable his humanity, which the most high divinity has united to itself."[20] See, he said both that the Word alone was made flesh, and that humanity was united to divinity.—AUGUSTINE, IN THE BOOK *ON THE TRINITY*. The same [Augustine] also said earlier that "the whole Trinity made the servile form which was taken by the Son alone."[21]

9. It is by now easy to recognize that authorities have handed down different and manifold views on the proposed question; and so those who came after them, reading these views, take occasion from the aforesaid to set forth various and contradictory opinions.

10. WHAT IS TO BE HELD CONCERNING THIS. Wishing to remove any sign of mendaciousness and contradiction from the sacred Pages, we agree with the orthodox Fathers and Catholic doctors who are untouched

[16]Cf. Phil. 2, 6.
[17]Fulgentius, *De fide ad Petrum*, c2 n19.
[18]Hilary, *De Trinitate*, bk 12 n6.
[19]Pelagius, *Libellus fidei ad Innocentium Papam*, n5.
[20]Fulgentius, *De fide ad Petrum*, c2 n23; cf. above, dist. 1 c3 n2.
[21]See above, dist. 2 c3 n2.

by any suspicion of evil understanding. And so we say that the person of the Son took on a human nature, and that a divine nature was united to a human nature in the Son, and that he united it to himself or took it, so that he is truly called incarnate.

11. DETERMINATION OF THE AUTHORITIES. But in saying that the Son alone took the form of a servant,[22] the divine nature is not thereby excluded from taking on a servile form, but the other two persons, namely the Father and the Holy Spirit, are.—Also, that other assertion, namely 'that which is proper to the Son alone, not that which is common to the Trinity, took human form,'[23] is to be understood as follows: that is, it was specifically in the hypostasis of the Son, not jointly in the three persons, that divine nature united the human one to itself.

12. JOHN OF DAMASCUS. This sense is confirmed by the words of John of Damascus, who clearly asserts that the whole divine nature became incarnate in one of the hypostases. He says: "In the Word of God becoming man, we say that the whole and perfect nature of the divinity became incarnate, that is, it was united to a human nature in one of the divine hypostases, and not a part to a part. For we say that the whole nature or substance of the divinity was united to the whole human nature."[24]—Also: "The same nature is in each of the hypostases, that is, of the persons. And when we say that 'the nature of the Word became incarnate,' according to the blessed Athanasius and Cyril, we are saying that the divinity was united to the flesh."[25] "And we confess that the one nature of the Word of God became incarnate."[26] "And the Word both possesses what is common to the substance, and has what is proper to the hypostasis, that is, to the person."[27]—From these words, it is manifestly shown that the divine nature became incarnate; and so the same nature is truly said to have taken on a human nature.

Chapter 2 (15)

1. WHETHER THE DIVINE NATURE OUGHT TO BE SAID TO HAVE BEEN MADE FLESH. But it is asked whether the same divine nature ought to be said 'to have been made flesh,' just as the Word is said to have been made flesh.[1] For if to become incarnate is the same as to be made flesh, it may seem that the divine nature ought to be said to have been made flesh, just

[22]Cf. Toledo XI, above, n4.
[23]Toledo VI, under the name of Toledo VIII, above, n4.
[24]John of Damascus, *De fide orthodoxa*, bk 3 c6.
[25]Ibid.
[26]Ibid., bk 3 c7.
[27]Ibid., bk 3 c6.

[1]Cf. Jn. 1, 14.

as it is said to have become incarnate.—RESPONSE. To which we say that, if that expression were to be found in sacred Scripture, it would be taken in the same sense as when the divine nature is called incarnate. But because authority passed over the matter in silence, and, what is more, the mode of speech would seem excessively bold if the divine nature were said to have been made flesh, I believe it better to be silent concerning this or to deny it than to assert it rashly, lest, if that were said, it might be held to signify the convertibility of the one nature into the other.—From the foregoing, it is indubitably clear that the person or nature of the Word took on a human nature, namely flesh and soul, but not a human person.

2. But if the divine nature took a human nature, why is it not said to have been made or to be man, as the Word of God is?—To which it can be said that the Son of God is said to have been made man or to be man not only because he took the form of a man, but because he took it into the unity and singularity of himself, that is, of his person. But although the divine nature did indeed take human form, that is, united the form of man to itself, it did not take it into the singularity and unity of itself. For the singularity of the person remained while the property and diversity of the two natures were preserved. And so the divine nature is not said to be man or to have been made man, in the same way as the Son of God is. But some grant both of these interchangeably.

Chapter 3 (16)

1. WHY [THE WORD] DID NOT TAKE THE PERSON OF A MAN, EVEN THOUGH IT TOOK A MAN. But [the Word] did not take the person of a man because that flesh and that soul which it would have taken were not united into the one person. For there was no person composed of those elements when the Word was united to them; indeed, they were united to each other at the same time as they were united to the Word. And yet the union by which those two, namely the soul and the flesh, were united was one thing, and the union by which they were united to the Word was another; because the first is the union of that soul to the flesh, the second is the union of the Word to that soul and flesh. And so the Word of God did not take the person of a man, but the nature, because there was no person composed of that flesh and that soul whom the Word took, but the Word united by taking, and took by uniting.

2. OBJECTION TO THIS, BY WHICH SOME WISH TO PROVE THAT A PERSON TOOK A PERSON. Here the objection is made by some that a person took a person: "For a person is a rational substance of an individual nature."[1] But that is what a soul is; and so, if the Word took a soul, it also took a

[1]Boethius, *Opusculum V: Liber contra Eutychen et Nestorium*, c3.

person.—But this does not follow, because the soul is not a person when it is united personally to another thing, but when it exists by itself. For when it is freed from the body, it is a person, like an angel. But that particular soul never existed without being joined to another thing; and so it was not the case that the taking of that soul was the taking of a person.

3. ANOTHER PROOF OF THE SAME. They also strive in another way to prove that the Word of God took a person: because it took a particular man. For it took the man Jesus Christ; and so [it took] a particular man.—AUGUSTINE. Augustine, in his *Exposition of the Creed*, under threat of anathema, hands down that the Word took the man Jesus Christ; he says: "If anyone has said and believed that the man Jesus Christ was not assumed by the Son of God, let him be anathema."[2] He also uses expressions taken from several passages of Scripture,[3] like the following: 'That man was assumed by the Word,' 'That man was made the Christ.' And the Prophet, speaking to God of the man Christ, says: *Blessed is he whom you have chosen and taken.*[4] From which it appears to follow that a particular man was taken by the Word, and in such way that a person was taken by a person.

4. RESPONSE DETERMINING THE ABOVE EXPRESSIONS. But because it is impious to say or hold this, the above expressions and others like them surely ought to be taken in the following sense: that the man Christ, or that man, or some man, is said to have been taken by the Word, or united to the Word, not because the person of a man was taken or united to the Word, but because that particular soul and that particular flesh were taken and united to the Word, and in them subsisted the person of God and of man: so that you look to the nature of man, not to the person, when Scripture, in phrases of this sort, says that some man or a particular man was taken or united.—And so, when it is asked without the support of authority whether some man or a particular man was taken by the Word or united to the Word, no response is here to be made without distinguishing what is meant because the aforesaid question is multifaceted. But once the limits of the questioner's intention have been determined, then, if you are asking about the person of the man, I answer: no; if about the nature of the man, I say: yes, indeed.

[2]Pseudo-Augustine, *Sermo 233*, n2 (rather, the Creed of the Council of Toledo I).
[3]See below, dist. 6 c2 n6.
[4]Ps. 64, 5.

DISTINCTION VI

Chapter 1 (17)

1. ON THE MEANING OF THESE EXPRESSIONS: GOD WAS MADE MAN, GOD IS MAN; WHETHER OR NOT BY THESE EXPRESSIONS GOD IS SAID TO BE MADE SOMETHING [ELSE] OR TO BE SOMETHING [ELSE]. But from the foregoing emerges a question which contains much usefulness, but also a great deal of difficulty and confusion. For since it is established from the foregoing and many other testimonies, and all Catholics unanimously profess, that God was made man, and that Christ is true God and true man, it is asked whether by these expressions: 'God was made man,' 'the Son of God was made son of man,' 'God is man' and 'man is God,' God is said to be made something [else], or to be something [else], or something is said to be God. And is it as suitable to say: 'Man was made God' and 'the son of man was made the Son of God,' as is it to state the converse. And if by these expressions God is not said to be made anything or to be anything [else], what is the meaning of these expressions and of others like them.

2. THAT THE LEARNED DIFFER IN THEIR EXPOSITION OF THIS QUESTION. The learned are found to differ very much in their plumbing of this depth and their exposition of this thorny question.

Chapter 2 (18)

1. HE REPORTS THE VIEW OF SOME. For some say that, in the very incarnation of the Word, some man was formed from a rational soul and human flesh: from these two, any true man is formed. And that man began to be God, not indeed by the nature of God, but by the person of the Word; and God began to be that man. They also grant that that man was assumed by the Word and united to the Word, and yet that he was the Word. And they hand down that it was for that reason that it is said that 'God was made man' or 'is man,' because God was made (that is, began to be) some substance subsisting from a rational soul and human flesh; and that substance was made (that is, began to be) God. And yet not by the passage of [one] nature into [another] nature, but, with the property of each nature being preserved, it was brought about that God be that substance and that substance be God. And so it is truly said that God was made man and man was made God, and that God is man and man is God, and that the Son of God is son of man and vice versa. And although they say that that man subsists from a rational soul and human flesh, yet they do not profess that he was composed from two natures, namely the divine and the human, nor that his parts are two natures, but only that they are soul and flesh.

2. He sets out authorities by which they defend their view. And lest they be held to speak only from their own understanding, they defend their view with several testimonies. For Augustine says, in the book *On the Trinity*: "When we read, *the Word was made flesh*,[1] by *the Word* I understand the true Son of God, by *flesh* I acknowledge the true son of man, and both at once one person, God and man, joined by the generous bestowal of ineffable grace."[2]

3. The same, in the *Enchiridion*: "Jesus Christ is God from God, but as man was born of the Holy Spirit from the Virgin Mary. By either substance, namely the divine and the human, he is the one Son of God the Father almighty, from whom the Holy Spirit proceeds."[3] "Both are one, but one on account of the Word, the other on account of the man; not two sons, God and man, but one Son of God: God without beginning, man from a certain beginning."[4]

4. Also in the same: "What did the human nature in the man Christ deserve, that it should be singularly taken into the unity of person of the one Son of God? What good will, what good works went before that this man should deserve to become one person with God? Had he been a man before, and had this singular benefit been given to him, so that he should be singularly worthy of being God? Assuredly not! As soon as he began to be man, this man did not begin to be anything other than the Son of God, and the only one; and so he began to be the Word of God, because the flesh that was made and taken in him is certainly God. And just as each man is one person, namely a rational soul and flesh, so Christ is one person, Word and man."[5]

5. The same [Augustine], in *On John*: "Let us acknowledge the twofold substance of Christ: namely the divine one, by which he is equal to the Father, and the human, by which the Father is greater; and yet Christ is both at once, not two, but one, lest God be not a trinity, but a quaternity. And through this, Christ is God, rational soul, and flesh."[6]

6. The same also in the book *On the Predestination of the Saints*: "Whence did that man deserve that, having been assumed into the unity of person by the Word coeternal with the Father, he be the only-begotten Son of God? What good of his preceded that he should come to such ineffable excellence? It was by the doing and taking of the Word of God that that man, from the moment that he began to be, began to be the only

[1]Jn. 1, 14.
[2]Augustine, *De Trinitate*, bk 13 c19 n24.
[3]Augustine, *Enchiridion*, c38.
[4]Ibid., c35.
[5]Ibid., c36.
[6]Augustine, *In Ioannem*, tr. 78 n3.

Son of God."[7]—Also: "Any man is made Christian by grace as that man by grace was made the Christ from the beginning."[8]

7. The same, in *On the Trinity*, book 13: "The grace of God is commended to us in the man Christ because it was not by any preceding merits that he deserved to be joined to God by such unity that the Son of God became one person with him. But as soon as he began to be man, he was also God. And so it is said: *The Word was made flesh.*"[9,10]

8. HILARY. Hilary too, in *On the Trinity*, book 10, says: "We do not doubt that Christ is God the Word; and neither are we unaware that the son of man was composed of soul and body."[11]

9. Those who say that some man, composed of a rational soul and flesh, was made God use these and other authorities. But it was by grace, not by nature. For it was by grace alone, and not by merits or nature, that that man had it to be God or Son of God, and to have all the knowledge and power which the Word has, with whom he is one person. In the foregoing, not only do we read that that man is one person with the Word and is the Word itself, but also that the same person is a rational soul and flesh and is both Christ and God.

Chapter 3 (19)

1. THE VIEW OF OTHERS. But there are also others who in part agree with the former, but they say that that man was not composed only of a rational soul and flesh, but also of a divine and human nature, that is, of three substances: divinity, flesh, and soul. They profess this Christ to be only one person; however, that person was simple only before the incarnation, but in the incarnation he was made into a person composed of divinity and humanity. Nor is he therefore another person than before, but what was before only a person of God, in the incarnation was also made a person of man: not so as to be two persons, but that the person of God and of man be one and the same. And so the person which before was simple and existed only in one nature, then subsists in and from two natures. And the person which was only God has also become true man, subsisting not only from soul and flesh, but also from divinity. And yet that person should not be said to have been made a person, although it is said to have been made a person of man. And so, as some would have it, that person was made into something subsisting from soul and flesh, but was not

[7]Augustine, *De praedestinatione sanctorum*, c15 n30.
[8]Ibid., c15 n31.
[9]Jn. 1, 14.
[10]Augustine, *De Trinitate*, bk 13 c17 n22.
[11]Hilary, *De Trinitate*, bk 10 n57.

made a person or substance or nature. And insofar as he is subsistent, the person is composite; but insofar as he is the Word, the person is simple.

2. HE ALSO SETS OUT THE AUTHORITIES WHICH PROVE THIS VIEW. Concerning this, Augustine, in the book of the *Sentences of Prosper*, says: "In all possible ways, we strive to prove that the Church's sacrifice consists of two things and is made from two things: the visible form of the elements, and the invisible flesh and blood of our Lord Jesus Christ, the sacrament and the thing of the sacrament, that is, the body of Christ. Similarly, the person of Christ consists in and is made from God and man, since Christ himself is true God and true man; because each thing contains in itself the nature and truth of the things from which it is made."[1]

3. On this same subject, John of Damascus: "In our Lord Jesus Christ, we acknowledge two natures, but one hypostasis composed from both."[2] —"And so Christ became flesh, taking the first-fruits of our mass from the Virgin,[3] so that the hypostasis itself, which is the hypostasis of God's Word, existed in the flesh, and the hypostasis of the Word, which had formerly been simple, was made composite: composed of two perfect natures, divinity and humanity, bearing both the characteristic and determining property of the divine filiation of the Word of God, according to which he is distinguished from Father and Holy Spirit, and the characteristic and determining property of the flesh, according to which he differs from his Mother and the rest of humankind."[4]

4. Also: "We confess the one hypostasis of the Son of God in the two complete natures of divinity and humanity, and that the same hypostasis became flesh; and that these two natures are preserved and remain in it after their union; nor do we hold that each of them is by itself and a part, but that they are mutually united in the one composite hypostasis. For we call this union substantial, that is, true, and not imaginary; but we say substantial not because the two natures produce something else, namely one composite nature, but that they are mutually united into the one composite hypostasis of the Son of God; and we determine that the difference of substance remains. For what was created remained created, and what was uncreated uncreated, and what was mortal mortal, and what was immortal immortal, and what was circumscribable circumscribable, and what was uncircumscribable uncircumscribable. And this shines out with wonders."[5]

5. On this Augustine, too, in the book *On the Trinity*, says: "In as much as the nature of Father and Son is one according to divinity, so also the

[1]These words are Lanfranc's, partially taken from Berengar, *De sacramento corporis et sanguinis Christi*, c10.

[2]John of Damascus, *De fide orthodoxa*, bk 3 c4.

[3]Cf. Rom. 11, 16.

[4]John of Damascus, *De fide orthodoxa*, bk 3 c7.

[5]Ibid., bk 3 c3.

nature of Mother and Son is the same according to humanity. From each substance, of the divinity and the humanity, one and the same is God, Son of God and man, Jesus Christ: as he is true God, so he is also true man."[6] —The same, in *On the Trinity*, book 13: "Human nature could be so joined to God that one person could be made from the two substances; and thereby already from three: God, soul, and flesh."[7]

6. It is with these and other authorities that they defend themselves who say that the person of Christ is composite, or made, consisting of either two natures or three substances.

Chapter 4 (20)

1. THE THIRD VIEW OF SOME OTHERS. There are even some others as well who not only deny [the existence of] a person composed of natures in the incarnation of the Word, but also say that there was not any man at all, or even any substance, there composed or made from soul and flesh. They say that these two things, namely soul and flesh, were united to the person or nature of the Word, not in such a way that any substance or person was made or composed from those two or these three things, but so that the Word of God might be clothed with those two as with clothing in order to appear suitably to the eyes of mortals.[1]

2. And so he is said to have been made true man because he took the truth of flesh and soul. And we read that he took these two into the singularity or unity of his person, not because those two, or anything composed from them, is one person with the Word or is the Word, but because the number of persons was not increased by the joining of those things to the Word so as to turn the Trinity into a quaternity because the very person of the Word, which before had been without this clothing, was not divided or changed by the taking on of clothing, but remained one, the same, and unchanged.

3. They also say that God was made man according to habit. For it is by taking on man that God is said to be made man: on the one hand, it is because of *the man taken* that God is said to be truly man; on the other hand, it is because of *God taking* that man is said to be God. Indeed, they say, if God were understood to be man, or man God, essentially, then, if God had taken human form in the female gender, the woman too would be God essentially, and vice versa. But God could have taken human form in the female gender; and so a woman could be God, and vice versa.

[6]Rather, Pseudo-Augustine, *Sermo 238*, n3.
[7]Augustine, *De Trinitate*, bk 13 c17 n22.

[1]Cf. Augustine, below, c6 n4.

Chapter 5 (21)

HE BRINGS FORTH AUTHORITIES BY WHICH THIS VIEW IS STRENGTHENED. Lest they appear to be expressing merely their own view, they also confirm what they say by the submission of authorities. For Augustine says, in the book *On the Grace of the New Testament*: "Just as the number of persons is not increased when flesh is joined to soul so that there be one man, so the number of persons is not increased when the man is joined to the Word so that there be one Christ. And so we read 'God man' in order to understand the singularity of this person, not to suspect a divinity changed into flesh."[1]

Chapter 6 (22)

1. FOUR KINDS OF HABIT ARE DISTINGUISHED. The same [Augustine], treating that statement of the Apostle: *He was found in the habit of a man,*[1] manifestly shows that God is said to have been made man or to be man according to habit; in the book of *84 Questions*, he says as follows: "We say 'habit' in many senses: a habit of the mind, as the mental grasp of a discipline established by usage; or a habit of the body, as when we say that one is more vigorous than another; or the habit of those things which are externally fitted to our limbs, as when we say that someone is clothed, shod, and suchlike. In all these kinds, it is manifest that habit is said with reference to a thing which is added to someone, so that he may also not have it. And this term is derived from the verb 'to have.' And so habit is said with reference to a thing which is added to us so that we may have it."[2]

2. FIRST KIND OF HABIT. "And yet what matters here is that some of those things which are added in order to produce a habit are not themselves changed, but they cause change while they remain whole and unassailable in themselves: and so wisdom, coming to a man, is not itself changed, but changes the man and, from a fool, makes him into a wise man."[3]—SECOND. "But some things are added so that they both change and are changed: like food which, losing its form, is changed into the body, and we, refreshed by the food, are changed from weakness and languor to strength and power."[4]—THIRD. "A third kind concerns those things which, on being added, neither change the things to which they are added, nor are they changed by them: like a ring placed on a finger; but this kind occurs very rarely."[5]—FOURTH. "A fourth kind is when those

[1]Augustine, *Epistola 140 (ad Honoratum)*, c4 n12.

[1]Phil. 2, 7.
[2]Augustine, *De diversis quaestionibus 83*, q73 n1.
[3]Ibid.
[4]Ibid.
[5]Cf. ibid.

things which, on being added, are not changed from their nature, but take on another shape and form. Such is the case with clothing which, once taken off and cast aside, does not have the same form which it had when it was worn, for when it is worn over the limbs, it takes on a form which it does not have when it is taken off."[6]

3. THE FOURTH KIND FITS THE COMPARISON HERE. This [last] kind fits the comparison here. For God the Son "*emptied himself*, not by changing his form, but *by taking the form of a servant*; nor was he changed or transmuted into a man, thereby losing his unchangeable stability, but the taker himself was *made in the likeness of men*, by taking a true man, and *he was found in the habit of a man*,[7] that is, by having human form, he was found as a man: not for himself, but for those to whom he appeared in his human form."[8] And in saying *of a man*, the text expresses the truth. "And so, by this term *habit*, the Apostle sufficiently signified what he meant by saying *made in the likeness of man*, because he was made a man not by way of transfiguration, but *by habit* when he was clothed with a human form. Uniting and conforming such form in some manner to himself, he made it a partaker of immortality and eternity. And so it is not fitting that the Word be understood to have changed by taking on human form, just as the limbs are not changed when they put on clothing, even though that taking has ineffably joined the one taken to the taker."[9]—By these words, Augustine appears to indicate clearly that God is said to have been made man according to habit.

4. AUGUSTINE: ON THE MANNER OF THE INCARNATION. Wishing to explain to questioners the manner of the incarnation itself, Augustine also says, in *On the Trinity*, book 4: "If it is asked how was the incarnation done: I say that the *Word* of God himself *was made flesh*,[10] that is, was made man; and yet, he was not changed or transformed into that which was made,"[11] "but he was clothed in flesh so that he might suitably appear to fleshly people."[12] "But certainly *made*, so that there is not only the Word of God and the flesh of man there, but also the rational soul of man; and all this is called both God because of God, and man because of man. And if this is difficult to understand, let the mind be cleansed by faith, by abstaining from sins and doing good works; for these are difficult things."[13]

[6]Augustine, *De diversis quaestionibus 83*, q73 n1.
[7]Phil. 2, 7.
[8]Augustine, *De diversis quaestionibus 83*, q73 n2.
[9]Ibid.
[10]Cf. Jn. 1, 14.
[11]Augustine, *De Trinitate*, bk 4 c21 n31.
[12]Augustine, *Epistolae ad Romanos inchoata expositio*, n4.
[13]Augustine, *De Trinitate*, bk 4 c21 n31.

5. The same in the book *On Faith to Peter*: "The Son of God, although he is eternal and true God, was made true and full man for our sake: true, because that God has a true human nature; but full, because he also took on a human flesh and a rational soul."[14]—Also: "That emptying of the most high God was nothing else than the taking up of the form of a servant, that is, of human nature. And so each form is in Christ, because each substance," namely the human and the divine, " is true and full in Christ."[15]

6. The same in the book *Against Maximinus*: "Although he was invisible in himself, he appeared visible in the human form which he deigned to take from a woman."[16]—The same in the same: "We believe that Christ the Lord took true human form: in it, he who was invisible appeared visibly to men; in it, he associated with men;[17] in it, he bore human things from human beings; in it, he taught men."[18]

7. Hilary too, in *On the Trinity*, book 10, says: "How was the Son of God born of Mary, if not that *the Word was made flesh*,[19] namely that the Son of God, *although he was in the form of God*, took *the form of a servant*?[20] And yet we profess him to be one and the same, not by the loss of divinity, but by the taking of humanity; and that he was found to be *in the form of God* through the divine nature, and in *the form of a servant* from the conception of the Holy Spirit according to the habit of a man."[21] "That was not nevertheless a man's habit, but as if a man's;[22] nor was that flesh sinful flesh, but *in the likeness of sinful flesh*."[23,24]—You have heard three views set out according to different proponents, and the testimonies brought forth for each of them.

DISTINCTION VII

Chapter 1 (23)

1. AFTER SETTING OUT THE VIEWS AND REPORTING THE TESTIMONIES, HE PURSUES THE MEANINGS OF THE PROPOSED EXPRESSIONS ACCORDING TO EACH VIEW, AND FIRST ACCORDING TO THE FIRST. According to the first,

[14]Fulgentius, *De fide ad Petrum*, c2 n10.
[15]Ibid., c3 nn20-21.
[16]Rather, Evodius, *De fide contra Manichaeos*, c22.
[17]Cf. Baruch 3, 38.
[18]Evodius, *De fide contra Manichaeos*, c26.
[19]Jn. 1, 14.
[20]Phil. 2, 6-7.
[21]Hilary, *De Trinitate*, bk 10 n22.
[22]Cf. Phil. 2, 7.
[23]Rom. 8, 3.
[24]Hilary, *De Trinitate*, bk 10 n25.

God is said to have been made man, and man to have been made God, because God began to be some rational substance which had not existed before, and that substance began to be God. And Christ had this by grace, not by nature or merits. Hence Christ, insofar as he is a man, is rightly said to be *predestined the Son of God.*[1]

2. WHAT OBJECTIONS ARE MADE TO THIS VIEW. The following objection is made to this view: If that substance began to be God, and God to be that substance, then some substance is God which was not always God; and some substance is God which is not the divine substance; and God is something which he not always was.—ORIGEN, *ON THE EPISTLE TO THE ROMANS.* Which they also grant, relying on the testimony of Origen, who says: "*He was made*, undoubtedly, that which he was not before," but adds: "*according to the flesh*; but according to God he was before, and he was not when he was not."[2]

3. Objection to their view also can be made in a variety of further ways, but we pass over them, leaving this studious exercise to the reader while we move on to the next view.

4. HERE HE EXPLAINS THE SECOND VIEW AND THE SENSES OF THOSE SAME EXPRESSIONS. But in the second view, the reason for this statement is as follows: that in saying 'God was made man,' Christ would be understood to have begun to be subsistent from two natures or three substances; and conversely 'man was made God,' because, subsisting in two natures, he began to be God.—Or rather, what is said is 'man was made God or vice versa,' because God took on man and the man was taken by God. Hence Augustine says, in the book *On the Trinity*: "For that taking was such as to make man God, and God man."[3]—But the meaning is changed in saying 'God is man' and 'man is God.' For God is said to be a person subsisting in and from two natures; and the person subsisting from two natures is said to be God, that is, the Word, or the divine nature. It is possible that a simple person or nature be predicated of a composite person; but, as John of Damascus says, it is not the same to say nature or person.[4]

5. IN WHAT SENSE THEY CALL CHRIST PREDESTINED. These say that Christ is predestined insofar as he is a man, that is, insofar as he is subsistent from two substances, namely soul and flesh; for insofar as the nature of the divinity is concerned, he is not predestined. And so it is not insofar as he subsists in it or by it that he is predestined; but insofar as he subsists in the other two substances, that is, in soul and flesh, that is, insofar as he is man.

[1]Cf. Rom. 1, 4.
[2]Origen, *In Epistolam ad Romanos* 1, n5; cf. Rom. 1, 3.
[3]Augustine, *De Trinitate*, bk 1 c13 n28.
[4]John of Damascus, *De fide orthodoxa*, bk 3 c4.

6. HOW THE AUTHORITIES OF THE FIRST VIEW WHICH APPEAR TO RUN COUNTER TO THIS SECOND VIEW ARE EXPOUNDED. They also determine the authorities which agree with the first view, and which appear to contradict this one, as when we read 'that man, assumed in the singularity of person by the Word,' or 'made one person with the Word,' this is understood of the human nature which is united to the Word in singularity of person, that is, in such a way that the same person which was before and was simple, remained without increase of number and unchanged, although [now] composite. But they say that the reason for this composition is other than what obtains in other men, because this man's composition proceeds from three substances, while that of others proceeds from two.

7. They also deny that the human nature is a person or the Son of God; and just as they say that man and God are one and the same, both the son of man and the Son of God are also one and the same, and not two different things, just as they are not two different beings.

8. HE SETS OUT SOME TEXTS WHICH APPEAR TO CONTRADICT THE FOREGOING. But these appear to be contradicted by what is contained in the chapters below. For Augustine, in *On John*, says: "The Word of God is one thing, the man another. But *the Word was made flesh*,[5] that is, man; and so it is not the case that there is one person of the Word, another of the man, because Christ is both and one person."[6]—The same, *To Felicianus*: "The Son of God is one thing, the son of man another thing, but not another being."[7]—Also: "The Son of God is one thing from the Father, another from the Mother."[8]—The same, in *On the Trinity*, book 1: "Although the Son is both God and man, one substance is God and another substance is man."[9]

9. HOW THEY RESPOND TO THESE [ARGUMENTS]. And they determine these [arguments] in the following way: that in saying 'the Word of God is one thing, the man another,' or 'one substance is God, another man,' Christ is signified to be of one nature insofar as he is man, and of another insofar as he is God; and one thing by the nature by which he is man, another thing by the nature by which he is God.—JOHN OF DAMASCUS. For, as John of Damascus says, "the two natures are mutually united without conversion or alteration; the divine nature does not depart from its proper simplicity, nor is the human one either changed into the nature of the divinity or reduced to non-existence, nor is one composite nature made from the two. For a composite nature cannot be *homousia* (that is, consubstantial) with either of the natures from which it is composed, but

[5]Jn. 1, 14.
[6]Augustine, *In Ioannem*, tr. 69 n3.
[7]That is, Vigilius of Thapse, *Contra Felicianum Arianum de unitate Trinitatis*, c11.
[8]Cf. ibid., c12.
[9]Augustine, *De Trinitate*, bk 1 c10 n20.

makes something else out of the other two, just as the body, which is composed of the four elements, is not called fire, nor air, nor earth, nor water, nor is it said to be *homousion* with any of these. And so if, as the heretics say, Christ was of one composite nature after the union, he was changed from a simple nature into a composite one, and is neither of the same simple nature as the Father, nor of the same substance as the Mother; and he will be called neither God nor man, but only Christ. And this name, namely Christ, will not be the name of the person itself, but, they say, of the one composite nature. But we do not teach that Christ is of one composite nature. And this name, namely Christ, we say of the person; it is not said monotropically (that is, in one way), but as signifying the two natures, namely divinity and humanity. For we confess that, from divinity and humanity, he is and is to be called perfect God and perfect man, from two natures and in two natures."[10]—And so the Son of God is said to be one thing, the son of man another thing, because he is of one substance or nature insofar as he is Son of God, of another insofar as he is son of man, not because the same Son of God and man is those two different things, that is, two different natures.

10. HE CONFIRMS THE DETERMINATION BY AUTHORITY. For Hilary says clearly, in *On the Trinity*, book 9: "Since the son of man is not one thing and the Son of God another thing: for *the Word was made flesh*;[11] and since he who is Son of God is also son of man, who, I ask, is glorified in this son of man."[12] He clearly says that the Son of God is not one thing and the son of man another thing; from this, the above determination is strengthened and approved.

11. IN ORDER TO MAKE A DETERMINATION, HE ALSO NOTES SOME OTHER WORDS OF THE AUTHORITIES. And what was said earlier, 'Christ is both and one person,'[13] may trouble the reader; as also that which Augustine says in *On the Trinity*, book 1: "Because the form of God took the form of a servant, both are God, both are man; but both God because it is God who takes, and both man, because it is man who is taken."[14] And that which the same says in the book *On the Good of Perseverance*: "He who is faithful believes that, when in Christ God the Word took a true human nature, he so raised it up that the one who took and that which he took were one person in the Trinity; by that taking, he ineffably brought about the truth of one person in God and man."[15] But if he who took and that which he took is one person, then the human nature is one person with the Word.

[10]John of Damascus, *De fide orthodoxa*, bk 3 c3.
[11]Jn. 1, 14.
[12]Hilary, *De Trinitate*, bk 9 n40; Jn. 13, 31-32.
[13]Above, n8.
[14]Augustine, *De Trinitate*, bk 1 c7 n14.
[15]Augustine, *De dono perseverantiae*, c24 n67.

12. HERE HE MAKES USE OF AN AUTHORITY TO CONFIRM THE DETERMINATION. But they hand down that all these things would have been said in the following sense: that Christ is said to be both and one person, because one Christ and one person subsist in both. And the taker is said to be one person with what is taken, because what is taken is joined to the taker in unity of person, that is, in such a way that the unity of person persisted, but not in such a way that flesh and soul are God. For as Jerome says, "the Word is God, not the flesh that was taken."[16] And Ambrose, in *On the Holy Spirit*, book 3, says: "The taker is one thing, and what was taken is something else."[17]

13. HERE HE SETS OUT AN AUTHORITY WHICH APPEARS TO BE MUCH OPPOSED TO THEIR VIEW. There is also another text which appears to run very much counter to this view. For Augustine says, in the book *Against Maximinus*: "Christ is one person of twofold substance, because he is both God and man. And God or man cannot be said to be part of this person: otherwise the Son of God was not wholly God before taking the form of a servant, and he attained that stature when man joined his divinity."[18] See, he says that God is not part of that person; and so it appears that that person is not comprised of God and man.

14. THEIR RESPONSE, WITH A DETERMINATION. To which also they say that that person does not consist from God and man as if a whole from its parts. For the parts of some whole come together in such a way that what was not before is composed of them. But it is not in such a way that the human and divine nature are united in Christ: for the order of this union, which is not a union of parts, is inexplicable.—ANOTHER SOLUTION. But some hold that the term 'God' there signifies person, because [Augustine] was speaking of the three persons, none of whom he said was a part of the Trinity, just as God is not a part of this person. But if it is understood of a person, then it is obvious, because a person is not a part of a person.

15. We have diligently set out the second view and the explanation for it. No objection, or almost none, arises to the second view from the authorities which are brought forward in the third view, to which we must now turn.

16. WHAT THE MEANING OF THE AFORESAID PROPOSITIONS IS ACCORDING TO THE THIRD VIEW. And so, in this view, 'God was made man' is said because he took human form; and 'man' is said because he has human form or because he is one who has human form; and 'man was made God,' because he was taken by God; and 'man is God,' because the one who has taken human form is God.

[16]Jerome, *Epistola 9 (ad Paulam et Eustochium)*, n12.
[17]Ambrose, *De incarnationis dominicae sacramento*, c6 n61.
[18]Augustine, *Contra Maximinum*, bk 2 c10 n2.

17. CASSIODORUS. And so, in saying 'God is man,' either the habit is predicated, or the person, but humanized. And Cassiodorus appears to show that a humanized person is what is being predicated, saying: "He was made, so to speak, a humanized God, who does not cease to be God, even in the taking of flesh."[19] Yet this may be taken in different ways: as to say 'God was made one who is humanized,' or 'Christ is made a God who is humanized'; for either of these may certainly be said. And so, when 'God was made man' is said, according to them, it has a manifold meaning: that he is understood to have taken human nature, or to have begun to be the Word humanized. Yet it does not follow that, if he began to be the Word humanized, that he would have begun to be the Word. Nor, if God is made the Word humanized, does it follow that he was made the Word. As when concerning someone we say: Today he began to be a good man or was made a good man, and yet he did not begin to be a man or was made a man today.

Chapter 2 (24)

1. IN WHAT SENSE, ACCORDING TO THEM, HE IS CALLED PREDESTINED. According to them, Christ, insofar as he is a man, is said to be predestined to be Son of God: because it was predestined by God from eternity, and it was conferred on him in time through grace, that he, being a man, be the Son of God. For he did not always have this, but took it in time through grace.

2. HE CONFIRMS THE EXPOSITION BY AUTHORITY.—AUGUSTINE. Augustine appears to have noted this in the book *To Prosper and Hilary*, saying: "Jesus was predestined so that he who was going to be the son of David according to the flesh, should be Son of God *in power*."[1]

3. And when Christ is said to be less than the Father according to his being a man, they understand this to be said according to habit, that is, insofar as he has a man united to himself. Hence Augustine, in *On the Trinity*, book 1: "God the Son is equal in nature with God the Father, but less in habit. For in *the form of a servant*, he is less than the Father; in *the form of God*, he is equal to the Father."[2]

4. WHY HE IS NOT CALLED A DEIFIED MAN. And because the manner of the incarnation is to be taken according to habit, therefore they hand down that he is called God made man, and not a deified man. Hence John of Damascus: "We do not call him a deified man, but God made man."[3]

[19]Cassiodorus, *Expositio Psalmorum*, Ps. 56, division.

[1]Augustine, *De praedestinatione sanctorum*, c15 n31.
[2]Augustine, *De Trinitate*, bk 1 c7 n14.
[3]John of Damascus, *De fide orthodoxa*, bk 3 c2.

Chapter 3 (25)

1. WHY HE IS NOT TO BE CALLED THE LORD'S MAN. And although he is called 'man God,' yet he is not fittingly called 'the Lord's man.' Hence Augustine in the book of *Retractations*: "I do not see whether he who is *the mediator of God and men, Christ Jesus*,[1] may rightly be called the Lord's man although he is entirely Lord; and that I might have used the expression, I found it in some Catholic writers. But wherever I have said this, I wish it unsaid. For afterwards I saw that it ought not to be said, although it may be defended with some reason."[2]

2. According to them, the person of the Son is also said to exist in or from two natures according to adherence and in-essence: for the one inheres in him, the other is in him.

3. THAT THE FOREGOING DO NOT SUFFICE FOR AN UNDERSTANDING OF THIS QUESTION. With sufficient diligence, I have treated the question posed above according to the views of different people, without prejudice or assertion of my own. And yet, in such a great matter and one so difficult to understand, I do not wish the reader to believe that our disputation should suffice. But let him also read other, perhaps better considered and argued, treatments. As for those things which may trouble him here, let him, if he can, examine them with a more careful and more discerning mind, always holding firmly that (*ON ECCLESIASTICAL DOGMAS*): "God took on man, man passed into God, not by a changeableness of nature, but by God's condescension: so that God is neither changed into human substance by taking on man, nor is man changed into the divine one by being glorified into God, because a transformation or changeableness makes for a diminution of nature and the abolition of substance."[3]

DISTINCTION VIII

Chapter 1 (26)

1. WHETHER THE DIVINE NATURE OUGHT TO BE SAID TO BE BORN OF THE VIRGIN. After the aforesaid, it must be considered whether it is to be granted concerning the divine nature that it was born of the Virgin, as it is said to have become flesh in the Virgin.—And it seems that it ought not at all to be said to be born of the Virgin, since it was not born of the Father: for a thing which is not begotten of the Father does not seem to be born of the Mother, lest some thing have the name of filiation as to humanity

[1]Cf. 1 Tim. 2, 5.
[2]Augustine, *Retractationes*, bk 1 c19 n8.
[3]Gennadius, *Liber seu diffinitio ecclesiasticorum dogmatum*, c2.

which it does not have as to divinity.—And yet it appears that it can be proved that it was born of the Virgin, for if for God to be born of the Virgin is this: namely to take on human form in the Virgin's womb, since the divine nature has been said above to have taken human form,[1] it appears that it must be said to have been born.

2. And concerning this, Augustine, in the book *On Faith to Peter*, speaks as follows: "The eternal and divine nature could not be conceived temporally and be born from human nature, unless, according to the taking of human truth, the ineffable divinity took into itself a true conception and birth in time. So the eternal God is truly conceived and born of the Virgin in time."[2]—It appears to be indicated by this authority that the divine nature is born and conceived of the Virgin; but if the words are diligently noted, it is seen to treat rather of the person: which without doubt must be said to be born of the Father and the Mother.

Chapter 2 (27)

ON THE TWOFOLD BIRTH OF CHRIST, WHO WAS BORN TWICE. It is also usual to ask whether Christ ought to be said to have been begotten twice, since he is called son of God and of man.—To which it can be said that Christ was born twice, and had two nativities. Hence Augustine, in the book *On Faith to Peter*: "God the Father, from his own nature, begot God the Son, equal and coeternal with himself. And this same only-begotten God was born twice: once from the Father, once from the Mother. For God the Word was born of the Father, and the Word made flesh was born of the Mother. And so one and the same Son of God is born before time, and is born in time; and each birth, namely the divine and the human, is of the one Son of God."[1]—JOHN OF DAMASCUS. John too says of this: "We revere the two nativities of Christ: one from the Father before time," which is "beyond cause and reason and time and nature; and one in the last times, for us, and like us, and above us. For us, because for our salvation; like us, because he was a man born of woman and in the [usual] time from conception," namely nine months; "above us, because it was not by seed, but by the Holy Spirit and the holy Virgin, transcending the law of conception."[2]—From these words, it is clearly apparent that there were two nativities of Christ, and that he was born twice.

[1]Dist. 5 c1 nn5-10.
[2]Fulgentius, *De fide ad Petrum*, c2 n14.

[1]Fulgentius, *De fide ad Petrum*, c2 nn10-11.
[2]John of Damascus, *De fide orthodoxa*, bk 3 c7.

DISTINCTION IX

Chapter 1 (28)

1. ON THE ADORATION OF CHRIST'S HUMANITY: WHETHER THE SAME ADORATION IS TO BE EXTENDED TO HIS HUMANITY AND TO HIS DIVINITY. Moreover, it is necessary to investigate whether the flesh and soul of Christ must be adored by one and the same adoration as the Word, namely that which is called *latria*. But *latria* is understood as the service or worship due to the Creator alone;[1] if it is extended to the soul or flesh of Christ, since the soul of Christ or his flesh is only a creature, that which is due to the Creator alone is extended to the creature. The charge of idolatry is made against one who does such a thing.

2. SOME SAY THAT IT IS NOT TO BE ADORED BY THE SAME ADORATION. And so it seems to some that the flesh or soul of Christ is not to be adored by the adoration which is *latria*, but by the one which is *dulia*.[2]—ON THE KINDS OF *DULIA*. Of the latter, they say that there are two kinds or modes. For there is one kind of *dulia* which may be extended to any creature; and there is another kind which may be extended to the humanity of Christ alone, and not to any creature, because the humanity of Christ is to be venerated and loved above all other creatures, and yet not so much as to extend to it the worship due to the divinity. This worship consists in love, the offer of sacrifice, and reverence: it is called 'piety' in Latin, and in Greek *theosebia*, that is, the worship of God; or *eusebia*, that is, good worship.[3]

3. THE VIEW OF OTHERS, WHO HAND DOWN THAT THE SAME ADORATION IS TO BE EXTENDED TO BOTH. But it pleases others that Christ's humanity is to be adored in one adoration with the Word: not for its own sake, but for the sake of him whose foot-stool it is, to whom it is united; not the mere or naked humanity itself, but with the Word to whom it is united; nor for its own sake, but it is to be adored for the sake of the Word. Nor is the one who does this liable to the charge of idolatry because he does not serve the creature alone, nor for its own sake; he serves the Creator with and in his humanity.

4. JOHN OF DAMASCUS. Concerning this, John speaks as follows: "There are two natures of Christ by reason and manner of their difference, but united according to the hypostasis. And so Christ is one, perfect God and perfect man, whom we adore with the Father and the Spirit in one adoration with his untainted flesh; we do not say that the flesh is not to be

[1]Cf., e.g., Augustine, *De Trinitate*, bk 1 c6 n13.
[2]Cf. Augustine, *Quaestiones in Heptateuchum*, bk 1 q61; bk 2 q94.
[3]Cf. Augustine, *Enchiridion*, c2.

adored: for it is adored in the one hypostasis of the Word, which hypostasis was begotten; we do not extend veneration to what was created. For we do not adore it as naked flesh, but as united to the divinity into the one hypostasis of the Word of God in whom the two natures come together. I fear to touch the coal because of the fire which is joined to the wood. I worship both natures of my Christ because of the divinity which is joined to the flesh. For I do not posit a fourth person in the Trinity, but I confess the one person of the Word and his flesh."[4] By these words, it seems to be indicated that the humanity of Christ is to be adored in one adoration with the Word.

5. AUGUSTINE. Augustine too speaks of this, commenting on the Lord's words: *Do not let your heart be troubled*;[5] he says as follows: "The heretics say that the Son is not God by nature, but a created thing. To them it is to be answered that, if the Son is not God by nature, but a creature, then he is not to be worshipped at all, nor to be adored as God, since the Apostle says: *They worshipped and served the creature rather than the Creator*.[6] But they will reply to this and say: Why is it that, although you do not deny his flesh to be a created thing, yet you adore it together with his divinity, and you serve it no less than his divinity? I adore the Lord's flesh, or rather the perfect humanity in Christ, because it has been taken up by the divinity and it has been united to the Godhead: so that I may confess the Son of God not as being two different things, but one and the same God and man. Indeed, if you severed the man from God, I would not under any circumstance believe in him nor serve him. If one finds the royal purple or diadem lying about, will he presume to adore them? But when the king has put them on, one who refused to adore them along with the king incurs the danger of death. So also, if anyone refused to adore in Christ the Lord his humanity—not alone or naked, but united to his divinity—namely the one Son, true God and true man, he will die eternally."[7]

6. The same on Psalm 98, where it says: *Adore his foot-stool, for it is holy*:[8] "It is to be known that in Christ there is earth, that is, flesh; which is adored without impiety. For he took on earth from earth, because flesh is from the earth, and he took flesh from the flesh of Mary. This flesh, which is taken by the Word of God, is adored by us without impiety because no one eats of his flesh without first adoring it; but one who adores it gazes not upon the earth, but rather upon him whose foot-stool it is and

[4]John of Damascus, *De fide orthodoxa*, bk 3 c8.
[5]Jn. 14, 1.
[6]Rom. 1, 25.
[7]Pseudo-Augustine, *De verbis Domini*, sermon 58 or sermon 246, n5.
[8]Ps. 98, 5.

for whose sake he adores it."[9]—By these authorities, the solution to the above inquiry is revealed.

Distinction X

Chapter 1 (29)

1. Whether Christ, according to his being a man, is a person or anything. It is also usual for some to ask whether Christ, according to his being a man, is a person, or even is anything.

2. Argumentation on each side of the question. There are arguments on each side of the question. That he is a person, they argue with the following reasons: If he is anything according to his being man, then he is either a person, or a substance, or something else. But he is not something else, so he is either a person or a substance. But if he is a substance, then he is either a rational one or an irrational one; but he is not an irrational substance, so he is a rational one. But if, according to his being man, he is a rational substance, then he is a person, because this is the definition of a person: "A rational substance of individual nature."[1] And so, if he is anything according to his being man, then he is a person according to his being man.—But conversely, if, according to his being man, he is a person, then either he is the third person in the Trinity or some other person; but he is not some other person; and so he is the third person in the Trinity. But if, according to his being man, he is the third person in the Trinity, then he is God.

3. Because of these and other unsuitable conclusions, some say that Christ, according to his being man, is not a person or anything else, unless perhaps 'according' is expressive of the unity of the person. For 'according' has a manifold function: at times it expresses the condition or property of the divine or human nature, at times the unity of the person; at times it denotes habit, at times a cause. Let the reader diligently ponder the reason for the distinction and store it in the innermost recess of his memory, lest his understanding of it be confused when the term occurs in regard to Christ.

4. Although Christ, according to his being man, is said to be a rational substance, yet it does not therefore follow that, according to his being man, he is a person. And yet, what was adduced in the above argumentation does not follow: that if Christ, according to his being man, is a rational substance, therefore he is a person. Indeed,

[9]Augustine, *Enarrationes in Psalmos*, on Ps. 98, n9.

[1]Boethius, as above, dist. 5 c3 n2.

even now the soul of Christ is a rational substance, and yet not a person because it does not speak by itself,[2] and, indeed, is joined to another thing. But that description of person is not given for those three persons [of the Trinity].

5. ANOTHER PROOF THAT CHRIST IS A PERSON. But they strive to prove in yet another way that Christ, according to his being man, is a person: because Christ, according to his being man, *was predestined* to be *Son of God.*[3] But he is that which he was predestined to be; and so, if according to his being man, he was predestined to be Son of God, then he is Son of God according to his being man.—RESPONSE. To which it can be said that Christ is that which was predestined to be: for he was predestined to be Son of God, and he truly is Son of God. But according to his being man, he was predestined to be Son of God, because he has this through grace according to his being man; and yet he is not Son of God according to his being man, unless perhaps 'according' is expressive of the unity of person, so that the sense is: he who is a man is the Son of God; but he has it through grace that, being a man, he be Son of God. But if cause is denoted, it is false; for it is not by reason of his being a man that he is Son of God.

Chapter 2 (30)

1. WHETHER CHRIST IS AN ADOPTIVE SON ACCORDING TO HIS BEING MAN OR IN SOME OTHER MANNER. But if it is asked whether Christ is an adoptive son according to his being man or in another manner, we answer that Christ is not an adoptive son in any manner, but only a natural one, because he is son by nature, not by grace of adoption.—But he is not called son by nature in the same way in which he is called God by nature: for he is not son by the same reason by which he is God, because he is son by the property of birth, God by the nature of divinity. And yet he is called son by nature or of nature because he is naturally a son, namely having the same nature as the one who begot him.[1]

2. WHY HE IS NOT AN ADOPTIVE SON. But he is not an adoptive son because he did not first exist and was afterwards adopted as a son, as we are called adoptive children because, although we were born *children of wrath,*[2] we were made *children of God*[3] through grace. But Christ was never not a son, and so he is not an adoptive son.

[2]Peter is punning here, in his definition of person (*persona*) as that which speaks by itself (*per se sonans*).
[3]Rom. 1, 4.

[1]Cf. Hilary, *De Trinitate*, bk 5 n37.
[2]Cf. Eph. 2, 3.
[3]Cf. Jn. 1, 12.

3. OBJECTION THAT HE IS AN ADOPTIVE SON. But the following objection is made to this: Christ is the son of man, that is, of the Virgin, either by grace, or by nature, or in both manners. But if by nature, then either by the divine or the human one; but not by the divine one: and so he is son of man either by human nature, or not by nature [at all]. If not by nature, then by grace alone; and even if by human nature, then no less by grace. But if he is son of the Virgin by grace, then he appears to be an adoptive son: so that the same one is the natural Son of the Father and the adoptive son of the Virgin.—RESPONSE. To which it can be said that Christ is the son of the Virgin by nature or naturally and by grace; and yet he is not the adoptive son of the Virgin because he is said to be son of the Virgin not by adoption, but by union. For he is called son of the Virgin because in the Virgin he took on human form into the unity of person; and this was a matter of grace, not of nature.—Hence Augustine, in *On John*: "That the only-begotten is equal to the Father is not a matter of grace, but of nature; but that a man was taken up in the unity of the person of the only-begotten is a matter of grace, not of nature."[4] And so Christ is the adoptive son neither of God, nor of man; he is naturally the Son of God, and he is son of man naturally and by grace.

4. Augustine, in the book *On Faith to Peter*, shows that he is naturally son of man: "He, namely God, was naturally made son of man who is naturally the only-begotten son of God the Father."[5]

5. But that he is not an adoptive son, and yet is a son by grace, is proved by the following testimonies. Jerome, in *On the Epistle to the Ephesians*, says: "It was written of Christ Jesus that he was ever with the Father, and the Father's will that he exist never preceded him. And what is more, he is son by nature; but we are sons by adoption. He was never not son; before being such, we were predestined, and then we received *the spirit of adoption*,[6] when we believed in the Son of God."[7]—Hilary too, in *On the Trinity*, book 3, says: "By saying, *Glorify your Son*,[8] the Lord attested that he was son not only in name, but also in property. We are sons of God, but not as he is son: for he is a true and proper son: by origin, not adoption; in truth, not in name only; by birth, not by creation."[9]—Augustine too, in *On John*, says: "We are sons by grace, not by nature; but the only-begotten is son by nature, not by grace. Is this also to be referred to the human form in the Son himself? Assuredly so."[10]—Ambrose also, in *On the Trinity*,

[4]Augustine, *In Ioannem*, tr. 74 n3.
[5]Fulgentius, *De fide ad Petrum*, c2 n14.
[6]Cf. Rom. 8, 15.
[7]Jerome, *In quattuor Epistolas Paulinas*, Eph. 1, 5.
[8]Jn. 17, 1.
[9]Hilary, *De Trinitate*, bk 3 n11.
[10]Augustine, *In Ioannem*, tr. 82 n4.

book 1, says: "Christ is son not by adoption, but by nature; we are called sons by adoption; he is such by the truth of nature."[11]—From these testimonies, it is clearly shown that Christ is not son by the grace of adoption. For it is the grace of adoption which is meant when Augustine asserts that he is not son by grace:[12] for the Son of God is son of man, and vice versa, by the grace of union and not by that of adoption.

Chapter 3 (31)

WHETHER THE PERSON OR THE NATURE WAS PREDESTINED. If it is then asked whether the predestination which the Apostle recalls[1] is of the person or of the nature, it can truly be said that the person of the Son, which existed always, was predestined according to the human form taken, namely that the same person, being man, be Son of God; and the human nature was predestined that it be united personally to the Word of the Father.

DISTINCTION XI

Chapter 1 (32)

1. WHETHER CHRIST IS A CREATURE, OR CREATED, OR MADE. It is also usual to ask whether it ought simply to be said and granted that Christ was made, or created, or is a creature.—To which it can be said that this is said less than suitably, if it is asserted simply and without determination; and if it happens that, for the sake of brevity, this is simply stated, yet it is never to be simply understood because, as Augustine shows, in *On the Trinity*, book 1, "when we speak of Christ, the prudent, diligent, and pious reader must understand what is being said, according to what, and on account of what."[1]

2. In *On the Trinity*, book 1, he also shows that Christ or the Son of God was not made and is not a creature; he speaks as follows: "*In the beginning was the Word*, and *the Word was made flesh*, and *all things were made through him.*[2] Now *all things* refers to the things that were made, that is, every creature. From this, it is clearly apparent that he himself was not made through whom all things were made. And if he was not made, he is not a creature. But if he is not a creature, he is of the same substance with the Father. For any substance which is not God is a creature; and

[11]Ambrose, *De fide*, bk 1 c19 n126.
[12]Just above, *In Ioannem.*

[1]Rom. 1, 4.

[1]Augustine, *De Trinitate*, bk 1 c13 n28.
[2]Jn. 1, 1, 14, and 3.

what is not a creature is God. But if the Son is not of the same substance as the Father, then he is a substance that was made; and if he is a substance that was made, all things were not made through him. But *all things were made through him*."[3] And so he is not a substance that was made, but he is one not-made substance with the Father.—Also, in the same place: "But if the Father made the Son, whom the Son himself did not make, all things were not made through the Son. But *all things were made through*[4] the Son; and so he himself was not made, so that with the Father he might make all things that were made."[5]

3. The same in the book of *84 Questions*: "A creature is anything which God the Father made through the Son; the latter cannot himself be called a creature because through him all things were made."[6]—Ambrose, in *On the Trinity*, book 1, says: "Let us prove that the Son of God is not a creature. For we have heard in the Gospel that the Lord commanded his disciples: *Preach the Gospel to every creature*.[7] In saying *every creature*, he is not excepting any. And where does that leave those who call Christ a creature? For if he were a creature, he would be commanding that the Gospel be preached to himself";[8] and he would be subject to vanity because, as the Apostle attests, *every creature is subject to vanity*.[9] "And so Christ is not a creature, but the Creator, who commands the disciples to teach the creature."[10]

Chapter 2 (33)

1. ON THE PERFIDY AND PUNISHMENT OF ARIUS.—AMBROSE, IN *ON THE TRINITY*, BOOK 1. We read that the perfidy of Arius consisted in the profession that Christ is a creature. And so "the bowels of Arius gushed out and he burst in the middle, falling on his face, polluting those foul lips with which he had denied Christ."[1]

2. IN WHAT SENSE CHRIST IS SAID TO HAVE BEEN MADE. From these and several other testimonies, we are instructed not to simply confess that 'Christ was made or is a creature'; but this may rightly be said with the addition of a determination, as if we were to say that he was made according to the flesh or according to his humanity, so that having been made is attributed to his humanity, not to God.—For as Ambrose says in *On the*

[3]Augustine, *De Trinitate*, bk 1 c6 n9.
[4]Cf. Jn. 1, 3.
[5]Augustine, *De Trinitate*, bk 1 c6 n12.
[6]Augustine, *De diversis quaestionibus 83*, q67 nn1-2.
[7]Mk. 16, 15.
[8]Ambrose, *De fide*, bk 1 c14 n86.
[9]Rom. 8, 20.
[10]Ambrose, *De fide*, bk 1 c14 n86.

[1]Ambrose, *De fide*, bk 1 c19 nn123, 124.

Trinity, book 1, "He was not made God, but God was born Son of God; but afterwards, he was made man from Mary according to the flesh. *For God sent his Son, made from a woman, made under the Law*.[2] He says *his* Son, namely not one out of many. In saying *his*, he designated the property of eternal generation. He asserted afterwards that he was *made from a woman* so that his being made might be ascribed not to his divinity, but to his putting on of a body. And so he says *made from a woman* for the taking on of flesh; *made under the Law* for the observance of the Law."[3] "Generation causes no prejudice to generation, nor flesh to the divinity."[4] "For the eternal God took up the sacrament of the incarnation not as divided, but as one, and as one in both, namely in divinity and a body. For he was not one thing from the Father and another from the Virgin, but was the same in one way from the Father and in another from the Virgin."[5] And he was made "according to the putting on of our nature, not according to the substance of eternal life."[6] Of him, "we read *first-born* and *only-begotten*: first-born, because there was none before him; only-begotten, because after him there was no one."[7]—From these words, it is clearly handed down in what sense it is to be taken when we say that Christ was *made*, whether simply or with a qualification, namely so that the being made or being a creature be referred not to the God who takes on, but to the humanity which is taken on.

3. For in God there cannot be a creature, as Ambrose says in *On the Trinity*, book 1: "Was Christ made by a word? Was Christ created by a command? But how can there be a creature in God? For God is of a simple nature, not of a conjoined or composite one; nothing can be added to him, and he has in his nature only that which is divine."[8]

4. And so, although Christ is called a creature according to his humanity, yet Christ is not simply to be called a creature. Nor does it follow that, because Christ is said to be a creature according to his humanity, one may proceed to argue as follows: If Christ is a creature according to his humanity, then either he is a rational one or not, or a creature which is God or not. This argument strives to prove that Christ is something not divine, because he is that which he is according to his humanity. And so, if, according to his humanity, he is some substance which is not divine, then he is certainly something which is not divine.—But there is no right way for an argument to proceed from figurative speech; and the expression is in-

[2]Gal. 4, 4.
[3]Ambrose, *De fide*, bk 1 c14 nn93, 94.
[4]Ambrose, *De incarnationis dominicae sacramento*, c5 n36.
[5]Ibid., c5 n35.
[6]Ibid., c5 n37.
[7]Ambrose, *De fide*, bk 1 c14 n89.
[8]Ibid., bk 1 c16 nn105-106.

deed a figurative one by which Christ is called a creature, whether simply or with qualification.

DISTINCTION XII

Chapter 1 (34)

1. WHETHER THAT MAN ALWAYS WAS OR BEGAN TO BE. After the above, it is asked whether that man began to be or always was, just as we simply say that Christ or the Son of God always was and did not begin to be.

2. Concerning this, Augustine speaks as follows, in *On John*: "There was a time when the Son of God had something which that same man and son did not yet have, because he had not yet become man."[1] Also, in the same: "Before the world was, neither we, nor the very *mediator of God and men, the man Christ Jesus,* existed."[2,3] The same on the Psalm: "Our Christ, although he is perhaps a recent man, yet he is eternal God."[4]—But elsewhere we read that "that child created the stars";[5] and Christ says that he is *the beginning*, and that he was *before Abraham.*[6]

3. And so, in no way departing from these authorities, we say that that man, insofar as he is a man, had a beginning; insofar as he is the Word, he always was. For here a response is not to be handed down without distinction. Indeed, Augustine himself makes use of this distinction in several places, saying that all things were made through Christ, insofar as he is the Word; but according to his being man, he himself was made and glorified. And so, if you look to the person, confidently say that that man always was; but if to the human nature, grant that he had a beginning.

Chapter 2 (35)

1. IF GOD COULD HAVE TAKEN ON ANOTHER HUMAN NATURE OR FROM OTHER THAN THE STOCK OF ADAM. It is also usual to ask whether God could have taken on another human nature or from other than the stock of Adam.

2. RESPONSE. To which it may certainly be said that he could have taken another soul and another flesh, because it was by grace alone that that soul and flesh were taken by the Word of God.—AUGUSTINE, IN *ON THE*

[1] Augustine, *In Ioannem*, tr. 106 n5.
[2] 1 Tim. 2, 5.
[3] Augustine, *In Ioannem*, tr. 105 n7.
[4] Augustine, *Enarrationes in Psalmos*, on Ps. 80, 10.
[5] Cf. Fulgentius of Ruspe, *Sermo* 4 nn6 and 8.
[6] Cf. Jn. 8, 25 and 58.

TRINITY, BOOK 13. For as Augustine says, "in those things which arise in time, that is the highest grace: that man is joined to God in the unity of person."[1] And so God could take another soul and another flesh.—And certainly he could have taken flesh other than from the stock of Adam. Hence Augustine, in *On the Trinity*, book 13: "God could certainly have taken from elsewhere a human form in which to be the mediator of God and men, and not from the stock of that Adam who bound humankind by his sin, just as he did not create Adam from the stock of another when he first created him. And so he was able, either in a similar way, or in any other way that pleased him, to create another by whom the conqueror of the first man might be overcome. But he judged it better to take human form through which to conquer the enemy of humankind from the very stock which had been conquered; and yet to take it from a virgin, whose conceiving was preceded by the Spirit and faith, and not by flesh and lust. Nor was there present that concupiscence of the flesh by which others are conceived who contract original sin. Holy virginity was made fruitful by belief, not by conjugal intercourse."[2] From these words, it is openly shown that God could have taken another human form and from another stock.

Chapter 3 (36)

1. IF IT WOULD HAVE BEEN POSSIBLE FOR THAT MAN TO SIN OR NOT BE GOD. And so, it is not undeservedly asked whether that man might have been able to sin, or not to be God. For if he could sin, then he could be damned; if he could be damned, he could not be God; and so, if he could sin, he could not be God, because to be God and to be able to will iniquity cannot exist together.[1]

2. RESPONSE. Here there is need to distinguish whether we are speaking of the person or of the nature. For if we are speaking of the person, it is manifest that he could not sin, nor was he able not to be God. But if we are concerned with the nature, then we must clarify whether we are speaking of it as united to the Word, or of it as if not united to the Word and yet a being; that is, whether of it according as it was united to the Word, or of it as according to its being able to be and yet not be united to the Word. For it is not in doubt that that soul, being united to the Word, is not able to sin; and it is also true without doubt that the same soul, if it existed and was not united to the Word, would be able to sin.

[1]Augustine, *De Trinitate*, bk 13 c19 n24.
[2]Ibid., bk 13 c18 n23.

[1]Interlinear gloss, on Ps. 5, 5.

3. THE OBJECTION OF SOME, THAT IT WAS ABLE TO SIN EVEN WHEN UNITED TO GOD. But some strive to prove that, even when united to the Word, it is able to sin because it has free choice and so can bend to either side. —But this is frivolous, since the angels also have free choice,[2] and yet they are so confirmed by grace that they cannot sin. And so how much more [free choice did] that man [have] to whom the Spirit was given without measure?[3]

4. THEY INVOKE AUTHORITY IN SUPPORT OF THE SAME POINT. They also adduce authority to prove the same point. For it is written in the book of Wisdom: *He could have transgressed and did not, could have done evil and did not.*[4]—But this is to be taken as referring to the members, or as partly to the head and partly to the members.[5] It refers to the head in saying: *he did not* transgress and he *did not* do evil; it refers to the members in saying: *he could have transgressed*, and *could have done evil.*

Chapter 4 (37)

WHETHER GOD COULD HAVE TAKEN HUMAN FORM IN THE FEMALE SEX. It is also usual for some to ask, if only for effect, whether God could have taken human nature according to the female sex.—Some judge that he could have taken human form in the female sex as he did in the male; but it was done more suitably and fittingly that he be born of a woman and take male form so that the liberation of both sexes might be shown. Hence Augustine, in the book of *84 Questions*: "The liberation of humankind had to manifest itself in each of the sexes. And so, because it was necessary that he take the form of a male, which is the more honourable sex, it followed that the liberation of the female sex manifest itself in the fact that that man was born of a woman."[1] "And so the Wisdom of God, which is called the only-begotten Son, declared the liberation of humankind by taking human form"[2] in the womb and from the womb of the Virgin.

[2]Cf. Bk 2 dist. 25 c3.
[3]Cf. Jn. 3, 34.
[4]Eccli. 31, 10.
[5]Cf. Augustine, *De doctrina christiana*, bk 3 c31 n44.

[1]Augustine, *De diversis quaestionibus 83*, q11.
[2]Ibid.

DISTINCTION XIII

Chapter 1 (38)

1. WHETHER CHRIST, ACCORDING TO HIS HUMAN NATURE, WAS ABLE TO, AND DID, MAKE PROGRESS IN WISDOM AND GRACE. Moreover, it is to be known that Christ, according to his human nature, received the fullness of grace from the moment of conception, for to him *the Spirit was not given according to measure,*[1] and in him *the fullness of the divinity dwells in bodily form.*[2]

2. HOW THE FULLNESS OF THE DIVINITY IS SAID TO DWELL IN CHRIST. But it dwells in such a way, as Augustine says in *To Dardanus*, that he is filled with every grace; it does not so dwell in the saints. Just as "in our body there is a sense in each of the members, but not so much as in the head: for in the head there is sight and hearing and smell and taste and touch, but in the others there is only touch,"[3] so also in Christ *dwells the fullness of the divinity*, because he is the head in which are all the senses; but in the saints there is, as it were, touch alone, for to them the spirit was given according to measure, when they took *from his fullness.*[4]—HOW 'WE TOOK FROM HIS FULLNESS,' IS TO BE UNDERSTOOD. But they took from his fullness not according to essence, but according to likeness, because they did not receive the same grace as to essence, but a like one.

3. And so that child was *filled with wisdom and grace*[5] from the moment of conception. Hence Jeremias rightly says: *The Lord will make something new upon the earth: a woman will encompass a man,*[6] because a perfect man came into existence in the Virgin's womb, and not only in regard to soul and flesh, but also in regard to the wisdom and grace with which he was filled.[7]

4. HE SETS OUT AN AUTHORITY WHICH SEEMS TO CONTRADICT [THIS]. But there appears to be a contradiction between this and what we read in the Gospel of Luke: *Jesus made progress in wisdom and age and grace before God and men.*[8] For if he made progress in wisdom and grace, it does not seem that he had fullness of grace without measure from the moment of conception.

[1] Jn. 3, 34.
[2] Col. 2, 9.
[3] Augustine, *Epistola* 187 c13 n40.
[4] Cf. Jn. 1, 16.
[5] Cf. Lk. 2, 40.
[6] Jer. 31, 22.
[7] Cf. interlinear gloss, on Jer. 31, 22.
[8] Lk. 2, 52.

5. DETERMINATION OF THE AUTHORITY. To which it can truly be said that, according to his humanity, he received from his conception such fullness of wisdom and grace that God could not confer it more fully upon him. And yet he is truly said to have made progress in wisdom and grace; indeed, not in himself, but in others, who made progress from his wisdom and grace while, increasing in age, he made more and more manifest to them his gifts of wisdom and grace.—GREGORY. Hence Gregory says in some homily: "He made progress in wisdom according to human nature: not that he, who remained filled with the spirit of wisdom from the first hour of his conception, became wiser by the passage of time, but that he gradually over time manifested to others that same wisdom with which he was filled. According to his human nature, *he made progress in age*: from infancy to youth; according to his human nature, *he made progress in grace*: not by he himself receiving in time what he did not have before, but by revealing the gift of grace which he had; *before God and men*: because, with his progress in age, the more he revealed to men the gifts of grace and wisdom which were in him, the more he moved them to the praise of God; and so he made progress for God the Father as to praise, and for men as to salvation."[9]—Therefore it was in others, not in himself, that *he made progress in wisdom and grace*. Hence in the same Gospel that child is shown to be *filled with wisdom and grace*.[10] And so he is said to have made progress in wisdom and grace in the same way as some ecclesiastical prelate is said to make progress in the care entrusted to him when others make progress by his industry.

6. WHAT AMBROSE SAYS APPEARS TO CONTRADICT WHAT WAS SAID ABOVE. And yet elsewhere it is found to have been written that he had made progress according to human senses, just as he made progress in human age. For Ambrose says as follows, in *On the Holy Spirit*, book 3: "God took on the perfection of human nature. He took human sense, but was not made proud by the senses of the flesh.[11] With human sense, he said that his soul was troubled;[12] with human sense, he was hungry and he prayed;[13] with human sense, he made progress, as it is written: *Jesus made progress in age and wisdom and grace*.[14] How did the wisdom of God make progress? There was a progress of age and a progress of wisdom, but of the human one. That is why he mentioned age, so that you would believe it to be said by reference to man: for age does not pertain to the

[9]Ordinary gloss, on Lk. 2, 52, under Gregory's name; but see Bede, *In Evangelia*, hom. 1.19.
[10]Cf. Lk. 2, 40.
[11]Cf. Col. 2, 18.
[12]Cf. Jn. 12, 27.
[13]Cf. Mt. 4, 2; Lk. 22, 32.
[14]Lk. 2, 52.

divinity, but to the body. And so, if he made progress in human age, he also made progress in human wisdom. But his senses made progress; and because his senses did, so did his wisdom."[15]—ON THE TWO SENSES OF CHRIST, NAMELY THE TWOFOLD WISDOM. "Which sense made progress? If the human one, then it was taken; if the divine one, then it is changeable through progress: for what makes progress is changed for the better. But what is divine is not changed;[16] and so what is changed is not divine. Therefore it was his human sense that made progress: it follows that he took a human sense."[17] "The power of God could not be made stronger, nor could God grow, nor could the depth of God's wisdom be filled.[18] And so the wisdom that was filled was not God's, but ours. For how could he be filled, who *came down in order to fill all things*?[19] And in what sense did Isaias say that the child knew neither his father nor his mother? For it is written: *Before the child knows his father and mother*, he will take *the spoils of Samaria.*[20] For future and hidden things do not escape God's wisdom; but a child who has not yet acquired knowledge, because of human ignorance, cannot know what he has not yet learned."[21]—"But we must be careful, I say, not to divide Christ by attributing to him two principal senses or a twofold wisdom. But do we divide Christ when we adore both his divinity and flesh? Do we divide him when we venerate in him God's image and the cross? Certainly, the Apostle, who said of him: *For although he was crucified from our weakness, yet he lives by the power of God,*[22] also said that *Christ is not divided.*[23] Do we divide him when we say that he took a rational soul capable of understanding as we do? For God the Word himself was not in his flesh as a substitute for a rational soul which was capable of understanding; but he was perfect man by taking a rational soul and capable of understanding, a human soul and of the same substance as our souls, and a flesh similar to ours and of the same substance as our flesh."[24]

7. ON THE MEANING OF THE ABOVE WORDS. These words of Ambrose are to be examined with pious diligence because in part they instruct and enlighten our human ignorance, but in part, if they are badly understood, provide an occasion for error.

[15]Ambrose, *De incarnationis dominicae sacramento*, c7 nn71-72.
[16]Cf. Num. 23, 19; Mal. 3, 6.
[17]Ambrose, *De incarnationis dominicae sacramento*, c7 n72.
[18]Cf. Lk. 2, 40; Rom. 11, 33.
[19]Eph. 4, 10.
[20]Is. 8, 4.
[21]Ambrose, *De incarnationis dominicae sacramento*, c7 nn73-74.
[22]2 Cor. 13, 4.
[23]1 Cor. 1, 13.
[24]Ambrose, *De incarnationis dominicae sacramento*, c7 nn75-76.

8. ON THE TWOFOLD WISDOM OF CHRIST: BEGOTTEN AND CREATED. And indeed, it is clearly handed down by these words that there are two principal senses, or a twofold wisdom, in Christ. Nor is the unity and singularity of the person divided on that account, but he has two wisdoms according to his two natures: the first, which is he himself, is begotten and not created; the second is not begotten, but created, and is conferred upon him by grace. Indeed, Isaias presages of him: *The spirit of wisdom and understanding shall rest over him*, etc.[25] And so, by the spirit of wisdom and understanding, that is, by the wisdom and understanding freely given through the Holy Spirit, Christ was wise as a soul; but as God, he was wise by the begotten wisdom which he is. And just as, insofar as he is God, he is good by the natural goodness which he is, and just by the natural justice which he is, so also he is wise by the natural wisdom which he is. But just as his soul is good and just by the freely given goodness or justice which he or it is not, so it is wise by the freely given wisdom which it is not. And although there is a twofold wisdom in Christ, yet the person is one and the same which, insofar as it is God, or insofar as it is the divine nature, is wise by the eternal wisdom,[26]

[ORIGINAL TEXT] namely by the begotten wisdom, that is, by itself, and by that wisdom which is not begotten that is common to the three persons; and yet not by a twofold wisdom, because there are not two different wisdoms, one begotten, which is the Son alone, and a wisdom which is the Father and Son and Holy Spirit in common.

[SECOND VERSION] namely by the unbegotten wisdom which is the Father, and by the wisdom which is not unbegotten, that is common to the three persons; and yet not by a twofold wisdom, because there are not two different wisdoms, one unbegotten, which is the Father alone, and a wisdom which is the Father and Son and Holy Spirit in common.

But insofar as the same person is man, that is, according to the humanity that was taken, or insofar as he subsists from soul and flesh, he is wise by a freely given wisdom. And so he is wise in a human and a divine sense.

9. HOW THAT [STATEMENT] IS TO BE UNDERSTOOD: HIS HUMAN SENSE MADE PROGRESS. But from what cause are we to take the meaning of that statement, namely 'his human sense made progress'? For Ambrose seems to indicate clearly that Christ had made progress according to his human sense, and that in his infancy he would have been lacking in knowledge, and would not have known his father and mother: which the Church does not accept, nor do the above authorities admit of such an understanding. But it can certainly be taken in this sense: that Christ may be said to have

[25]Is. 11, 2.
[26]See above, Bk 1 dist. 32 cc2-5, esp. c5.

made progress in the sight of men and in what he revealed of his own senses. And so the human sense made progress in him according to what he revealed and in the opinion of other men. In the same way, he is also said not to have known his father and mother in his infancy because he acted and bore himself as if he were lacking in this knowledge.

DISTINCTION XIV

Chapter 1 (39)

1. WHETHER THE SOUL OF CHRIST HAD WISDOM EQUAL TO GOD'S AND WHETHER IT KNOWS ALL THINGS THAT GOD KNOWS. Since Christ's soul was wise by a freely given wisdom, here it is necessary to ask whether it had wisdom equal to God's, or whether it had or has knowledge of all things, that is, whether it knows all the things which God knows.

2. THE OPINION OF SOME. It pleases some to hold that it neither has equal knowledge with God, nor knows all things which God does, "because the creature is in no way equated to the Creator."[1]—THEY SET FORTH A REASON. And so, since that soul is a creature, it is in no way equated to the Creator; and so it is not equal in wisdom. Therefore it does not have an equal wisdom with God, nor knows all things which God does.—Also, if that soul has equal wisdom with God, then it is not the case that God has a greater sufficiency than his creature with regard to any good.—THEY ALSO SET FORTH AUTHORITIES. They also set forth authorities to prove the same point. For the Prophet says, in the person of the man taken up: *Your knowledge has been made wonderful to me, and I am not able to grasp it.*[2] Expounding this, Cassiodorus says: "The truth of the human condition is shown here, because the man taken up cannot be equated to the divine substance in knowledge or in anything else."[3]—The Apostle too says: *No one knows the things that are God's, other than the Spirit of God, who alone searches all things, even the deep things of God.*[4]—It is in these and several other reasons and authorities that they find support who assert that the soul of Christ neither has an equal knowledge with God, nor knows all things which God knows; for if it knows all things which God knows, then it knows how to create the world, and so it also knows how to create itself.

[1]Walter of Mortagne, *Epistola ad Hugonem de S. Victore*; cf. Augustine, *De natura et gratia*, c33 n37.
[2]Ps. 138, 6.
[3]Cassiodorus on Ps. 138, 6.
[4]1 Cor. 2, 10-11.

3. RESPONSE TO THE QUESTION CONTAINING A DEFINITIVE SENTENCE. Responding to them, we say that the soul of Christ, through a freely given wisdom, in the Word of God, to which it is united and which perfectly understands, knows all things which God knows, but cannot do all the things that God can do. Nor does it grasp all things as clearly and sharply as God does, so that it is not equated to its Creator in knowledge, even though it knows all things that he knows; nor is its wisdom equal to God's wisdom because the latter is much worthier and comprehends all things more worthily and perfectly than the wisdom of that soul. And so, even with regard to knowledge, God has a greater sufficiency than that soul, which is worthier than any creature.

4. But as for that text of the Apostle which they adduce: *No one knows the things that are God's, other than the Spirit of God, who alone searches all things,*[5] it supports our view. For the Apostle immediately adds: *But we have the Spirit of God,*[6] in order to show that, through the Spirit whom he had, he understood *the deep things of God*. But that soul had the Spirit of God more than all others, since, as John the Evangelist says, to it *the Spirit was not given according to measure*;[7] and so it had the gifts of the Holy Spirit without measure; hence it also had wisdom. It follows that that soul knew all things. For if it knew some things, but not others, then it did not have knowledge without measure. But it did have knowledge without measure; and so it knows all things.

5. In some sermon of his, Fulgentius also adduces many arguments to assert that that soul has knowledge of all things;[8] he appeals to the authority of the Apostle, who says: *In whom are hidden all treasures of wisdom and knowledge.*[9]—The point may also be proved by reason, as follows: One knows nothing of which one's soul is ignorant; but, as everyone grants, Christ knows all things; and so his soul knows all things.

6. But as to their saying, 'If it knows all things, then it knows how to create the world or itself,' we respond that it has the knowledge to create the world, but not the power. So also with regard to the creation of the soul: it knows how God created it; and so it has knowledge of itself as created, but not of itself as creating, because it is not creating, but is already created.

[5] 1 Cor. 2, 10-11.
[6] 1 Cor. 2, 12.
[7] Jn. 3, 34; cf. above, dist. 13 nn1-2.
[8] Fulgentius, *Epistola 14 (ad Ferrandum)*, q3, n29.
[9] Col. 2, 3.

Chapter 2 (40)

1. WHY GOD DID NOT GIVE TO THAT SOUL THE POWER OVER, AS WELL AS THE KNOWLEDGE OF, ALL THINGS. But if it is asked why God did not give to it the power of making all things, as he did knowledge of them, it may be answered that it was naturally capable of knowledge, and so that of which it was naturally capable was suitably given to it without measure. It was not given to it to be able to do all things which God does, however, lest it be thought to be omnipotent and, for this reason, God. But perhaps it was even the case that God could not grant to it the power to do all things, although he could grant the power to do some things which it is not able to do.—And so Christ's soul knows all things which God knows in the Word of God, and contemplates more clearly and immediately than any creature as united to the Word; in the same Word, the angels too know the things which are God's and those which are future.[1]

2. HOW SOME WORDS OF AMBROSE ON LUKE ARE TO BE UNDERSTOOD. But if that soul does not have as much power as God, nor does the man assumed have as much power as God, how then is to be understood Ambrose's statement on the text of Luke, where the angel says of the Son who is to be born of the Virgin: *He shall be great and will be called Son of the Most High*?[2] For Ambrose says: "He will not be great in the sense that he was not great before the Virgin gave birth, but in the sense that the man was going to receive in time that power which the Son of God has naturally, so that man and God may be one person."[3] See, he says plainly that the man was going to receive in time that power which the Son of God had naturally.

3. But if the man was going to receive that power, then either his person or his nature [was going to do so]. But not his person, because it always had and has it; and so his nature. But if the nature, then the soul; for concerning the flesh, it is established that it cannot receive [that power]. —To this we say that the text is to be taken as concerning the person, but not insofar as it is God's, but rather insofar as it is the man's person. For the person of God and man, and of the Son of God and the son of man is one. Insofar as this is God's person, it always and naturally had omnipotence; but insofar as it is a man's person, it did not always exist. And so that person, which had always been God's, was going to become a man's person; and as it was going to become a man's person in the future, it was going to receive in time the power which it had always and naturally had as God's person.—That text and others like it can be rightly understood in

[1]See Bk 2 dist. 11 c2, esp. nn8-10.
[2]Lk. 1, 32.
[3]Ordinary gloss, on Lk. 1, 32, under the name of Ambrose and Bede, but the text is Bede's, *In Evangelia*, hom. 1.3.

accordance with this distinction, which is necessary in [resolving] several articles of questions against the cryptic wordiness of some people. But "when things are well established, it is pointless to engage in controversy concerning words."[4]

Distinction XV

Chapter 1 (41)

1. Of man's defects which Christ assumed in his human nature. It is also not to be passed over that the Son of God took a human nature that was capable of suffering: a soul capable of suffering, and flesh that was capable of suffering and mortal. And so that he should be shown to have a true body, he took on the defects of the body: hunger and thirst and suchlike; and so that he should be shown to have a true soul, he took on the defects of the soul, namely sadness, fear, pain, and suchlike.

2. Augustine. But every sense pertains to the soul: for it is not the flesh that senses, but the soul which uses the body as an instrument. Hence Augustine, in *On Genesis*, book 12: "It is not the body that senses, but the soul through the body, which the soul uses as a messenger to confirm within itself what is announced outside of it."[1] And so, just as the soul sees or hears through the body as its instrument what is outside itself, so also it feels through the body some evils which it would not feel without the body, such as hunger and thirst and suchlike; hence it is not unjustly that they are called defects of the body. But it feels some other evils not through the body, indeed even without the body, as is the case with fear and suchlike. Therefore the soul senses sufferings, but some through the instrument of the body and others not.

3. And just as Christ took on a true human nature, so also he took on the true defects of man, but not all of them. For he assumed the defects of punishment, but not those of fault; and yet not all the defects of punishment, but all those which it was suitable for him as man to assume and which did not derogate from his dignity. For just as he was made man for the sake of man, so also for his sake he took on man's defects. He took of what was ours to confer on us what was his and so as to take away what was ours. For he took the ancientness [of our nature] in order to infuse his newness in us. He took a single ancientness, that is, the one of punishment, in order to destroy our twofold one, that is, of punishment and of fault.

[4]Cf. Augustine, *Contra Academicos*, bk 2 c10 n24; c11 n25.

[1]Augustine, *De Genesi ad litteram*, bk 12 c24 n51.

4. HOW THAT WHICH POPE LEO SAYS IS TO BE TAKEN. Authority hands down that "our Lord assumed in himself all that pertained to our infirmity, apart from sin."[2] But unless this is taken to refer only to those things which it was suitable, and not indecent, for him to bear on our behalf, it shall be proven to be false.—For he did not take on any ignorance, even though there is an ignorance which is a defect and not a sin, namely invincible ignorance. And indeed, vincible ignorance is a sin, but only if it concerns those things which it is profitable for us to know: for there are some things whose knowledge does not assist, or whose ignorance does not stand in the way of, salvation, and perhaps the ignorance of such things is not a defect.[3]

5. But it is also evident that in us there are an ignorance and a difficulty to will and do the good, and these pertain to our misery. And so Augustine, in *On Free Will*, book 3, says: "To approve falsehoods as if they were truths, so as to err unwilling, and to be unable to refrain from lustful acts because of the painful throes of a carnal bond, this is not the nature of man as he was originally established, but his punishment after his condemnation."[4] "From this misery, which was most justly inflicted on sinners, God's grace brings freedom because man was able to fall by his own free will, but he could not also rise. To this misery pertain the ignorance and obduracy [to will and do the good] which every man suffers from the beginning of his life, nor is anyone freed from this evil other than by God's grace."[5]—See, Augustine clearly says here that the ignorance by which anyone unwillingly approves falsehoods as if they were truths, and the weakness by which one cannot restrain oneself from evil, pertain to our misery and are a punishment of man. But Christ did not have these; and so he did not take on all the defects of our infirmity apart from sin.

6. THAT SUCH AN IGNORANCE AND DIFFICULTY IS NOT A SIN. But perhaps someone will say that these are sin.—But opposed to this is Augustine's assertion, namely that God could have placed these blamelessly in man before sin, at the beginning of his establishment, so that they would be natural endowments of his. In the book of *Retractations*, he says: "Even if ignorance and difficulty had been among man's natural primordial endowments, God would not be deserving of blame, but of praise."[6] But if man had naturally had these things in the beginning, would these be a defect and punishment in him? No; [because] if a defect or punishment had been placed in him before sin, God would appear to deal unjustly with him, if man experienced the punishment before the fault.—Because of this, we

[2]Leo, *Sermo 63*, c4.
[3]On vincible and invincible ignorance, see Bk. 2 dist. 20 c5 n4 and 22 c5 nn. 1-2.
[4]Augustine, *De libero arbitrio*, bk 3 c18 n52.
[5]Augustine, *Retractationes*, bk 1 c9 n6.
[6]Ibid.

rightly say that such things would not have been defects or punishments, if they had naturally been placed in man; in the same way, it was not a defect or punishment for man to be unable to make progress before sin, when he had not yet received grace. But after he received grace, through which he was able to make progress, and for a time he did indeed make progress, and afterwards he lost it by his own fault, he simultaneously lost the power to make progress, and it was a defect and punishment for him not to be able to make progress, namely to reject evil and do good.

7. And so, apart from sin, Christ took all our defects which were suitable for him to take and profitable for us. For there are several kinds of illnesses and defects of the body from which he was entirely free. As for the defects which he did have, he took them either to demonstrate his true humanity: such as fear and sadness; or to fulfill the work for which he had come: such as the capacity to suffer and die; or to raise our hope from our despair of immortality: such as death.

8. THAT HE TOOK THOSE DEFECTS BY HIS WILL ALONE, NOT BY THE NECESSITY OF HIS CONDITION. And he took these defects not by the necessity of his condition, but by the will of his compassion. And so he had true defects, as we do, but not from the same cause. For we derive these defects from original sin, as the Apostle indicates, saying: *The body is dead because of sin,*[7] that is, it has in itself the necessity of dying. But Christ did not have defects from such sin, because it was without sin that he was conceived and born and lived on earth. It was entirely from the will of his compassion that he transferred true infirmity from what was ours to himself, just as he also took true flesh; and he could have taken it without any infirmity, just as he took it without any fault.

9. AGAINST SOME WHO DENY THIS, HE PROVES WITH AUTHORITIES THAT CHRIST, ACCORDING TO HIS HUMANITY, TRULY FELT PAIN AND WAS AFRAID. A few are found to have thought wrongly concerning sensation in the suffering of the humanity of Christ. They assert that the man Christ bore a likeness and semblance of suffering and pain, but did not at all endure pain or suffering [itself]. Let us remove all doubt from what we said above by convicting them by the testimonies of authorities.

10. The Prophet Isaias says: *Truly, he has borne our weaknesses, and he has carried our sorrows.*[8] And Truth itself says in the Gospel: *My soul is sorrowful even unto death;*[9] where we also read: *Jesus began to be dismayed and distressed.*[10] The Prophet too, in the person of Christ, says: *My soul is filled with evils.*[11] Expounding this text, Augustine says: "The

[7]Rom. 8, 10.
[8]Is. 53, 4.
[9]Mt. 26, 38.
[10]Mk. 14, 33.
[11]Ps. 87, 4.

soul of Christ was filled not with vices and sins, but with the evils of humanity, that is, it was filled with sorrows, in which it suffers together with the flesh. For there can be no suffering of the body without the soul; but the soul can suffer even without the body's pain. He took on these affects of human infirmity, as he did the flesh itself and death, not by the necessity of his condition, but by the will of his compassion."[12]

11. Ambrose too, in *On the Trinity*, book 3, says as follows: "It is written: *Father, if it is possible, let this cup pass from me.*[13] And so Christ is afraid; while Peter is not afraid, Christ is afraid. Peter said: *I lay down my life for you;*[14] Christ said: *My soul is troubled.*[15] Each statement is true and each is fully reasonable: both that the one who is lower is not afraid, and that the one who is greater suffers this feeling of fearfulness."[16]—The same, in the same place: "As a man, he is troubled; as a man, he sheds tears; as a man, he is crucified."[17] "It was through his human nature that he both was distressed and rose from the dead."[18] "Neither his power, nor his divinity is troubled, but *his soul is troubled*:[19] it is troubled in accordance with his having taken human frailty. Indeed, by taking a soul, he took also the soul's capacity to suffer, for insofar as he was God, he could not be troubled or die."[20]—The same, in the same place: "He took my sadness. With confidence I call it sadness because I preach the cross. As a man, he suffered sadness, which he bore with my capacity to suffer: he takes pity on me; he is sad in me; he suffers in me. And so he who had no reason to suffer for himself suffered for me and in me. And so, Lord Jesus, you suffer my wounds, not your own, because you suffer not for your own sake, but for mine."[21]

12. Jerome, too, in his *Explanation of the Faith*, says: "We say that a passible humanity was taken by the Son of God in such a way that the divinity remained impassible. For the Son of God suffered truly, and not putatively, all the things which Scripture attests according to that which was able to suffer, namely according to the substance that was taken. For although the person of the Son had taken a humanity that was able to suffer, yet by such indwelling it suffered nothing according to its own substance, as neither did the whole Trinity, whom we must necessarily

[12]Augustine, *Enarrationes in Psalmos*, on Ps. 87, 4, n3.
[13]Mt. 26, 39.
[14]Jn. 13, 37.
[15]Jn. 12, 27.
[16]Ambrose, *De fide*, bk 2 c5 nn41, 43-44.
[17]Ibid., bk 2 c7 n56.
[18]Ibid., bk 2 c8 n59.
[19]Jn. 12.27.
[20]Ambrose, *De fide*, bk 2c7 nn56.
[21]Ibid., bk 2 c7 nn53-54.

profess to be impassible."[22]—By these and other authorities, it is made very clear that Christ took a humanity that could suffer truly, and that in it he took the defects and affects of our infirmity, but by his own will and not by the condition of necessity.

13. HERE HE SETS OUT SOME ASSERTIONS WHICH APPEAR TO OPPOSE THE FOREGOING. But some statements are found in the treatises of the saints which appear to oppose the foregoing. Indeed, commenting on that place in the Psalm: *I have called out, and you will not hear me*,[23] Augustine appears to assert that Christ neither truly feared, nor was truly saddened; he states: "How does he say this, *who committed no sin, nor was deceit found in his mouth*?[24] But he says this of us, his body; for he spoke in the person of his body, that is, the Church. In the same way, when he said elsewhere: *Let this cup pass from me*,[25] he speaks for us. Unless perhaps one holds that he feared to die. But the Lord, who was to rise on the third day, did not truly fear to suffer, since Paul burned [with desire] *to be dissolved and be with Christ*.[26] For the soldier is not stronger than his commander. Does the soldier, who is to receive the crown, rejoice in dying, while his Lord, who is to crown him, fears death? No; he said these things to point out our weakness, for his weak ones, who fear to die: he was their voice."[27]—Jerome too says: "Let them blush, who hold that the Saviour feared death, and that it was in fear of suffering that he said: *Let this cup pass from me*."[28,29]

Chapter 2 (42)

1. DETERMINATION OF THE AUTHORITIES. But lest it be thought that there is any irreconcilable contradiction in the sacred texts, we say that the words of these authorities are to be taken in the following way: they are to be understood to take away from Christ not the truth or 'propassion' of fear and sadness, but rather the necessity and passion of his fear and sadness.—For Christ in his human nature had true fear and sadness, but not as we do, who are his members. For by reason of our sin, we are of necessity subject to these defects, and these defects exist in us according to both propassion and passion; but they are in Christ only according to propassion.

[22]Pelagius, *Libellus fidei ad Innocentium Papam*, n5.
[23]Ps. 21, 3.
[24]1 Pt. 2, 22.
[25]Mt. 26, 39.
[26]Phil. 1, 23.
[27]Augustine, *Enarrationes in Psalmos*, on Ps. 21, n4.
[28]Mt. 26, 39.
[29]Jerome, *In Matthaeum* 26, 1.

2. ON THE PROPASSION AND PASSION OF FEAR OR SADNESS. For just as propassion and passion constitute degrees in sins, so also they are found in these emotions which are the punishment for sin. For one is at times affected by fear or sadness, but not in such a way that the mind's understanding is as a consequence removed from righteousness or the contemplation of God, and then it is propassion. But at times it is removed or troubled, and then it is a passion.

3. JEROME. But Christ was not so troubled in his soul by fear or sadness as to fall away in any way from righteousness or the contemplation of God; it is in this sense that the assertion that he was not fearful or sad is understood. Hence Jerome, in *On Matthew*, where we read: *He began to be sad and sorrowful*,[1] says: "He was truly saddened so as to prove how truly he had taken on humanity; but this passion did not dominate his spirit and, in truth, is propassion. Hence it says: *He began to be sad*.[2] And indeed, it is one thing to be sad, another to begin to be sad,"[3] that is, one is saddened in one way by propassion, in another way by passion. And so it is in accordance with this distinction that at times Christ is said not to have been truly afraid, at times that he was indeed afraid, because he felt true fear and sadness, but not according to passion, nor from the necessity of his condition.

4. AUGUSTINE, ON THE PSALM. Hence Augustine, wishing to interpret some statements in accordance with these reasons, asserts that Christ was not truly afraid or sad, but immediately adds that he had true sadness. He says: "It is by way of signifying in his own person those who are weak that the Lord says: *Father, if it may be, let this cup pass from me*.[4] For the Lord, who was to rise on the third day, did not truly fear to suffer, since Paul burned [with desire] *to be dissolved and to be with Christ*.[5] Does he rejoice, who is to receive the crown, while the Lord, who is to crown him, is sad?"[6] See, here he seems to remove sadness and fear from Christ.— But he immediately added: "But he took on sadness as he did flesh. For he was sad, as the Gospel says. Indeed, if he was not sad, even though the Gospel says: *My soul is sad*, etc.,[7] then he did not sleep when it says: *Jesus slept*,[8] and he did not eat when it says: *He ate*.[9] And so nothing is left solid, so that it can even be said that his body was not a true one. Therefore whatever was written of him is true, and hap-

[1]Mt. 26, 37.
[2]Ibid.
[3]Jerome, *In Matthaeum* 26, 37.
[4]Mt. 26, 39.
[5]Phil. 1, 23.
[6]Augustine, *Enarrationes in Psalmos*, on Ps. 93, 15, n19.
[7]Mt. 26, 38, Mk. 14, 34.
[8]Mt. 8, 24.
[9]Lk. 14, 1

pened truly. And so he was sad; but he took up true sadness willingly, just as he took true flesh willingly."[10]—You can clearly see that he would be contradicting himself in these assertions, if he did not distinguish the different causes from which the meaning of these statements is to be drawn. But if the cause of the meaning of the above words is discerned, there is no hint of contradiction.

Chapter 3 (43)

1. ON SOME RATHER OBSCURE CHAPTERS OF HILARY WHICH APPEAR TO CONTRADICT THE COMMON OPINION. And yet some words of Hilary appear to be more troublesome and to pose a more difficult question, because he appears to say that the blows and wounds fell upon Christ in such a way that they did not inflict the pain of suffering. Just as a spear drawn through water, or fire, or air does all the same things as when it is drawn through animate bodies, because it pierces and wounds, and yet does not inflict pain, because those things are not capable of pain, in the same way, he says that the body of Christ received the force of pain without the sensation of pain because, just as our body does not have a nature such as to be able to walk on water, so he says that Christ's body did not have the nature of our pain because it did not have a nature for suffering.

2. He says as follows, in *On the Trinity*, book 10: "The only-begotten God, without ceasing from his divinity, took true humanity according to the likeness of our humanity. And although a blow struck him, or a wound befell him, or ropes bound him, or he was lifted up, and these carried the force of the passion, yet they did not inflict the pain of the passion. Some spear which pierces water, or penetrates fire, or wounds the air, does indeed inflict all these sufferings which its nature can: it pierces, it penetrates, it wounds. But the suffering inflicted on these things does not retain its nature because it is not in its nature that water be pierced, or fire penetrated, or air wounded, even though it belongs to the nature of the spear to wound and pierce and penetrate. So too, Christ does indeed suffer when he is struck, when he is lifted up, when he dies; the suffering which rushed into his body indeed was suffering, yet it did not act in accordance with the nature of suffering. Even as the pain savagely struck in the mystery of the punishment, yet that body's power bore the force of the pain that savagely struck it without feeling it. And certainly, that body of the Lord had the nature of our pain, if our body were of such a nature as to tread on the waves and walk upon the waters and find closed doors not to be an obstacle. (PAY ATTENTION HERE!) But if it is the nature of the Lord's body alone to be borne in the waters, and to stand upon the waves, and to pass through walls, how can we judge the flesh conceived by the

[10]Augustine, *Enarrationes in Psalmos*, on Ps. 93, 15, n19.

Spirit by comparison with the nature of the human body? That flesh is from heaven, and that man is from God. He had a body able to suffer, and he suffered, but he did not have a nature able to feel pain."[1]

3. The same, in the same: "Let us see whether the sequence of his sufferings allows us to discern in the Lord the weakness of bodily pain. Deferring a discussion of the reasons why heretics ascribe fear to the Lord, let us consider the events themselves as they occurred. For it cannot be that his words signify fear whose deeds demonstrate such confidence. Does it seem, o heretic, that he feared to suffer? But Peter became a *Satan* and a *scandal* because he erroneously held this through ignorance.[2] Was Christ afraid, who went forth to meet his armed captors? And was there weakness in his body, at whose approach the ranks of his pursuers broke as they fell down to the ground?[3] (NOTE WELL!) And so what weakness do you believe to have overcome this body, whose nature had such great power? Perhaps he feared the pain of his wounds? But tell me, you who assert the Lord's weakness, how he feared the flesh-piercing nail, who by his mere touch restored the ear that was cut off ?[4] Does this hand, which creates an ear, feel the pain of the nails? And does he feel the wound, who did not leave another to feel the pain of a wound? Is he sad through fear of the piercing of his own flesh, by whose touch that flesh is healed which has been cut off?"[5]

4. Also: "And so, we have considered the powers of his words and deeds. We have clearly shown that there was no weakness of a bodily nature in the nature of his body, and that even though that suffering was inflicted upon his body, yet it did not inflict upon that body the nature of pain because, although the form of our body was in the Lord, yet the form of our sinful weakness was not in the body which the Virgin brought forth by the conception of the Holy Spirit."[6]

5. O reader, you have heard Hilary's words, by which he seems to deny [Christ's] suffering. But set aside all opinionated and impious obtuseness. If you note with diligence what is said above and explore the context of what was written, you will then be able to understand as best you can the reason and power of what was said and will not try to fault its meaning. For it is clear that he said that there was no pain of suffering in Christ, and that the power of Christ's body received the force of pain without feeling it because Christ did not have in himself the cause of pain or deserve to feel it. This seems to have been pointed out when he says: 'he did

[1] Hilary, *De Trinitate*, bk 10 n23.
[2] Cf. Mt. 16, 23.
[3] Cf. Jn. 18, 4-6.
[4] Cf. Lk. 22, 51.
[5] Hilary, *De Trinitate*, bk 10 nn26-28.
[6] Ibid., bk 10 n35.

not have a nature able to feel pain.'[7] And so his flesh is not to be judged according to the nature of our body. Nor did suffering have dominion over him. Hence he also did not have a nature to fear or to be sad, because he did not have such a nature as might contain a cause of fear or sorrow. Therefore in him there was no necessity to fear, as there is in us; nor was there in him a nature of suffering, as there is in us.

6. Hilary, in the book *On the Synod*: "Although these kinds of suffering affect the weakness of the flesh, yet God the Word, made flesh, could not become changeable by suffering. Indeed, although the Word that was made flesh subjected himself to the passion, he nevertheless was not changed by the passibility of suffering. For he was able to suffer, and yet was not able to be passible, because passibility pertains to a weak nature; but passion is the bearing of those things which are inflicted."[8]

Chapter 4 (44)

ON CHRIST'S SORROW AND ITS CAUSE ACCORDING TO THE SAME.—HILARY. And yet, he next asserts that there was sorrow in Christ, but that the cause of it was not his own death, but the failure of Peter and the other Apostles.—For he says that Christ was sorrowful not because of his own death, but unto death; he states as follows: "I ask what it means to be sorrowful *unto death*.[1] To be sorrowful 'because of death' cannot mean the same as 'unto death' because, when the sorrow is 'because of death,' then death is the cause of the sadness; but when sorrow is 'unto death,' then death is not the cause of the sorrow, but its end. And so this sorrow was not taken up because of death in order to be removed through death."[2] "Therefore it is not for himself that he is sorrowful, but for those who were going to be scandalized because of the weakness of the flesh: he admonishes them to pray, lest they be lead into temptation,[3] who earlier had promised that they would not be scandalized."[4,5]

[7]Above, n2.
[8]Hilary, *De synodis*, n49.

[1]Mt. 26, 38.
[2]Hilary, *De Trinitate*, bk 10, n36.
[3]Mt. 26, 41.
[4]Mt. 26, 33-35.
[5]Hilary, *De Trinitate*, bk 10, n37.

DISTINCTION XVI

Chapter 1 (45)

1. WHETHER IN CHRIST THERE WAS THE NECESSITY TO SUFFER AND DIE, WHICH IS A GENERAL DEFECT. Here arises a question which draws its origin from the foregoing. For it was said above that Christ took in himself our defects, other than sin.[1] But there is a general human defect which is not sin, namely the necessity to suffer and die: hence our body is called not merely mortal, but even *dead*,[2] because it has not only a capacity for dying, but also a necessity. And so the question of whether there was such a necessity in Christ's body arises.—THAT MORTALITY WAS NOT A DEFECT IN MAN BEFORE SIN. Insofar as the capacity for dying is concerned, there is no doubt that it was present in him. This capacity was in man even before sin, when there was no defect in him, and so that mortality was not then a defect in him because it was natural to him.—WHETHER IT IS NOW A DEFECT IN US. And so some say, not without justification, that the defect in us is not mortality as such, but the necessity of dying or suffering, which is also called mortality or passibility. For man is now said to be passible or mortal not only by way of capacity, but also because of necessity.—WHETHER THE SOUL OF CHRIST HAD THE NECESSITY OF SUFFERING. But was this defect in Christ's flesh? And since his soul was passible before death, did it have the necessity of suffering? No, for if the necessity of suffering or dying was in Christ, it does not seem that he took our defects only by the will of his compassion.

2. SOLUTION. To which it may be said that Christ took these defects, as he did the others willingly, and not by the necessity of his nature, namely the necessity of suffering in his soul together with that of suffering and dying in the flesh. Truly, he did not have this fate from the necessity of his condition, since he was immune from sin, but took of our infirmity by his will alone, placing *his tabernacle in the sun*,[3] that is, under [the rule of] temporal mutability and labour.—Hence authority says, in *On the Epistle to the Hebrews*, that "as *it was established* for other men by right and law of nature, *that they die once*, so *Christ*, by the same necessity and right of nature, *was offered once only*, and not several times."[4] Nor was it because he had taken this defect by the nature of his condition that it says 'by right of nature'; this defect does not come to us from nature as it was first instituted, but as it was vitiated by sin. And so it is here called a natural defect because, shared by all, it has almost become our nature.

[1] Above, in dist. 15 c1 n3.
[2] Cf. Rom. 8, 10.
[3] Cf. Ps. 18, 6.
[4] Interlinear gloss, on Heb. 9, 27-28.

Chapter 2 (46)

OF THE STATES OF MAN, AND WHAT CHRIST TOOK FROM EACH OF THEM. It is here to be noted that Christ, who came to save all,[1] took something from each of the states of man. There are four states of man: first before sin, second after sin and before grace, third under grace, fourth in glory. From the first state, he took immunity from sin. Hence Augustine, expounding that phrase of John the Evangelist, *He who comes from above, is over all*,[2] says: "Christ came from above, that is, from the loftiness of human nature before sin, because it was from that height that the Word of God took on human nature; he took its punishment without taking its fault."[3] But he took the punishment and other defects from the second state; from the third, he took the fullness of grace; from the fourth, he took the inability to sin and the perfect contemplation of God. Indeed, he took simultaneously some of the goods of the wayfarer and some of the goods of the fatherland, as he took also some of the evils of the wayfarer.

DISTINCTION XVII

Chapter 1 (47)

WHETHER EVERY PRAYER OR WILL OF CHRIST WAS FULFILLED. After the above, it is good to consider whether Christ willed or prayed for anything which was not done. This may be thought to be the case because he himself said: *Father, if it is possible, let this cup pass from me. But not my will, but yours, be done.*[1] Indeed, here he seems to be separating his own will from the Father's.

Chapter 2 (48)

1. ON THE WILLS OF CHRIST ACCORDING TO HIS TWO NATURES. In regard to this, it is not to be doubted that in Christ there were different wills according to his two natures, namely a divine will and a human one. And human will is a disposition of reason or a disposition of sensuality. The disposition of the soul is one thing according to reason, another according to sensuality, and yet each of these is called human will. By the disposition of reason, he willed the same as by his divine will, that is, to suffer and die; by the disposition of sensuality, he did not will this—indeed, he wanted to flee it.

[1]Cf. Mt. 18, 11.
[2]Jn. 3, 31.
[3]Ordinary gloss, on Jn. 3, 31.

[1]Mt. 26, 39.

2. Nor was it the case that in him the flesh lusted against the spirit or against God, because, as Augustine says, "there is some vice when *the flesh lusts against the spirit*."[1,2] "And the flesh is said to lust because the soul does this according to the flesh, just as the soul hears through the ear and sees through the eye."[3] "For the flesh lusts only through the soul; but it is said to lust when the soul with carnal concupiscence struggles against the spirit,"[4] "finding carnal pleasure by and from the flesh, in opposition to the pleasure which the spirit has. The cause of this carnal concupiscence is not in the soul alone, nor in the flesh alone; it comes from both, and this pleasure is not felt without both."[5] Such a struggle and contention could in no way be in Christ's soul, because carnal concupiscence has no place there. It was even God's will and consonant with reason that Christ should so will according to the flesh, in order that the truth of the humanity in him should be proved. For he who took on human nature had to suffer what pertains to such a nature.

3. And so, just as there is in us a double disposition, namely of the mind and of sensuality, so there had to be in him also a double disposition: by the disposition of the mind, he was willing to die, and by the disposition of sensuality he was not, and the same is true in holy men. For Truth itself says to Peter: *When you are old, you will stretch out your hands, and another will gird you and lead you where you do not want to go*,[6] that is, to death. Expounding this, Augustine says that Peter "was unwillingly led to that burden; he came unwillingly, but he willingly overcame it, and left behind the disposition of infirmity by which no one is willing to die; such a natural disposition is this, that even old age had not removed it from Peter. And so even the Lord says: *Father, let this cup pass from me*;[7] but the power of love overcame him."[8] And so in Christ too, according to his humanity, and in [us] his members, there is a twofold disposition: one of reason, informed by charity, by which one is willing to die for the sake of God; another of sensuality, connected and joined to the infirmity of the flesh, by which death is fled.—For as Augustine says: "A pious person, by the reason of his mind, desires *to be dissolved and to be with Christ*;[9] but by the sensation of the flesh, he flees and rejects this."[10]

[1]Gal. 5, 17.
[2]Augustine, *De civitate Dei*, bk 19 c4 n3.
[3]Augustine, *De Genesi ad litteram*, bk 10 c12 n21.
[4]Augustine, *De continentia*, c8 n19.
[5]Augustine, *De Genesi ad litteram*, bk 10 c12 n20.
[6]Jn. 21, 18.
[7]Mt. 26, 39.
[8]Augustine, *In Ioannem*, tr. 123 n5.
[9]Phil. 1, 23.
[10]Augustine, *Epistola 150* (*ad Honoratum*), c6 n16.

"Human disposition does this because it loves life and hates death."[11] According to this disposition, Christ was not willing to die, nor did he obtain what he asked for in accordance with this disposition.

4. BY MEANS OF AUTHORITIES, HE PROVES THAT THERE ARE DIVERSE WILLS IN CHRIST. And it was from his human disposition, which he derived from the Virgin, that he wanted not to die, and prayed that the cup should pass.—BEDE. And so Bede: "He prays that the cup should pass, because he is a man, saying: *Father, if it is possible, let this cup pass from me.*[12] See, here you have the express human will. But see also the righteous heart: *But not my will, but yours be done.*[13] And so elsewhere: *I did not come to do my will*, namely the one which I took in time from the Virgin, *but the will of the one who sent me*,[14] namely the one which I, the eternal one, shared with the Father."[15] Here he says clearly that there were two wills in Christ, and that he willed different things according to each.

5. JEROME. Jerome too, on that place: *The spirit is ready, but the flesh is weak*,[16] gives it to be understood that the two wills are expressed here, and says as follows: "This is against the Eutychians, who say that in Christ there was only one will. But here he shows a human will, which rejects the passion because of the weakness of the flesh, and a divine one, which is ready to carry out the divine plan."[17]

6. AUGUSTINE, ON PSALM 31. Augustine too asserts that there are two wills in Christ, saying: "As far as God is from man, that is how far the will of God is from the will of man. And so Christ, bearing his humanity, gave evidence of a private human will, which stood for both his and our will, for he is our head and we are, as it were, his members. *Father*, he says, *if it is possible, let this cup pass from me.*[18] This was a human will, desiring something of its own and, as it were, private. But because he wants to be a righteous man who is entirely directed toward God, he adds: *But not my will, but yours, be done*,[19] as if to say: See yourself in me, because you are able to will something of your own, even as God wills something else. This is allowed to human frailty."[20]—THE SAME, ON PSALM 88. The same, elsewhere: "Christ in his passion expressed the two wills that were in him according to his two natures; and so he said:

[11]Augustine, *Sermo 344*, n4.
[12]Mk. 14, 35.
[13]Mk. 14, 36.
[14]Jn. 6, 38.
[15]Bede, *In Marcum* 14, 35-36.
[16]Mk. 14, 38.
[17]Ordinary gloss, on Mk. 14, 38.
[18]Mt. 26, 39; Mk. 14, 35.
[19]Mk. 14, 36.
[20]Augustine, *Enarrationes in Psalmos*, on Ps. 32, 1, n2.

Father, if it is possible, let this cup pass from me.[21] Here you have a human will; turning it immediately toward the divine one, he added: *But not my will, but yours, be done.*"[22]

7. AMBROSE. Ambrose too, in *On the Trinity*, book 3: "It is written: *Father, if it is possible, let this cup pass from me.*[23] The words are Christ's, but consider the manner and the form in which they are spoken: he bears the substance of man, he has taken human disposition. And so he does not speak as God, but as man."[24] "He did indeed take up my will. It was my will which he called his own, when he said: *But not my will, but yours, be done.*"[25,26] "But when he said: *All things that the Father has are mine,*[27] because nothing is excepted, it is certain that the Son has the same will as the Father has. Christ's will is the same as the Father's."[28] "And so one and the same will is the Father's and the Son's. But the human will is one thing, and God's another, so that you may know that what the human will desires is life; but what the divine will desires is the passion of Christ, that he should suffer for us."[29]

8. By these testimonies, it is clearly taught that there were two wills in Christ; because Archbishop Macarius denied this, he was condemned at the Metropolitan Synod.[30]—It was by the human disposition of sensuality, and not of reason, that he willed and asked for something which he did not obtain. Nor did he ask in such a manner as to obtain it, because he knew that God was not going to do that; nor did he want it to be done by the disposition of reason, or by his divine will.

9. WHY HE PRAYED AS HE DID. Why, then, did he ask? In order to give an example to [us] his members, when difficulties loom, of calling upon the Lord and subjecting one's will to God's: if they too are saddened by pressing trouble, to pray for its removal and, if they cannot avoid it, to say what Christ did.—CASSIODORUS. "So it was not pointless that Christ, in calling out, is not heard in regard to his bodily safety";[31] he asked for a good, namely that he should not die, but it was better that he should die, and this came to pass.

[21]Mt. 26, 39; Mk. 14, 35-36.
[22]Augustine, *Enarrationes in Psalmos*, on Ps. 93, 15, n19.
[23]Mt. 26,39; Mk. 14.35; Lk. 22.42.
[24]Ambrose, *De fide*, bk 2 c5 nn41-42.
[25]Mt. 26, 39.
[26]Ambrose, *De fide*, bk 2 c7 n53.
[27]Jn. 16, 15.
[28]Ambrose, *De fide*, bk 2 c6 n51.
[29]Ibid., bk 2, c7 n52.
[30]Macarius, patriarch of Antioch, was condemned at the Sixth Ecumenical Council (680-681).
[31]Cassiodorus, *In Psalmum* 21.3.

Chapter 3 (49)

1. ON AMBROSE'S ASSERTION THAT CHRIST DOUBTED BY HUMAN DISPOSITION. Yet we are troubled not a little by the words of Ambrose, in which he seems to say that Christ, according to his human disposition, doubted the Father's power; he says, in *On the Trinity*, book 3: "Whom does he doubt? Himself, or the Father? Surely, by his human disposition, he doubts him to whom he says: *Let this pass.*[1] For God does not doubt the Father, nor is he fearful of death. The Prophet also does not doubt, who asserts that nothing is impossible with God.[2] Will you treat God as if he were a man? The Prophet does not doubt, and you believe the Son doubts? And so it is as man that he doubts, and as man that he speaks."[3] These words seem to suggest that Christ doubted not insofar as he was God or Son of God, but by his human disposition insofar as he is man.—IN WHAT SENSE THE STATEMENT IS TO BE TAKEN. The statement may be taken not in the sense that he himself doubted, but that he took on the manner of a doubter and seemed to men to doubt.

2. WORDS OF HILARY EXPRESSING A VIEW VERY DIFFERENT FROM THE ABOVE. Neither are we to pass over Hilary's assertion that Christ prayed not for himself, but for his own [disciples], when he said: *Let this cup pass from me*, etc.,[4] just as it was not for himself, but for his own [disciples] that he feared; nor was it the case that he wished to avoid his own passion, but that the cup of the passion should pass from his own [disciples]. Hilary says: "If his passion was to glorify him, as Jesus said when Judas went out: *Now is the Son of Man glorified*,[5] how could fear of it have made him sad? Unless perhaps he was so irrational that he feared to suffer the death which, in his suffering it, was to glorify him? But perhaps he may be thought to have feared to the point of praying that the cup might pass him by, saying: *Father, let this cup pass from me.*[6] But how could he, because of fear of suffering, pray for the removal from himself of that which, in his zeal for God's dispensation, he was hastening to fulfil?[7] It is not fitting that he should be unwilling to suffer that which he was willing to suffer; and since you acknowledge that he was willing to suffer, it would have been more reverent to confess this to be the case than to rush out into impious folly by asserting that he prayed to avoid suffering, whom you acknowledge to be willing to suffer."[8] "And so it is

[1]Mk. 14, 36; Lk. 22, 42.
[2]Cf. Job 10, 13; Dan. 4, 6.
[3]Ambrose, *De fide*, bk 2 c5 nn43 and 42.
[4]Mt. 26, 39.
[5]Jn. 13, 31.
[6]Mt. 26, 39.
[7]Cf. Jn. 13, 27.
[8]Hilary, *De Trinitate*, bk 10 nn29-30.

not for himself that he is sad, nor for himself that he prays that the cup should pass, but for his disciples, lest the cup of suffering should fall to them; he prays that it may pass from him, so that it should not remain with them. ... Nor does he pray that it may not be with him, but that it may pass from him. Then he says: *But not my will, but yours, be done.*[9] In this manner, he signifies his fellowship with human anxiety, but without dissociating himself from the decree of the will which he shares with the Father."[10] "And so it is for the sake of men that he wills that the cup may pass, because all the disciples were to be tested by this cup; therefore he prays for Peter *that his faith may not fail.*"[11,12] "Knowing that all these things will cease after his death, he is sad *unto death,*[13] and he knows that the cup cannot pass, unless he drinks it, and so he says: *My Father, this cup cannot pass, unless I drink it; your will be done;*[14] he knows that, with the consummation of his passion, the fear of the cup would pass, which could not pass unless he drank it. Nor would the end of that fear come to pass before the same consummation, because after his death, the scandal of the apostles' weakness would be removed by the glory of his powers."[15]—Reader, understand these words with pious diligence, lest they become to you *vessels of death.*[16]

DISTINCTION XVIII

Chapter 1 (50)

1. WHETHER CHRIST MERITED FOR HIMSELF AND FOR US, AND WHAT FOR HIMSELF, WHAT FOR US. On Christ's merit, it must not be passed over that some say he merited not for himself, but only for his members.

2. For his members, he merited redemption from the devil, from sin, from punishment, and the opening of the kingdom so that, with the removal of the flaming sword,[1] access might be freely available. But for himself, he merited the glory of impassibility and immortality, as the Apostle says: *Christ for us became obedient unto death, even death on a cross; because of this, God exalted him, and gave him a name which is above all other*

[9]Mt. 26, 39.
[10]Hilary, *De Trinitate*, bk 10 n37.
[11]Cf. Lk. 22, 32.
[12]Hilary, *De Trinitate*, bk 10 n38.
[13]Mt. 26, 38.
[14]Mt. 26, 42.
[15]Hilary, *De Trinitate*, bk 10 n39.
[16]Cf. Ps. 7, 14.

[1]Cf. Gen. 3, 24; Apoc. 2, 12.

names.[2] The Apostle plainly says that Christ was therefore exalted by the glory of impassibility because he was humbled by the obedience of the passion. And so the humility of the passion was deserving of his exaltation, and the exaltation was the reward of humility.

3. AUGUSTINE, *ON JOHN*. Hence Augustine, expounding the said chapter, says: "In order that Christ might be made lustrous by his resurrection, he was first humbled by the passion; humility merits glory, and glory is the reward of humility. But all this was done *in the form of a servant*;[3] glory, on the other hand, was and shall ever be in the form of God."[4]—AMBROSE. Ambrose too, treating the same chapter, says: "Here is shown what and how much humility deserves."[5]

4. THAT HE ALSO MERITED IMPASSIBILITY OF SOUL. By these testimonies, it becomes evident that Christ, through the humility and obedience of the passion, merited the glorification of his body, and not this alone, but also impassibility of soul. For his soul was capable of suffering before his death, and his flesh mortal; but after his death, by merit of his humility, his soul had become impassible and his flesh immortal.

5. WHEN CHRIST'S SOUL WAS MADE IMPASSIBLE. Authority offers us no certainty as to whether the soul became impassible when the flesh became immortal, namely at the very moment of the resurrection; but the soul was endowed with impassibility either soon after separation from the flesh, or at the resurrection, when *the flesh again blossoms*.[6]

Chapter 2 (51)

1. THAT CHRIST MERITED FOR HIMSELF THE SAME THINGS FROM HIS CONCEPTION AS THROUGH HIS PASSION. Nor did Christ merit these things only when he submitted to the cross in obedience to the Father, but also from his very conception. From the moment when he became man, through charity, justice, and the other virtues, in whose fullness he was established according to his humanity, he merited for himself as much as he did afterwards by his suffering martyrdom. For there was such fullness of spiritual charisms in him, that he could not make any increase in them, and so his soul could not become better than it had been from the beginning of his establishment, because he could not make any progress in merits. For as Gregory says, "according to the merit of the soul, there was no way in which Christ could make progress; but in his members, which we are, he

[2]Phil. 2, 8-9.
[3]Cf. Phil. 2, 6-7.
[4]Augustine, *In Ioannem*, tr. 104 n3.
[5]That is, Ambrosiaster on Phil. 2, 9.
[6]Cf. Ps. 27, 7.

makes progress every day."[1]—And so Christ did not merit more for himself through his suffering on the cross than he had merited through the grace of his virtues from his conception. Therefore he did not make progress in regard to the merit of the soul as to the power of the merit. But he did make progress as to the number of merits. For he had more merits in his passion than in his conception; but the more were not of greater power to merit than the fewer had been before.

2. And so from his conception he merited not only the glory of impassibility and bodily immortality, but also impassibility of soul. By what means? By his perfect obedience and will, which he did not begin to have, or to have to a greater extent, only when he began to suffer and die; indeed, as man, he was perfectly obedient and good from the moment when he became man.

3. That soul, then, had some good in it after death which it had not had before. Was it not better or more blessed than before? Let us not say that it would have been better because it was not holier, nor more full of grace. Nor was it more blessed in the contemplation of God, in which blessedness principally consists. Nevertheless it may be said that it was more blessed in this: that it was now immune from all misery; it cannot be simply inferred from this that it would have been more blessed.

Chapter 3 (52)

1. CONCERNING THAT TEXT: HE GAVE TO HIM THE NAME WHICH IS ABOVE ALL OTHER NAMES.[1] Nor did he merit only the glory of impassibility and immortality, but also that to him should be given *the name which is above all other names*,[2] namely the honour that he is called God. Yet he had this name before his death: for the Son of God, insofar as he is God, had this name by nature from all eternity; but insofar as he was made man, he had it in time through grace.

2. AUGUSTINE, IN THE BOOK *AGAINST MAXIMINUS*: THAT THAT NAME WAS GIVEN TO A MAN, AND NOT TO GOD. Augustine says, however, that "that name was given to a man, and not to God, because he already had that name when he was only in the form of God. But when it is said: *Because of this, God exalted him, and gave him a name which is above all other names*,[3] it is sufficiently apparent for what reason he exalted him, namely because of obedience; and in what form he was exalted: for the form in which he was crucified was the form in which he was exalted,

[1]Ordinary gloss, on Ex. 25, 31; from Gregory, *In Ezechielem 1*, hom. 6 n8.

[1]Phil. 2, 8-9.
[2]Ibid.
[3]Phil. 2, 9.

and in the same was the name given to him, so that the only-begotten Son of God be named with the very form of a servant."[4] "That name was given to him as man which he already had as God."[5] And so he took this name through grace that, as a man or while subsisting in the form of a servant, that is, in soul and flesh, he should be named and be God.

3. IN WHAT SENSE IS THIS TO BE TAKEN. But did he merit this? For it was said above that this man did not merit so great a good.[6] How then is it said here that 'because of obedience, this name was given to him'?—This is to be taken according to that manner of speaking, so very frequent in Scripture, by which a thing is said to be done when it becomes known. "Truly, after the resurrection, what was before was now made manifest, so that men and demons might know it."[7] And so, after the resurrection, God granted to him the manifesting of that name, but he merited it by the obedience of his passion; because he obeyed in suffering, he was exalted in his rising again, and through this the name was made manifest.—He made use of this same manner of speaking even after the resurrection, when he said: *All power in heaven and on earth has been given to me*:[8] it was not that he then first took it, but that the power which he had had before was made manifest at that time.

4. AMBROSE: THAT THE NAME WAS GIVEN TO GOD, NOT TO A MAN. But Ambrose says that that name was given to God, not to a man;[9] and according to the surface of the words, he seems to contradict Augustine. But it is not in opposition in its meaning, even though it sounds discordant. For Ambrose understands that statement as concerning the natural gift, by which the Father, eternally begetting, gave to the Son *the name which is above all other names*, namely to be God by nature, because he begot from all eternity the Son, who is full and co-equal God. And yet the Apostle says that this name was given to Christ because of the obedience of his passion; but this is to be taken according to the manner of speaking discussed above.

Chapter 4 (53)

1. WHETHER CHRIST COULD HAVE HAD THOSE THINGS WITHOUT ANY MERIT. If we ask whether Christ, without any merit, could have had that glory of immortality and impassibility and that manifesting of the name of God, it may rightly be said that he could have taken as glorious a human

[4]Augustine, *Contra Maximinum*, bk 1 c5.
[5]Ibid., bk 2 c2.
[6]See above, dist. 6 c2 nn4, 6-7.
[7]Ordinary gloss, on Phil. 2, 9.
[8]Mt. 28, 18.
[9]Ambrosiaster, on Phil. 2, 9.

nature as happened at the resurrection, and he could also have manifested his name to men in some other way; but he could not have been a passible man as he was and come to that glory without merit.

2. But he could indeed have come to it without the merit of the passion because, after using up his mortality, he could have become clothed in the glory of immortality; yet he could not have done so without the merit of justice, charity, and the other virtues. For Christ could not have been a man in whom there would not have been the fullness of virtues and grace; nor could the virtues have been in him, once he had taken on the sackcloth of mortality, without his acquiring merit by them. Therefore, since he had these virtues according to his being a passible and mortal man, he could not but have merited the glory of immortality. And so, after becoming mortal, he could not without merit have achieved the glory of impassibility and immortality and the manifesting of the name of God. But he could have obtained these without the merit of the passion, because through his passion he merited nothing for himself which he had not already merited earlier through his virtues.

Chapter 5 (54)

1. ON THE CAUSE OF THE DEATH AND PASSION OF CHRIST. To what end, then, did he will to suffer and die, if his virtues were sufficient for him to merit those things? For your sake, not for his own. How for my sake? So that his passion and death should be a model and cause to you: the model of virtue and humility, the cause of glory and liberty;[1] the model of being obedient to God even unto death,[2] and the cause of your liberation and blessedness. For by his bearing his death and passion, he merited for us what he had not merited by the foregoing, namely entrance to paradise, and redemption from sin, punishment, and the devil.[3] And through his death we have acquired these things, namely redemption and adoption as children of glory.[4] Indeed, by his death, he was made the victim offered for our liberation.

2. HOW HE REDEEMED US BY HIS DEATH AND OPENED THE ENTRANCE TO THE KINGDOM, AND FIRST, OF THE OPENING OF THE ENTRANCE. But how did he, through his death, redeem us from the devil and sin, and open the entrance to glory? God had decreed "in mystery," as Ambrose says,[5] that man, because of the first sin, should not be allowed into paradise, that is, should not be admitted to the contemplation of God, unless

[1]Cf. Jn. 8, 36.
[2]Phil. 2, 8.
[3]Cf. Col. 1, 13-14; Heb. 5, 9.
[4]Cf. Rom. 8, 15, Gal. 4, 5.
[5]Ambrosiaster, on Rom. 5, 14.

so much humility should be found in one man which might suffice for all who follow him, just as in the first man was found such pride as to harm all who followed him. Among men, none was found through whom this might be fulfilled, except *the lion of the tribe of Juda*,[6] who opened *the book* and broke *the seals*, fulfilling *all justice* in himself,[7] that is, the most complete humility, than which there can be no greater. Other men were debtors, and each one's virtue and humility was scarcely sufficient for himself. And so none of them could offer a sacrificial victim sufficient for our reconciliation. But the man Christ was a sufficient and perfect victim; he was much more humbled in tasting the bitterness of death[8] than Adam had become proud in his guilty pleasure through his eating of the forbidden tree.[9] And so, if the latter's pride was ruin to all, expelling him from paradise and closing its doors to others,[10] much more able was Christ's humility, by which he tasted death, to open the entrance of the heavenly kingdom to all who follow him, by the fulfillment of God's degree, for it cancelled *the chirograph of the decree*.[11]

3. AMBROSE ON THE EPISTLE TO THE HEBREWS. For as Ambrose says, "so great was our sin, that we could not be saved, unless the only-begotten Son of God should die for us, who were debtors of death; but in this way, he made us worthy of the covenant and of the promised inheritance."[12]—This is not to be understood as if he could not have saved us in any other way, except through his death, but that through no other victim could the entrance of the kingdom be opened to us and our salvation achieved, except through the death of the only-begotten, whose humility and patience, as has been said, were so great that by his merit the entrance of the kingdom should lie open to those who believe in him. And so great things were granted to us in the death of the only-begotten, so that we should be allowed to return to the fatherland, just as formerly, at the death of the high priest, those who had fled to the city of refuge could now safely return to their own lands.[13]—See, we have seen to some extent how entry to the kingdom was readied for us by Christ's death.

[6]Apoc. 5, 5.
[7]Cf. Mt. 3, 15.
[8]Cf. Heb. 2.9.
[9]Cf. Gen. 3, 6.
[10]Cf. Gen. 3, 23-24.
[11]Col. 2, 14.
[12]Ambrosiaster (rather Alcuin), *In Hebraeos* 9.15.
[13]Cf. Num. 35, 25 and 28; Jos. 20.6.

DISTINCTION XIX

Chapter 1 (55)

1. HERE HOW, BY HIS DEATH, HE REDEEMED US FROM THE DEVIL AND SIN. And so now let us ask how, by his death, we are redeemed from the devil, from sin, and from punishment.—We are freed by Christ's death from the devil and sin because, as the Apostle says, *in his blood we are justified*;[1] and since we are justified, that is, released from our sins, we are freed from the devil, who kept us in the bonds of our sins.

2. QUESTION. But how are we released from our sins by his death? —SOLUTION. Because by his death, as the Apostle says, God's charity toward us is commended,[2] that is, God's charity toward us is revealed as most excellent and commendable, since he handed over his Son to death for the sake of us sinners.[3] Since token of such great love toward us has been shown, we are moved to, and kindled with, love of God, who has done so much for us; in this way, we are justified, that is, we are released from our sins, and so we are made just. Indeed, Christ's death justifies us, as by it charity is kindled in our hearts.

3. We are also said to be justified by Christ's death in another way, because by faith in his death we are cleansed from sins. Hence the Apostle: *The justice of God* is *by the faith of Jesus Christ*;[4] and also: *Whom God has proposed as a propitiator, through faith in his blood*,[5] that is, by faith in his passion, as once those who looked at the bronze serpent hanging from a pole were healed from the bites of serpents.[6] In the same way, if we look with right faith upon him who hung from a pole for our sake,[7] we are released from the devil's bonds, that is, from sins. And we are so freed from the devil, that even after this life he cannot find anything to punish in us.—AUGUSTINE. "For by his death, by the one most true sacrifice, Christ extinguished whatever fault there was, by which the devil held us bound to suffer tortures,"[8] so that he should no longer overcome us in this life by temptation. For though he still tempts us after Christ's death in the same ways in which he did before, yet he cannot overcome us as he did before. And so Peter, before Christ's death, terrified by the slave-girl's voice, denied him;[9] after Christ's death, led before kings and governors,

[1]Rom. 5, 9.
[2]Cf. Rom. 5, 8.
[3]Cf. Rom. 8, 32.
[4]Rom. 3, 22.
[5]Rom. 3, 25.
[6]Cf. Num. 21, 9; Jn. 3, 14-15.
[7]Cf. Gal. 3, 13.
[8]Augustine, *De Trinitate*, bk 4 c13 n17.
[9]Cf. Mk. 14, 66-72; Lk. 22, 56-60.

Peter did not yield.[10] Why? Because *a stronger one*, that is, Christ, coming *into the house of a strong one*, that is, into our hearts, where the devil had an abode, *bound the strong one*,[11] that is, restrained him from the seducing of the faithful, so that seduction should not follow the temptation which is still allowed him.

4. AUGUSTINE, *ON THE CHRISTIAN COMBAT*. And so in the blood of Christ, who restored what he did not steal,[12] we are redeemed from sin, and so also from the devil. For as Augustine says, in him "are vanquished the invisible powers which are inimical to us, as are vanquished our invisible lusts."[13]—AUGUSTINE, IN THE BOOK *ON THE BAPTISM OF CHILDREN*. "Once that blood was shed without fault, the chirographs of all faults are cancelled, by which they who now believe in him were formerly held bound by the devil, hence: *Which is shed for many*."[14,15]

5. AUGUSTINE, IN THE BOOK *ON THE BAPTISM OF CHILDREN*. And so we were redeemed by him in whom the prince of this world found nothing.[16] Hence Augustine, conveying the cause and manner of our redemption, says: "The devil found nothing in Christ by which he should die, but Christ willed to die for the Father's will; he had no cause for death from sin, but tasted death from obedience and righteousness, and by it delivered us from slavery to the devil."[17] "For we had fallen in with the prince of this world, who seduced Adam and turned him into a slave, and had begun to possess us as if we were slaves of his household. But the Redeemer came, and the deceiver was defeated. And what did the Redeemer do to our captor? He set a mouse-trap for him, which was his own cross, and he set his own blood as if bait for him. It was not a debtor's blood that he shed and by which the devil departed from his debtors. Christ shed his own blood so that he might erase our sins. And so the source of our bond to the devil was erased by the blood of the Redeemer, for it was by nothing else than the bonds of our sins that he bound us.[18] These were the captives' chains. Christ came and *bound the strong one*[19] by the bonds of his passion; he entered *into his house*, that is, in those hearts in which the devil had made his abode, and took out *his vessels*, that is, ourselves, which the devil had filled with his bitterness. But our God took those vessels and made them his own, poured out the bitterness and filled them

[10]Cf. Mt. 10, 18; Act. 5, 27-29.
[11]Cf. Lk. 11, 22; Mt. 12, 29.
[12]Cf. Ps. 68, 5.
[13]Augustine, *De agone christiano*, c2 n2.
[14]Mt. 26, 28.
[15]Augustine, *De peccatorum meritis seu de baptismo parvulorum*, bk 2 c30 n49.
[16]Cf. Jn. 14, 30.
[17]Augustine, *De peccatorum meritis seu de baptismo parvulorum*, bk 2 c31 n51.
[18]Cf. Prov. 5, 22; 2 Tim. 2, 25-26.
[19]Mt. 12, 29.

with sweetness,"[20] redeeming us from our sins by his death and granting us adoption as children of glory.

Chapter 2 (56)

WHY GOD MAN AND DEAD. And so he was made a mortal man, in order to vanquish the devil by dying. "For unless it was a man who vanquished the devil, then it would not seem to be by justice, but by violence, that man, who had freely subjected himself to the devil, would be taken from him; but if it was a man who vanquished him, then the devil lost man by manifest right. And in order that a man might vanquish him, it is necessary that God should be in him, in order to make him immune from sin. For if it had been only a man, or an angel in human form, he would easily have sinned, since it is well-known that each of these natures, on its own, had fallen."[1] And so the Son of God took on passible human form, in which he tasted even death;[2] by this, he opened heaven to us and redeemed us from slavery to the devil, that is, from sin (for sin is slavery to the devil), and from punishment.

Chapter 3 (57)

HOW AND FROM WHAT PUNISHMENT DID CHRIST REDEEM US BY HIS DEATH. From what punishment? From the temporal and the eternal one: from the eternal one, by the abolition of our debt; from the temporal one, he will entirely free us in the future, when *death, the very last enemy, will be destroyed.*[1] For we still await *the redemption of our body.*[2] But according to our souls, we are already redeemed in part, not in total, from our fault, not from our punishment, nor entirely from fault: for we are not entirely redeemed from fault so that it no longer exists, but that it no longer dominates us.[3]

Chapter 4 (58)

HOW HE BORE OUR PUNISHMENT. Also, he is said to have borne *our sins*, that is, the punishment of our sins, *in his body on the cross*,[1] because, by the pain which he bore on the cross, all temporal punishment due for sin

[20] Augustine, *Sermo 130*, n2; cf. also *Sermo 263*, n1 (2).

[1] Ordinary gloss, on Heb. 2, 11.
[2] Heb. 2, 9.

[1] 1 Cor. 15, 26.
[2] Rom. 8, 23.
[3] Cf. Rom. 6, 6.

[1] 1 Pt. 2, 24.

is entirely forgiven to the convert in baptism, so that no such punishment is exacted from the baptized. The same punishment is lessened in penance, for the punishment by which the Church binds the penitent would not suffice without the aid of Christ's pain, which he suffered for our sake.[2] The sins of the just who lived before Christ's coming, according to the Apostle, were *in the divine forbearance* until Christ's death, *for the manifestation of his justice in this age.*[3]—See, it has been partially explained how and what Christ, by his death, merited and accomplished for us.

Chapter 5 (59)

WHETHER CHRIST ALONE IS TO BE CALLED REDEEMER, AS HE ALONE IS CALLED MEDIATOR. And so he is truly called redeemer of the world and mediator of God and men. The Son alone is called mediator in Scripture.[1] But at times the Father also or the Holy Spirit is called redeemer;[2] but this is so only by reference to the use of power, not as an example of humility and obedience. According to the use both of power and of obedience, the Son is properly called redeemer because he both fulfilled in himself those things by which we are justified, and worked that same justification by the power of the Godhead with the Father and the Holy Spirit. And so, he is redeemer insofar as he is God, by the use of power, insofar as he is man, by the effect of humility. And he is more frequently called redeemer according to his humanity, because according to it and in it he took up and fulfilled those sacraments which are the cause of our redemption. And so the Son is properly called redeemer.

Chapter 6 (60)

1. ON THE [TITLE] MEDIATOR. He alone is called mediator, and not the Father or the Holy Spirit. As the Apostle says of him: *There is one mediator of God and men, the man Christ Jesus,*[1] that is, according to his humanity, he is, as it were, the arbiter placed in the middle for the making of peace, that is, to reconcile men with God. He is the arbiter whom Job awaits: *Would that there were an arbiter between us.*[2]

[2]Cf. Ps. 68, 5.
[3]Rom. 3, 26.

[1]Gal. 3, 19-20; 1 Tim. 2, 5; Heb. 9, 15.
[2]Cf. Ps. 18, 15 and 77.35; Is. 41, 14; 49, 7 and 26; 60, 16; 63, 16.

[1]1 Tim. 2, 5.
[2]Job 9, 33.

2. AUGUSTINE, *ON JOHN*. For as the Apostle says, *we have been reconciled to God by Christ's death*:[3] "This is not to be understood as if Christ reconciled us to God in such a way that he now began to love those whom he used to hate, as an enemy is reconciled to an enemy, so that afterwards they become friends who previously hated each other; but we were reconciled to God who already loved us. For he did not begin to love us from the moment when we were reconciled to him by the blood of the Son, but from before the creation of the world, before we were anything at all."[4]—How then were we reconciled to God, who already loved us? "Because of sin, we were enemies to God, who had only love toward us, even when we acted on our enmity by working iniquity against him."[5] —AUGUSTINE, IN HIS BOOK *ON THE TRINITY*: "And so we were enemies to God, as sins are enemies to righteousness; once sins are remitted, such enmities come to an end, and they whom he himself justifies are reconciled to the just one."[6]

3. And so Christ is called mediator because, as intermediary between God and men, he reconciles them to God. He reconciles by removing the offences of men from God's sight, that is, by taking away the sins by which God was offended and we were his enemies.

4. QUESTION. But since it is not the Son alone, but also the Father and the Holy Spirit, who takes away sins, remission of which serves to reconcile us with God, why is the Son alone called mediator? For concerning the Father, it is read that he reconciled the world to himself. As the Apostle says: *God was in Christ, reconciling the world to himself*.[7] And so, since the Father reconciles, why is he not called mediator?—ANSWER. Because he is not an intermediary between God and men, nor did he have in himself those sacraments by faith in, and imitation of, which we may be justified, that is, reconciled with God. And so, it was the whole Trinity that reconciled us by the use of power, namely by the erasure of sins; but the Son alone did so by the fulfillment of obedience, in whom, according to his human nature, were accomplished those things through which those who believe and imitate him are justified.

Chapter 7 (61)

1. ACCORDING TO WHICH NATURE IS HE MEDIATOR. And so he is called mediator according to his humanity, not according to his divinity. "For

[3]Rom. 5, 10.
[4]Augustine, *In Ioannem*, tr. 110 n6.
[5]Ibid.
[6]Augustine, *De Trinitate*, bk 13 c16 n21.
[7]2 Cor. 5, 19.

he is not mediator between God and God, since *God is one*;[1] but between God and man, as between two extremes, because there can only be an intermediary between two different things."[2]—AUGUSTINE, IN SOME SERMON: "And so he is mediator insofar as he is man; for insofar as he is God, he is not mediator, but equal to the Father, the same as the Father, and one God with the Father."[3] And so he mediates between men and the triune God according to his human nature, in which he bore those things by which we are reconciled to the triune God.—AUGUSTINE, IN HIS BOOK OF THE *CONFESSIONS*: And according to the same nature, "he has something like God, and something like men," which was fitting for a mediator, "lest being in all things like men, he should be far from God; or if in all things like God, he should be far from man, and so would not be a mediator. And so Christ appeared, as the true mediator between mortal sinners and the immortal just one: mortal with men, just with God."[4] "By his infirmity, he was close to us, ... by righteousness, to God. And so rightly is he called mediator, because between the immortal God and mortal man there is the God man, reconciling man to God: insofar as he is man, he is mediator; insofar as he is the Word, he is not an intermediary, because he is one with God the Father."[5]

2. VIGILIUS, *AGAINST EUTYCHES*: "And so, o heretics, if Christ, according to you, only had one nature, how shall he be in the middle? Unless he is intermediate in such a way that he is God according to the nature of his divinity and man according to the nature of his humanity, how will human realities be reconciled to the divine ones in him? For in his coming, he first joined human and divine realities in himself by the joining of the two natures in one person; then, by his death, he reconciled all the faithful with God,"[6] so that "those who, by believing, loved Christ's humility and, by loving, imitated it, were healed from impiety."[7]

3. HE MAKES A BRIEF SUMMATION OF THE MEANING OF WHAT HAS BEEN EXPLAINED ABOVE. See, we have here come to see to some extent why Christ alone is called mediator of God and men; and according to which nature he mediates, namely the human one; and with whom he mediates, namely the triune God. For he reconciled us to the Trinity by his death, by which he also redeemed us from slavery to the devil. As Peter says, we

[1]Gal. 3, 20.
[2]Augustine, *In Epistolam ad Galatas*, n24.
[3]Augustine, *Sermo 293*, n7.
[4]Augustine, *Confessiones*, bk 10 cc42-43, nn67-68.
[5]Augustine, *Enarrationes in Psalmos*, 2, on Ps. 29, n1.
[6]Vigilius, *Contra Eutychen*, bk 5 n15.
[7]Augustine, *In Epistolam ad Galatas*, n24.

were *redeemed not by corruptible gold and silver, but by the precious blood of the spotless Lamb.*[8]

DISTINCTION XX

Chapter 1 (62)

THAT HE COULD HAVE FREED US IN SOME OTHER MANNER, AND WHY RATHER BY THIS ONE.—AUGUSTINE, IN BOOK 13, *ON THE TRINITY*. But if it is asked whether God could have freed man in some other manner than by Christ's death, we say that "another manner was possible to God, to whose power all things are subject, but that there would not have been, nor would it have been proper that there be, any other manner more fitting to cure our misery."[1]

Chapter 2 (63)

1. THE REASON WHY IN THIS MANNER. "For what so raises up our minds and frees them from despair of immortality, than that God rated us so highly that the Son of God, unchangeably good, remaining in himself what he was, and taking from us what he was not, deigned to enter into fellowship with us in order to bear our evils by his death?"[1]

2. ANOTHER REASON.—AUGUSTINE, IN THE SAME PLACE. There is also another reason why he willed to free us in this manner rather than in another: "because in this way the devil is overcome by righteousness, not by power";[2] "and how this was done, I shall explain as I am able."[3] "By some justice of God, humankind was delivered into the power of the devil, with the sin of the first man being transmitted originally into all and binding all by his debt. And so all men are by their origin in subjection to the devil; hence the Apostle says: *By our nature, we were children of wrath*:[4] namely by our nature as it was depraved by sin, not as it was created upright from the beginning. But the manner in which man was given into the power of the devil ought not to be so understood as if God did it, or commanded it to be done, but that he only allowed it, and yet justly. Once God had abandoned the sinner, the author of the sin immediately invaded

[8]1 Pt. 1, 18-19.

[1]Augustine, *De Trinitate*, bk 13 c10 n13.

[1]Augustine, *De Trinitate*, bk 13 c10 n13.
[2]Ibid., bk 13 c13 n17.
[3]Ibid., bk 13 c11 n15.
[4]Eph. 2, 3.

him. And yet God did not hold back *his mercies in anger*,[5] nor did he dismiss man from the law of his own power, when he allowed him to be in the power of the devil, since the devil himself is not separated either from the power of God, or from his goodness. For he would not subsist by any kind of life at all, except through him who gives life to all things. And so God did not abandon man so as not to show himself to him as God, and among penal evils, he also granted many good things to bad men. Remission of sin, granted by the blood of Christ, at last rescued man from the devil—the same man whom the commission of sins had made subject to the devil—, so that in this way the devil should be overcome by righteousness, not by power."[6]

Chapter 3 (64)

1. BY WHAT RIGHTEOUSNESS WAS THE DEVIL OVERCOME. "But by what righteousness? Jesus Christ's. And how was he conquered by it? Because, although he found in Jesus nothing worthy of death,[1] yet he killed him. And so it is entirely just that those debtors whom he held bound should be set free, if they believe in him whom he killed without any debt."[2] "But God did not will to overcome the devil by power because the devil, by the vice of his own perversity, is a lover of power and a forsaker and assailant of righteousness; men imitate him all the more in this as they pursue power, neglecting or even hating righteousness, and as they either rejoice in the attainment of power, or are inflamed by the lust for it. And so it pleased God to rescue man, overcoming the devil not by power, but by righteousness, so that man might learn to imitate God in this."[3] "But afterwards, at the resurrection, power followed, because he who had died was alive again, never to die again."[4]

2. QUESTION. "But would the devil not have been overcome by a most just right, if Christ had willed to deal with him by power alone? Surely, but Christ held back what he could have done, in order that he might first do what was fitting."[5] And so he freed man by the righteousness of his humility, whom he might most equitably have freed by power alone.

[5]Ps. 76, 10.
[6]Augustine, *De Trinitate*, bk 13 cc12-13 nn16-17.

[1]Cf. Lk. 23, 15.
[2]Augustine, *De Trinitate*, bk 13 c14 n18.
[3]Ibid., bk 13 c13 n17.
[4]Ibid., bk 13 c14 n18.
[5]Ibid.

Chapter 4 (65)

1. ON THE LITIGATION AMONG GOD, MAN, AND THE DEVIL. And if those three should come to court, namely God, man, and the devil, the devil and man would have no objection to make against God. For the devil would be convicted of the injury which he did to God by fraudulently stealing and violently retaining his servant, namely man. Man also would be convicted for having done injury to God by holding his commands in contempt and submitting himself to another's dominion. The devil would also be convicted of the injury done to man because first he deceived him with a false promise, and then harmed him by subjecting him to many evils. And so the devil, on his own part, unjustly kept man in bondage, but man justly was so kept; the devil never merited to have power over man, but man, by his fault, merited to suffer the tyranny of the devil.

2. And so, if God, who ruled over both of the others, had wanted to free man by force, he could most righteously free man by the power of his command alone; but for the cause set out above,[1] he willed to make use of the justice of humility.—AUGUSTINE, IN BOOK 13, *ON THE TRINITY*. And while he was crucified in his mortal flesh, we were justified, that is, we were taken away from the power of the devil by the remission of sins, and so the devil is overcome by Christ through justice, and not through power.[2] As to how our sins were remitted in his blood, there is an explanation above.[3]

Chapter 5 (66)

1. ON THE HANDING OVER OF CHRIST, WHICH IS SAID TO HAVE BEEN DONE BY THE FATHER, THE SON, JUDAS, AND THE JEWS. And so Christ is the priest, as he is also the victim and the price of our reconciliation.[1] He offered himself on the altar of the cross not to the devil, but to the triune God, and he did so for all with regard to the sufficiency of the price,[2] but only for the elect with regard to its efficacy, because he brought about salvation only for the predestined.

2. And we read of him that he was handed over by the Father,[3] and that he handed himself over,[4] and that both Judas and the Jews handed him over.[5] He handed himself over, because he freely came to his passion; and

[1]Above, c3 n2.
[2]This paraphrases Augustine, *De Trinitate*, bk 13 c14 n18.
[3]Dist. 19 c1 nn1 and 4.

[1]Cf. Hebr. 9, 25; Rom. 5, 10.
[2]Cf. Heb. 5, 9.
[3]Cf. Rom. 8, 32.
[4]Cf. Gal. 2, 20; Eph. 5, 2
[5]Cf. Mt. 26, 25; 26, 48; 27, 18.

the Father handed him over, because he suffered at the will of the Father and, indeed, of the whole Trinity; Judas handed him over by betraying him, and the Jews by their instigation. And the act of Judas and the Jews was evil, that of Christ or the Father good. The work of Christ and the Father was good, because the will of Christ and the Father was good; the work of Judas and the Jews was evil, because their intention was evil.

3. The deeds or works there differed, that is, the acts were different; but there was one thing or deed, namely the passion itself. And so the doctors at some times join together in that deed the Father, the Son, Judas, and the Jews; at some times, they make a distinction among them. For in examining the passion, they call the work of all of them one; attending to intentions and acts, they distinguish different deeds.—AUGUSTINE, *ON THE EPISTLE OF JOHN*. Hence Augustine: "There was," he says, "a handing over by the Father; there was a handing over by the Son; there was a handing over by Judas: the thing done is one. What, then, makes for distinctions among them? The Father and the Son did this in love, but Judas in betrayal. You see that one must consider not what a man does, but with what will. We find God in the same deed as Judas; we bless the Father, but detest Judas, because God considered our salvation, Judas considered the price for which he sold the Lord, and the Son the price which he gave for us. And so the diverse intention makes the deeds diverse, even though the thing is one."[6] See how he says that there was one thing, but diverse deeds, because there was one passion, but the acts were diverse; and the acts of Judas and the Jews were evil, by which they brought about Christ's passion, which itself is good and the work of God.

Chapter 6 (67)

1. THAT CHRIST'S PASSION IS TERMED THE WORK OF GOD AND OF THE JEWS, AND HOW. And so the passion is termed the work of Christ and of the Jews, because it comes about by their acts; and also the work of God, because it happened with God as its author, that is, by his will. Hence Augustine: "No one takes Christ's soul from him, because he has the power of laying it down and taking it up;[1] here you have the author of the work. He lays down his soul: here you have the author's work. To draw a general conclusion: whenever Christ suffers anything in the flesh, the deed is the author's; but because he suffers by his own will, and not at the compulsion of another, he is the deed's author."[2]

[6]Augustine, *In I Ioannis* 4, 9, tr. 7 n7.

[1]Cf. Jn. 10, 17-18.
[2]Vigilius, *Contra Felicianum Arianum de unitatem Trinitatis*, c14.

2. WHETHER THE JEWS DID A GOOD DEED IN THIS. But since Christ's passion is the work of God, and so good, and since Judas and the Jews brought it about, the question is raised whether it is to be granted that their deed in this matter was good.—Here a distinction is to be drawn: for it can be said that they did a good deed, because from their acts derived a good thing, that is, Christ's passion; but it may also be said that they did not do a good deed, but an evil one, because their action was not good, but evil.

DISTINCTION XXI

Chapter 1 (68)

1. WHETHER AT CHRIST'S DEATH THERE WAS A SEPARATION IN HIM OF SOUL OR FLESH FROM THE WORD. After the foregoing, we must consider whether, at death, the soul or flesh was separated from the Word.

2. THE OPINION OF SOME, WHO ASSERT THAT THE FLESH WAS SEPARATED FROM THE GODHEAD. Some have held that as the flesh was separated at death from the soul, so also it would have been separated from the Godhead. For if, they say, the Godhead united the flesh to itself by means of the soul, as has been set out above,[1] it follows that, once the flesh is separated from the soul, it is also separated from the Godhead, because it could not be sundered from the soul through which it was united to the Word, without also being separated from the Word.—AUGUSTINE. And it was separated from the soul at death, otherwise there would have been no true death there since, as Augustine says, "the death which men fear is the separation of the soul from the flesh, and the death which they do not fear is the separation of the soul from God; at the devil's persuasion, each of these has been given to man."[2] And so, if in the man Christ there was true death, the soul was there divided from the flesh, and so also thereby from the Godhead.

3. THEY ADDUCE AN AUTHORITY.—AMBROSE. To this probable opinion of theirs, they add the witness of authority. For Ambrose, treating the abandonment of Christ, who, on the cross and *in a loud voice*, called out and said: *My God, my God, why have you abandoned me?*,[3] says: "The man, when about to die, cries out at the separation from the Godhead; for since the Godhead is free from death, most certainly death could not be there, unless life first departed, for the Godhead is life."[4] Here he appears

[1]Dist. 2 c2.
[2]Augustine, *Enarrationes in Psalmos*, on Ps. 48.15, sermon 2, c2.
[3]Mt. 27, 46.
[4]Ambrose, *In Lucam* 10 n12.

to assert that, at death, the Godhead was separated from the man, and that unless it had departed, that man could not have died. They refer this to the flesh, which they say had been separated from God.

4. RESPONSE. To them we respond that that separation is to be taken in the same way as we understand the abandonment which is signified by those words: *Why have you abandoned me?* And so how was Christ abandoned by the Father, when he called himself abandoned on the cross? God had not departed from the man in such a way as to dissolve the union of God and man, otherwise there would have been a time when Christ, who was still alive, was man and not God, for he was still alive when he called himself 'abandoned,' and not 'about to be abandoned.' And so, if that abandonment is understood as a dissolution of the union, a severance of God and man took place before Christ had died. But who would say this? So let us profess that God abandoned that man at death in some way, because for a time he exposed him to the power of his persecutors; God did not defend him by displaying his power so that he would not die. The Godhead severed itself because it took away its protection, but did not dissolve the union; it separated itself outwardly so that it was not there to defend him, but was not absent inwardly in regard to the union. If at that time the Godhead had not held back its power, but had displayed it, Christ would not have died. Christ died because the Godhead receded, that is, did not manifest the effect of its power in his defence.—This is the scapegoat which, after the other goat had been sacrificed, was sent *into the wilderness*, as we read in Leviticus.[5] For the two goats are taken to signify the humanity and divinity of Christ. And so, once his humanity had been offered up, the divinity went into the wilderness, that is, into heaven.—HESYCHIUS, *ON LEVITICUS*. Hence Hesychius: "*Into the wilderness*, that is, into heaven; the Godhead at the time of the passion is said to have departed, not by change of place, but by holding back its power in some way, so that the impious ones might consummate the passion. And so it departed, that is, held back its power; and he bore our *iniquities*,[6] not to keep them, but to consume them, for *God is a consuming fire*."[7,8] From this, it is sufficiently shown that the above words of Ambrose are to be taken as we said earlier.

5. THEY ADDUCE ANOTHER AUTHORITY.—ATHANASIUS. Others who say that the Godhead at the death withdrew from the man according to the flesh also support themselves with authority. For Athanasius says: "He is accursed who does not confess that the whole man, whom the Son of God took, rose again from the dead on the third day after being taken

[5]Lev. 16, 8-10.
[6]Cf. Lev. 16, 22.
[7]Deut. 4, 24.
[8]Hesychius, *In Leviticum* 16, 10.

once more or delivered. Let it be so, let it be so."[9]—HOW THEY PROCEED TO ARGUE FROM THIS AUTHORITY. They say that, if the man whom he had taken at the incarnation was taken up again at the resurrection, then he had laid him down at death; and so, at death, the Godhead was separated from the humanity.

6. RESPONSE. To these we answer that, if by these words such a taking up which is according to union is understood, then it was not the flesh alone, but the whole man, that is, the soul and the flesh, that he united to himself once more at the resurrection, because he does not simply say that 'the man' was taken, but 'the whole man.' And so it was the whole man that he laid down in his death, that is, soul and flesh. But who, except an enemy of truth, will say that the soul was laid down by the Word? And yet, unless they profess this, namely that the whole man was taken, that authority will not support them, because it speaks of the whole man.

7. DETERMINATION OF THE AUTHORITY. And so it is to be understood that Athanasius spoke as he did against the perfidy of those who denied Christ's resurrection, believing that he was held by death who alone is *free among the dead.*[10] And so Athanasius curses anyone who does not confess that the resurrection was of the whole man taken again, that is, that Christ again joined the soul to the body; in both again conjoined at the resurrection, he was truly alive according to his humanity, as he had been before his death. For in death the soul is severed from the flesh, hence Christ is truly said to have been dead; but neither was severed from the Word of God.

8. BY AUTHORITIES, HE CONCLUDES THAT THE FLESH WAS NOT SEVERED FROM THE WORD IN DEATH. This is what Augustine teaches, in *On John,* in treating that saying of the Lord: *I lay down my soul in order to take it up again. No one takes it from me, but it is I who lay it down; I have the power to lay it down and to take it up again.*[11] (ON THE TEXT: I LAY DOWN MY SOUL, ETC.) Here he says that the soul was let go. By whom was it let go? Not by itself, because it did not lay itself down. Nor was it the Word that laid down the soul or the flesh. Therefore it was the flesh that laid down the soul, but by the power of the Godhead residing in it; and so it was by the power of the Godhead that the soul was severed from the flesh, but neither [was severed] from the Word of God. Hence Augustine: "From the time that the Word took on humanity, that is, flesh and soul, he never laid down his soul in such a way that the soul was severed from the Word; the flesh did lay down the soul when it expired, but at the soul's return the flesh rose again. And so death separated flesh and soul for a

[9]That is, Eusebius of Vercelli, *De Trinitate*, c6.
[10]Ps. 87, 6.
[11]Jn. 10, 17.

time, but neither was severed from the Word of God. Therefore the flesh lays down and takes up the soul, and this not by its own power, but by the power of the Godhead inhabiting the flesh."[12] Here it is plainly handed down that neither the flesh, nor the soul, was divided at death from the Word of God in any way by which their union would have been dissolved.

9. AUGUSTINE, IN THE EXPOSITION OF THE CATHOLIC FAITH. Hence Augustine, *Against Felicianus*: "Far be it that Christ should have felt death in such a way that all that is life in him should lose life. If it had been so, the source of life would have dried up. And so he felt death by participation of the human disposition which he had freely taken up; he did not lose that power of his nature by which he gives life to all things. Therefore, in dying with it, he did not desert his flesh in the tomb as he had formed it in being born with it in the Virgin's womb. And so he did not die by the abandonment of life, just as he did not suffer by the perishing of power. No one took his soul from him because he has the power of laying it down and taking it up again."[13] See, you have here too that Christ did not abandon his flesh in death, and that life did not abandon the one who had died; also, that he freely gave up his spirit, and no one took it from him.

10. AMBROSE, *ON THE HOLY SPIRIT*, BOOK 3. Hence Ambrose: "Christ *gave up his spirit*,[14] and yet, as if he were the arbiter of whether his body would be spared or hung, he gave up his spirit, he did not lose it. He hung on the cross, and moved all things."[15] But from where did he give it up? From the flesh. To where did he send it? To the Father.

Chapter 2 (69)

1. FOR WHAT REASON CHRIST IS SAID TO HAVE DIED AND SUFFERED. But as the soul withdrew, Christ's flesh died; and because the flesh is dead, Christ is dead. For just as God is said to be dead when the man is dead, so the man is said to be dead when the flesh is dead. The separation of the soul was the death of the flesh. And so, because the flesh, which is united to the Word, was dead, God is said to be dead; and because both flesh and soul felt pain, God is said to have suffered, even though the Godhead had no share of any pain.

2. AUGUSTINE, ON PSALM 129. Hence Augustine: "*And the Word was made flesh*,[1] so that by this flesh the heavenly bread should come to the children. And in a similar way, the Word was crucified, but was not

[12]Augustine, *In Ioannem*, tr. 47 nn10-11.
[13]That is, Vigilius of Thapse, *Contra Felicianum Arianum de unitate Trinitatis*, c14.
[14]Mt. 27, 50.
[15]That is, Ambrose, *De incarnationis dominicae sacramento*, c5 n39.

[1]Jn. 1, 14.

changed into a man; the man was changed into the Word, so that he should become better than he was. And so, because he was man, God died; and because he was God, man was roused and rose again. Whatever the man suffered, God cannot be said not to have suffered, because God was man; in the same way, you cannot say that you have suffered no injury, if your clothing is torn, even though your clothing may not be you. Much more, then, whatever the flesh united to the Word suffers, God also must be said to suffer it, even though the Word may neither die, nor be subject to corruption or change. But whatever of these things he suffered, he suffered it in the flesh."[2]

3. Regarding this, Ambrose too says, in *On the Holy Spirit*, book 3: "What the Word's flesh suffered, the Word remaining in the flesh referred to himself because of having taken a body; and so he may be said to suffer because the flesh suffered, as it is written: *Christ suffered in the flesh*."[3,4] —Here is taught for what reason God or the Son of God is said to have suffered or died: not because he felt death insofar as he is God, but because the flesh united to him died.

4. AUGUSTINE, IN A SERMON ON FAITH. It is according to this reason that Augustine says: "If anyone should say and believe that God the Son of God suffered, let him be anathema."[5] Expounding the reason for this statement, from which we are to gather its meaning, he adds in the same place: "If anyone should say that God the Son of God felt pain in the passion, and not only the flesh with the soul which he had taken to himself, let him be anathema."[6]

5. And so it may rightly be said that God died and did not die, that the Son of God suffered and did not suffer, that the third person suffered and did not suffer, that the Word was crucified and was not crucified. According to the one nature he suffered, and according to the other he was unable to suffer.—Hence Ambrose: "This is the common faith: that Christ is the Son of God and was born of the Virgin. The Prophet describes him as if he were a giant,[7] because the one person is of a twofold nature, partaker of divinity and bodiliness. And so he at the same time suffered and did not suffer, died and did not die, was and was not buried, rose and did not rise again. He rose again according to the flesh which had died, but not according to the Word, which remained ever with the Father."[8]

[2]More accurately, Augustine, *Enarrationes in Psalmos,* on Ps. 130, 2, nn9-10.
[3]1 Pt. 4, 1.
[4]Ambrose, *De incarnationis dominicae sacramento*, c5 n44.
[5]Pseudo-Augustine, *Sermo 233*, n2 (Creed of the Council of Toledo I).
[6]Ibid.
[7]Cf. Ps. 18, 6.
[8]Ambrose, *De incarnationis dominicae sacramento*, c5 nn35-36.

DISTINCTION XXII

Chapter 1 (70)

1. WHETHER CHRIST WAS A MAN IN DEATH. Here it is asked whether Christ was a man during the three days of his death.

2. THE OPINION OF SOME PEOPLE. To some, this does not seem to be the case, because he was dead, and a dead man is not a man.—They also add that, if he was then a man, then either he was a mortal or an immortal one; but he was not mortal, because already dead, nor immortal, because this would be so only after the resurrection.

3. RESPONSE, BY WHICH IT IS CONFIRMED THAT, AND HOW, HE WAS A MAN. To them we answer that, although he was a dead man, yet God was man in death; and he was neither mortal, nor immortal, and yet truly a man. For those kinds of quibbles have their place in the case of creatures, but the mystery of faith is free from philosophical arguments.—AMBROSE. Hence Ambrose: "Put aside your arguments, where faith is required. Let dialectic be silent, even in her own schools. We believe fishermen, not dialecticians."[1]—And so we say that in Christ's death God was truly man, and yet the man was dead; and this man was neither mortal, nor immortal, because he was united to the severed soul and flesh. It is for a different reason that God is called man, or man God, than [a man is called] Martin or John. For the man is called God, and vice versa, because of the taking on of the man, that is, of the soul and flesh.—AUGUSTINE. Hence Augustine: "Such was that taking as to make God to be man, and man to be God."[2] And so, since that taking was not undone by death, and God continued to be united to the man and the man to God as before, truly God was then still man and vice versa, because he was united to soul and flesh. But the man was dead, because the soul was divided from the flesh. He was dead because of the separation of the soul from the flesh, but a man because of the union of the two in himself.—For he was not a man in such a way as to exist from conjoint soul and flesh, which is the reason why anyone else is called a man; perhaps he was a man in this way too before his death, and then again after the resurrection. But in his death he was a man only because of the union of soul and flesh in himself, and he was dead because of the division between those two.

[1]Ambrose, *De fide*, bk 1 c13 n84.
[2]Augustine, *De Trinitate*, bk 1 c13 n28.

Chapter 2 (71)

1. WHETHER IN DEATH CHRIST WAS A MAN ANYWHERE, AND WHETHER HE IS A MAN WHEREVER HE IS. Here it is asked whether in death Christ was a man anywhere, and whether, wherever he is, he is a man.—To which we say that it was not everywhere he was that he was a man; neither is he a man now wherever he is, because he is everywhere according to the Godhead, nor is he everywhere a man, because he is not everywhere united to the man. But wherever he is according to his humanity, there he is a man. At the time of his death, he was everywhere according to the Godhead, in the tomb according to his humanity, and in hell also according to his humanity; but he was in hell according to the soul and in the tomb according to the flesh.[1] And so the man was in the tomb, because he was united to his humanity, although not to all of it, because only to the flesh; and the man was in hell, because he was united to his humanity, although not to all of it, because only to the soul.

2. OBJECTION. But if in hell he was united to the soul alone, and in the tomb to the flesh alone, then he was not united to soul and flesh either in hell, or in the tomb. How then may the man be said to be either here or there? What is the reason for this assertion?—EXPOSITION OF ITS CAUSE. Because it was by one and the same union that he was united to the soul in hell and to the flesh in the tomb; and he was as united to those two, which had then become severed, as he had been to them before their separation, that is, before death.

3. OBJECTION. The following objection is made to this: If Christ had taken only a soul or only flesh, he would not have been true man; it was because he had taken both that he was true man. In the same way, then, where he did not have flesh and soul united to himself, there he was not true man. But at the time of his death he did not have those two in union anywhere, because neither in the tomb, nor in hell, nor anywhere else; therefore nowhere was he true man.—To which we say that Christ would certainly not have been true man, if he had not taken flesh and soul. And yet, because he never laid down either of them after he had taken them, but instead unceasingly continued the same union with each of them which he had contracted when he had taken them, not unsuitably do we say that wherever he is united to the soul or the flesh or both, there he is said to be true man, because there he has taken on human form.[2] And so the man was in the tomb, and the man was in hell, because in each place Christ had taken on human form and had one and the same union with soul and flesh, even though these were now separate. And at one and the same time, Christ lay in the tomb and descended into hell, but he lay in

[1]Cf. Fulgentius, *De fide ad Petrum*, c2 n11.
[2]Cf. above, dist. 7 c1 n17.

the tomb according to the flesh alone, and he descended into hell according to the soul alone.—AUGUSTINE, *ON JOHN*. Hence Augustine: "Who is he *who was not abandoned in hell*?[3] Christ, but only according to his soul. Who lay in the tomb? Christ, but only according to his flesh. Christ is in each of these; we confess Christ in all of these, jointly and severally."[4]

4. From all this, it is plainly shown that Christ was united to the flesh lying in the tomb, as he was to the soul in hell. Otherwise, if he had not been united to the dead flesh, he would not be said to have lain in it in the tomb. And so the soul descended into hell, the flesh lay in the tomb, and Wisdom remained with each of them. As Ambrose says, "this Wisdom shed the light of eternal life over them who were placed in hell. There shone the true light of Wisdom; it illuminated hell, but was not enclosed by it. For what sort of place is the place of Wisdom? Concerning it, it is written: *Man does not know its ways, nor is it found among men*, and of which *the abyss says: It is not in me; the sea says: It is not with me*.[5] And so Wisdom is neither in time, nor in place. Neither is death to be attributed to it":[6] "for it was the flesh that hung on the tree, and not that divine substance which works all things."[7] Yet we confess that Christ hung on the tree and lay in the tomb, but according to the flesh, and that he was in hell, but according to the soul alone.

Chapter 3 (72)

1. THAT THE WHOLE CHRIST IS EVERYWHERE, YET NOT WHOLLY, JUST AS HE IS WHOLE MAN OR GOD, YET NOT WHOLLY. In any case, the whole Christ was at the same time in hell, in heaven, and everywhere. For that eternal person was not greater where he had both body and soul united to himself than where he had only one of them; nor was he greater where he had both together or only one of them united to himself, than where he had neither of them. And so Christ was whole and perfect everywhere.—AUGUSTINE, IN THE *EXPOSITION OF FAITH AGAINST FELICIAN*. Hence Augustine: "Christ did not abandon the Father when he came into the Virgin: he was everywhere whole, everywhere perfect. And so at one and the same time he was whole in hell, whole in heaven. In the netherworld, he was the resurrection of the dead; in the heavens, he was the life of the living. Truly dead, truly alive: in him, the acceptance of mortality drew out death, and the Godhead did not give up life."[1] "And so the Son of God

[3]Act. 2, 31.
[4]Augustine, *In Ioannem*, tr. 78 n3.
[5]Job 28, 13-14.
[6]Ambrose, *De incarnationis dominicae sacramento*, c5 nn41-42
[7]Ibid., c6 n50.

[1]That is, Vigilius of Thapse, *Contra Felicianum*, c14.

did not bear death in his soul, nor suffer it in his majesty; but only by participation"[2] in infirmity "was the King of glory crucified."[3]

2. From this, it is plain that Christ was at the same time whole in the tomb, whole in hell, whole everywhere, just as now he is whole everywhere he is, and yet not wholly. Although whole, he was not wholly in the tomb, nor in hell, just as Christ is whole God, Christ is whole man, but not wholly, because he is not only God or man, but both God and man. For 'wholly' is referred to the nature, but 'whole' to the hypostasis, just as 'something' and 'something else' are referred to the nature, 'someone' or 'another' to the person.—THE DAMASCENE. Hence John: "Christ is whole and perfect God, and yet he is not wholly God, for he is not only God, but also man. And he is whole and perfect man, but not wholly man, for he is not only man, but also God. For 'wholly' here refers to nature, but 'whole' to hypostasis, just as 'something' refers to nature, but 'someone' to hypostasis";[4] and the same is true of similar terms.

Chapter 4 (73)

1. WHETHER THOSE THINGS WHICH ARE SAID OF GOD OR OF THE SON OF GOD CAN BE SAID OF THAT MAN OR OF THE SON OF MAN. It is also usual to ask whether it may suitably be said that the son of man or that man descended from heaven or is everywhere, just as we say that the Son of God or God came from heaven and is everywhere.

2. To which we say: If the meaning of the statement is referred to the unity of the person, then it may rightly be said; but if to the distinction of natures, then it is not at all to be granted.—AUGUSTINE, *AGAINST MAXIMINUS*. Hence Augustine: "Christ is one person, God and man. And so it is said: *No one ascended to heaven, unless he who descended from heaven*, etc.[1] If you attend to the distinction of substances, the Son of God descended and the son of man is crucified; but if to the unity of the person, then the son of man descended and the Son of God is crucified. Because of the unity of the person, not only did he say that the son of man had descended from heaven, but also that he was in heaven while he spoke on earth."[2,3]—AUGUSTINE, *ON THE TRINITY*, IN THE FIRST BOOK. Because of this same unity, "the God of glory is said to have been crucified, who yet was crucified only in the form of a servant, and not according to his being God of glory, in which capacity he glorifies his own. And yet the God of

[2]Vigilius of Thapse, *Contra Felicianum*, c16.
[3]Augustine, *De Trinitate*, bk 1 c13 n28.
[4]John of Damascus, *De fide orthodoxa*, bk 3 c7.

[1]Jn. 3, 13.
[2]Cf. ibid.
[3]Augustine, *Contra Maximinum*, bk 2 c20.

glory is said to have been crucified, and rightly: not by the power of his divinity, but by the infirmity of the flesh. And so, what is said on account of what, and what according to what, let the prudent, diligent, and pious reader discern."[4]

3. Let these things about the bindings of the Lord's shoe[5] suffice, lest *the bones of the king of Idumea* be consumed *even unto ashes*.[6]

DISTINCTION XXIII

Chapter 1 (74)

1. WHETHER CHRIST HAD FAITH AND HOPE, AS HE HAD CHARITY. Since it has been shown above[1] that Christ was filled with grace, it is not pointless to inquire whether he had faith and hope, as he had charity. If he lacked these, it does not seem that he had the fullness of graces.

2. HERE THESE THREE ARE TO BE DISCUSSED, AND FIRST FAITH. In order that this question may be discussed more plainly, some things are to be put forth with regard to each of them; and first of faith, according to whose measure the Apostle commands each one to be wise.[2]

Chapter 2 (75)

1. WHAT IS FAITH. Faith is the virtue by which unseen things are believed. And yet this is not to be taken of all things that are unseen, but only of those things which, as Augustine says, "it pertains to religion"[1] to believe. For there are many things which, "if the Christian ignores them, there is no reason to fear," because he does not thereby deviate from religion.

Chapter 3 (76)

1. ON THE WAYS IN WHICH THE TERM FAITH IS USED. The term faith is taken in three ways, namely for that by which one believes, and it is a virtue; also, for that by which one believes, and it is not a virtue; also, for that which is believed, which is different from that by which one believes. —AUGUSTINE, *ON THE TRINITY*, BOOK 13. Hence Augustine says: "The things which one believes are one thing, the faith by which they are be-

[4]Augustine, *De Trinitate*, bk 1 c13 n28.
[5]Cf. above, dist. 2 c2 n2.
[6]Cf. Amos 2, 1.

[1]Dist. 13 n1.
[2]Cf. Rom. 12, 3.

[1]Augustine, *Enchiridion*, c9.

lieved is another. The former consist in things which are said either to be, or to have been, or to be about to be; but the latter is in the believer's spirit, and is apparent to him alone whose it is."[1] And yet each of these is called faith, namely that which is believed, and that by which it is believed. That which is believed is called faith, as in: "This is the Catholic faith; whoever does not believe it faithfully and firmly cannot be saved."[2]

2. The faith by which one believes, if it is joined to charity, is a virtue, because, as Ambrose says, "charity is the mother of all virtues";[3] it informs all of them and without it there is no true virtue. And so faith working *through love*[4] is the virtue by which unseen things are believed.

3. AUGUSTINE, IN THE BOOK *ON FAITH AND WORKS*. This is the foundation which cannot be changed, as the Apostle says;[5] if it is placed as the foundation, it will allow no one to perish. Hence Augustine: "The foundation is Christ Jesus, that is, faith in Christ, *which works through love*,[6] through which Christ lives *in our hearts*,[7] and which allows no one to perish. None other is the foundation."[8]

4. AUGUSTINE, *ON THE EPISTLE OF JOHN*: "For faith without love is empty. Faith with love pertains to the Christian; the other kind is the demon's, for *the demons also believe and tremble*."[9,10]—AUGUSTINE, ON THE LORD'S WORDS: "But it matters much whether one believes Christ, or in a Christ, or in Christ, for the demons too believed that he was Christ,[11] but they did not believe in Christ."[12]

Chapter 4 (77)

1. WHAT IT IS TO BELIEVE GOD, OR IN A GOD, OR IN GOD.—BEDE; AUGUSTINE: "For it is one thing to believe in God, another to believe in a God, and yet another to believe God. To believe God is to believe that what he says is true, which the evil ones also do; we also believe a man, but not in a man. To believe in a God is to believe that he is God, which the evil ones also do. To believe in God is to love by believing, to go to him by believing, to adhere to him by believing and to be incorporated in-

[1]Augustine, *De Trinitate*, bk 13 c2 n5.
[2]Athanasian Creed.
[3]Ordinary gloss, on Rom. 14, 5; cf. Ambrosiaster, on Rom. 14, 5.
[4]Cf. Gal. 5, 6.
[5]Cf. 1 Cor. 3, 11.
[6]Gal. 5, 6.
[7]Cf. Eph. 3, 17.
[8]Augustine, *De fide et operibus*, c16 n27.
[9]James 2, 19.
[10]Augustine, *In I Ioannis*, tr. 10 n2.
[11]Cf. Mk. 3, 11-12; Lk. 4, 34.
[12]Augustine, *Sermo 144*, c2 n2.

to his members."[1] [—AUGUSTINE, ON THE PSALM:] "By this faith, the impious is justified, so that thenceforth faith itself begins to work through love. For those works alone are to be called good which are done through the love of God."[2]—AUGUSTINE, *ON JOHN*: "Even love itself is called the work of faith."[3]

2. And so the faith which demons and false Christians have is a quality of the mind, but it is formless, because it is without charity. That the evil ones too have faith, even as they lack charity, is shown by the Apostle who says: *If I should have all faith, but do not have charity*, etc.[4] But this faith too can be called a gift of God, because even in those who are evil there are some gifts of God.[5]

Chapter 5 (78)

WHETHER THAT FORMLESS QUALITY OF MIND, WHICH IS IN THE EVIL CHRISTIAN, BECOMES A VIRTUE WHEN HE BECOMES GOOD. But if it should be asked whether that formless quality, by which the evil Christian believes all the same things as the good Christian, remains and becomes a virtue with the coming of charity, or whether it is removed and replaced by another quality, which is a virtue, either view may be held without danger. But it seems to me that the same quality which was there earlier remains and becomes a virtue with the coming of charity.

Chapter 6 (79)

1. IN WHAT SENSE FAITH IS SAID TO BE ONE. Although faith is spoken of in different ways, yet it is to be professed that there is one faith, as the Apostle says: *One Lord, one faith.*[1] Indeed, whether faith is taken for that which is believed, or for that by which one believes, faith is rightly said to be one.

2. AMBROSE. If it is taken for that which is believed, it is said to be *one faith* in this sense, because "we are commanded to believe the same thing,"[2] and "that which is believed" by all the faithful "is one and the same";[3] that is why the faith is called 'Catholic,' that is, universal.

[1]Partly from ordinary gloss, on James 2, 23; Bede on James 2, 19; Augustine, *In Ioannem*, tr. 29 n6.
[2]Augustine, *Enarrationes in Psalmos*, on Ps. 67, 32-33, n41.
[3]Augustine, *In I Ioannis*, tr. 10 n1.
[4]1 Cor. 13, 2.
[5]Cf. above dist. 20 c1 n2.

[1]Eph. 4, 5.
[2]Ordinary gloss, on Eph. 4, 5 .
[3]That is, Ambrosiaster, on Eph. 4, 4.

3. But if faith is taken for that through which belief occurs, then faith is said to be one not by reason of its being one in number in everyone, but by its kind or likeness.—AUGUSTINE, IN BOOK 13, *ON THE TRINITY*. Hence Augustine: "That faith, which they who have it are called the faithful, and those who do not unbelievers, is common to all the faithful, in the same way in which a face is said to be common to many men, and yet each of them has his own. For faith is not one in number, but in kind; as it is in one, so it is in others, and yet not the very same one, but a similar one, and because of the similarity we speak of one faith rather than of many. In the same way, the will of those who will the same thing is said to be one, even though each has his own will, and the face of two people who are very like to each other is said to be one."[4]

Chapter 7 (80)

1. THAT FAITH PROPERLY CONCERNS THINGS WHICH ARE NOT SEEN, AND YET IT ITSELF IS SEEN BY THE ONE IN WHOM IT IS. It is also to be noted that faith properly concerns only things which are not seen.—GREGORY, IN SOME HOMILY. Hence Gregory: "Visible things do not require faith, but knowledge."[1]—THE SAME, IN A DIALOGUE. The same: "Although Paul says: *Faith is the substance of things to be hoped for, the evidence of things that do not appear,*[2] that is truly said to be believed which cannot be seen, for it is impossible to believe that which can be seen."[3] "Thomas saw one thing, and believed another: he saw a man, but he confessed [him to be] God, saying: *My God and my Lord.*"[4,5]

2. AUGUSTINE, IN BOOK 13, *ON THE TRINITY*. Concerning this same matter, Augustine too says: "Each one sees faith itself to be in his own heart, if he believes, or not to be there, if he does not believe. But not in the same way as we know those bodies which we see with our bodily eyes, and think about even when absent through their images which we retain in our memory. Nor even as those things which we have not seen, and which we shape in our thought from those which we have seen, and commit them to memory. Nor as a man, whose soul we do not see, and yet conjecture [its existence] from our own; and we also recognize him from the motions of his body, as we have learned them from looking at him. This is not the way in which faith is seen in the heart in which it is, by him whose it is; but he holds on to it with a most certain knowledge. And

[4]Augustine, *De Trinitate*, bk 13 c2 n5.

[1]Gregory, *In Evangelia*, hom. 26 n8.
[2]Hebr. 11, 1.
[3]Gregory, *Dialogi*, bk 4 c6.
[4]Jn. 20, 28.
[5]Gregory, *In Evangelia*, hom. 26 n8.

although we are commanded to believe because we cannot see that which we are commanded to believe, yet we see faith itself in ourselves, when it is in us; because faith even in absent things is present, and faith in outward things is itself within, and faith in things which are not seen is itself seen. Faith itself comes into the hearts of men in time; and if, from being faithful they become unbelievers, it perishes from them."[6]

3. With these words, it is plainly taught that faith in man's heart itself is seen by the man himself, and not corporeally or in the imagination, but intellectually. And yet faith itself concerns absent things and those which are not seen. For as Augustine says elsewhere, "we believe in order to know; we do not know in order to believe. For what is faith, except to believe what you do not see? Faith, then, is to believe what you do not see; truth, to see what you have believed."[7]

4. And so faith is rightly called the *evidence* or conviction of things that *do not appear*,[8] because if there is faith, then on its account there is conviction and proof that there are some things which do not appear, since faith concerns only things that do not appear.

Chapter 8 (81)

1. DESCRIPTION OF FAITH. For the Apostle says: *Faith is the substance of things to be hoped for, the evidence* or conviction *of things that do not appear*,[1] because those things for which we are to hope subsist in us even now through faith, and they will subsist in the future through experience. And it is the proof and conviction *of things that do not appear* because, if anyone should doubt concerning these, they are proven by faith, as even now the future resurrection is proven because the Patriarchs and other saints believed it to be so. Or it is the proof and certitude that there are some things which do not appear, as was said above.[2] But faith is properly called *the substance of things to be hoped for* because it 'stands under' the things to be hoped for, and because it is the foundation of good things and no one can change it.

2. WHETHER THAT DESCRIPTION [OF FAITH] IS SUITABLE FOR HOPE. But if it is asked whether this description is suitable for hope, either view may freely be granted. For if it is said to be suitable, there are also many other things in which faith and hope differ.[3] But it would not be wrong to say that it is only suitable for faith, and not for hope, because faith alone is

[6]Augustine, *De Trinitate*, bk 13 c1 n3.
[7]Augustine, *In Ioannem*, tr. 40 n9.
[8]Cf. Hebr. 11, 1.

[1]Hebr. 11, 1.
[2]See above, c7 n4.
[3]See below, dist. 26 c3.

called the foundation,[4] not because faith can be a virtue without hope and charity.—AUGUSTINE, IN THE *ENCHIRIDION*. Hence Augustine: "Faith working *through love*[5] certainly cannot exist without hope, nor love without hope, nor hope without love, nor either without faith, and faith without love *avails nothing*."[6,7]

3. And yet something may be believed which is not hoped for; but nothing can be hoped for which is not believed. And so to believe, which is an act of faith, naturally precedes hoping, which is an act of hope, because unless something is believed, it cannot be hoped for; but something is believed which is not hoped for. That is why in Scripture it is frequently found that faith precedes hope, and hope follows faith;[8] not that the virtue of faith precedes the virtue of hope temporally or causally, but because the act of faith naturally precedes the act of hope. Some even grant this of the virtue of faith itself, that it precedes hope naturally, and not in time.

Chapter 9 (82)

1. WHY FAITH ALONE IS CALLED THE FOUNDATION. And so faith is rightly alone called the foundation of all virtues and good works.

2. And yet it is not the foundation of charity, because faith is not the cause of charity; it is rather charity which is the cause of the virtue of faith itself. For charity is the cause and mother of all virtues.[1] (AUGUSTINE, *ON JOHN*:) "If it is wanting, in vain do we have other things; if it is present, we have all other things."[2] For charity is the Holy Spirit, as has been set out above.[3] And so it is the cause of all virtues, and no other virtue is the cause of it, because it excels all gifts. Hence Augustine: "Look at the gifts of the Church, and you will acknowledge that the gift of charity is more excellent than all the others";[4] "like oil, charity cannot be pressed to the bottom, but springs to the top."[5] And so faith is not the cause or foundation of it.

3. GREGORY. Nevertheless Gregory, in *On Ezechiel*, says "that unless faith is held first, no progress is made toward spiritual love. For charity does not precede faith, but faith charity, because no one can love what he

[4]See above, c3 nn2-3.
[5]Cf. Gal. 5, 6.
[6]Cf. 1 Cor. 13, 3.
[7]Cf. Augustine, *Enchiridion*, c8.
[8]1 Cor. 13, 13.

[1]See above, c3 n2.
[2]Augustine, *In Ioannem*, tr. 9 n8.
[3]Bk 1 dist. 17.
[4]Augustine, *Enarrationes in Psalmos,* on Ps. 103, 3, sermon 1 n9.
[5]Augustine, *In Ioannem*, tr. 6 n20.

has not believed,"[6] just as he cannot hope for it.—But this can be taken to be said of that faith which is not a virtue, for it frequently precedes hope and charity. Or of the act of faith, which perhaps naturally precedes the act of charity, as it does the act of hope. Indeed, the words quoted, if rightly noted, seem to indicate this, as do the ones which he adds, saying: "Unless you believe the things which you hear, you are not enflamed to love them,"[7] which concerns only things not seen, as we said earlier.[8]—JOHN CHRYSOSTOM. Hence Chrysostom: "Faith makes to exist in our soul those things which are not seen,"[9] with which faith is properly concerned; as to things which are seen, it is not faith, but knowledge.

DISTINCTION XXIV

Chapter 1 (83)

1. HOW THAT TEXT: WHEN IT COMES TO PASS, YOU MAY BELIEVE, IS TO BE UNDERSTOOD. Here it is asked: if faith is only of things not seen, how did Truth say to the Apostles: *I tell you now, before it comes to pass, so that when it comes to pass, you may believe*,[1] where it seems to be indicated that their faith concerned things done and seen?

2. AUGUSTINE, *ON JOHN*. In commenting on this text, Augustine raises the question and answers it as follows: "What can he mean by this: *So that when it comes to pass, you may believe*? The praise of faith is this: if that which is believed is not seen. Indeed, even Thomas—to whom it was said: *Because you have seen*, and *you have believed*[2]—did not believe that which he saw. For he saw and touched the living flesh, which he had seen dying, and he believed God to be hidden in that flesh. And so he believed with the mind what he did not see by that which was apparent to the senses of his body. Although things that are seen are said to be believed, just as every one says that he believes his own eyes, this is not the same faith which is built up in us; but from the things that are seen, it happens in us that we believe those which are not seen."[3]—From these words, it is plainly understood that faith properly is not of things which are apparent; nor is the faith by which we are built up in Christ that by which we say, in customary speech, that we believe what we see.

[6]Gregory, *In Ezechielem*, bk 2 hom. 4 n13.
[7]Ibid.
[8]In c7, above.
[9]John Chrysostom, *In Hebraeos*, hom. 21 n2.

[1]Jn. 14, 29.
[2]Jn. 20, 29.
[3]Augustine, *In Ioannem*, tr. 79 n1.

3. THAT FAITH IS ALSO SAID OF PRESENT THINGS, BUT IMPROPERLY. But Augustine says elsewhere that faith can be of things present: that shall be the case in the future, when we shall see God face to face; and yet this is not properly called faith, but truth.—AUGUSTINE, IN THE BOOK OF *QUESTIONS ON THE GOSPELS*. He says: "There is a faith by which are believed the things which are not seen; but there is also a faith in things, when we believe not in words, but in the very things present to us: that shall be the case when God's wisdom shall openly offer itself to the saints for contemplation face to face."[4]—But this is not properly called faith, but the reward of faith to which one will come by believing, so that from "faith in words" the just one may pass "into faith in things."[5]

Chapter 2 (84)

1. WHETHER PETER HAD FAITH IN THE PASSION WHEN HE SAW THAT MAN SUFFER. But if it is asked whether Peter had faith in the passion, when he discerned with his own eyes that the man Christ suffered, we say that he had faith in the passion not in that he believed that man to suffer because he saw this, but in that he believed that the one who suffered was God. For it was not the virtue of faith to believe that the man suffered and died, which even the Jewish bystander believed, but to believe that it was God who suffered.

2. Hence Augustine, on that place in the Psalm: *He answered him in the way of his power*: "The praise of faith is not that he believes that man to be dead, which even the pagan believes, but that he believes him to be glorified"[1] and true God. And so faith believes that God died and man was glorified. Therefore it was not [a matter of] faith for Peter to believe that that man was dying, which he could see with his own eyes, but to believe that it was God who was dying. Nor do we gain any merit by our faith, if we believe that the man died, which even a Jew believes, but because we believe that it was the man-God who died.

Chapter 3 (85)

1. WHETHER SOME THINGS WHICH ARE BELIEVED ARE KNOWN. After these matters, it is usual to ask, since faith concerns things that are not apparent and not seen, whether it is also only of things which are unknown, for if it concerns only things which are unknown, it appears to concern only things of which we are ignorant.

[4]Augustine, *Quaestiones Evangeliorum*, bk 2 q39.
[5]Ibid.

[1]Augustine, *Enarrationes in Psalmos*, on Ps. 101, 24, sermon 2 n7.

2. THAT FAITH IS NOT COMPREHENDED BY ANY SENSE. But it is to be known that, since there is an inner vision and an exterior one, faith is not among the things subject to the exterior vision; and yet it is among the things which are in some manner grasped by the interior gaze. And some things are certainly grasped so as to be understood, even if not as they will be in the future; others are not. And since faith comes *from hearing*,[1] but in an interior way, and not an exterior one, it cannot concern something of which one is entirely ignorant. Augustine sets down that faith does not pertain to a bodily sense; he says: "Although faith comes to us *from hearing*, yet it does not pertain to that sense of the body which is called hearing, because it is not a sound; nor to any other sense of the body, because it is a thing of the heart, and not of the body."[2]

3. AUGUSTINE, *ON OCTONARY* 10. And so some things are believed by faith which are understood by natural reason, but some are believed which are not so understood. Hence the Prophet: *Unless you believe, you will not understand*.[3]—Which Augustine plainly distinguishes, saying: "There are some things which, unless we understand them, we will not believe; there are others which, unless we believe them, we will not understand."[4] "But no one can believe in God unless he understand something, since faith comes from the hearing of preaching."[5]—The same, in the book *On the Trinity*: "A sure faith is in some manner the beginning of knowledge; but this knowledge is not made sure, except after this life."[6]—*ON OCTONARY* 10. Ambrose too says: "Where there is faith, knowledge does not immediately follow; where there is knowledge, faith has gone before."[7]—From these words, it is apparent that some things are believed which are not understood or known unless they are first believed; but some things are sometimes understood even before they are believed.

4. And yet they are not now understood as they will be known in the future; and even now they are better understood through faith, by which hearts are cleansed, because unless God is loved through faith, the heart is not cleansed to know him.—AUGUSTINE, IN BOOK 8 OF *ON THE TRINITY*. Hence Augustine: " But what is it to know God, except to behold him in our mind and to perceive him firmly? But even before we are able to behold and to perceive God as he is perceived by the pure in heart, unless he is first loved by faith, the heart will not be cleansed so as to be fit to see

[1]Cf. Rom. 10, 17.
[2]Augustine, *De Trinitate*, bk 13 c2 n5.
[3]Is. 7, 9, Septuagint.
[4]Ordinary gloss, on Ps. 118, 73; from Augustine on the same text, *Enarrationes in Psalmos*, sermon 18 n3.
[5]Ibid.
[6]Augustine, *De Trinitate*, bk 9 c1 n1.
[7]Ambrose, *Expositio de Psalmo 118*, sermon 10 n31.

him."[8] See, you have it plainly stated here that God cannot be known, unless he is first believed in love.

5. THAT SOME THINGS WHICH ARE NOT KNOWN YET ARE BELIEVED AND LOVED. But above it was said that no one can believe in God unless something is first understood.[9] And so we gather that some things which are to be believed cannot be known and understood unless they are first believed, and some are not believed unless they are first understood, and then they are understood more deeply through faith. Nor are those things entirely unknown which are believed before being understood, since faith comes *from hearing*;[10] and yet they are partly unknown, because they are not understood. And so something is believed which is not known, but not entirely, as also something is loved which is not known.—*ON THE TRINITY*, BOOK 8. Hence Augustine: "Something may be known and not loved; but I ask whether it is possible that something which is not known be loved. If it cannot, then no one loves God before knowing him. But where are those three, faith, hope, and charity, unless in a soul which believes what it does not yet know, and which hopes for and loves that which it believes? And so even that is loved which is not known, but yet it is believed."[11]

DISTINCTION XXV

Chapter 1 (86)

1. ON THE FAITH OF THE ANCIENTS. In addition to the foregoing, we must address the sufficiency of faith for the salvation of those who lived before the coming of Christ and of those who come after. It appears that faith made progress with the passage of time, just as knowledge did. And so faith is called great because of knowledge and the quantity of articles, or because of constancy and devotion. But there is some measure of faith without which salvation was never possible. Hence the Apostle: *The one who comes to God must believe that God is, and that he is the rewarder of those who hope in him.*[1]

2. THAT THERE WOULD NEVER HAVE BEEN SALVATION WITHOUT FAITH IN THE MEDIATOR. But it is asked whether, before the coming [of Christ] or before the Law, belief in these things would have been sufficient for salvation. For in the time of grace, it is most certain that this does not suffice, because it is necessary to believe all that is contained in the Creeds.

[8] Augustine, *De Trinitate*, bk 8 c4 n6.
[9] In n3.
[10] Cf. Rom. 10, 17.
[11] Augustine, *De Trinitate*, bk 8 c4 n6.

[1] Hebr. 11, 6.

—But it seems that this did not suffice either before the coming [of Christ] or before the Law, because the authorities of the saints attest that, without faith in the mediator, no man would have been saved, either before or after.

3. AUGUSTINE. Hence Augustine, *To Optatus*: "That faith is sound by which we believe that no man, of whatever little or great age, is freed from the contagion of death and the burden of sin, which he has contracted by his first birth, except through *the one mediator of God and men, Christ Jesus*.[2] It is by this most sound faith in this same man and God that even those just ones were saved who, before he came in the flesh, believed that he was going to come. For one and the same faith is theirs and ours."[3] "Therefore, since all the just, whether before the incarnation or after, lived and live only by faith in the incarnation of Christ, as indeed it is written, *there is no other name under heaven by which we can be saved*,[4] this same faith has had the power to save humankind from the very time that it became vitiated in Adam."[5]

4. IN THE BOOK *ON CORRECTION AND GRACE*. The same [Augustine]: "No one is freed from the condemnation which came about through Adam, unless through faith in Jesus Christ."[6]—IN THE BOOK *ON MARRIAGE AND CONCUPISCENCE*. The same [Augustine]: "The same faith in the mediator which saves us also saved the just ones of ancient times, both small and great. As we believe that Christ came in the flesh, so they believed that he would come; as we believe that he died, they believed that he would die; and as we believe that he rose again, so they believed that he would rise again. Both we and they believe that he will come to judge the living and the dead."[7]

5. Gregory, *On Ezechiel*: "*And those who went before, and those who followed, called out, saying: Hosanna to the son of David*, etc.,[8] because all the elect, who could have been in Judea, or those who are now in the Church, believed and believe in the mediator of God and men."[9]—By these and many other testimonies, it is taught very plainly that no one has ever received salvation, except through faith in the mediator. And so, *The one who comes to God must believe* what the Apostle said above,[10] but it is not sufficient.

[2] 1 Tim. 2, 5.
[3] Augustine, *Epistola 190*, c2 nn5-6.
[4] Act. 4, 12.
[5] Augustine, *Epistola 190*, c2 n8.
[6] Augustine, *De correptione et gratia*, c7 n11.
[7] Augustine, *De nuptiis et concupiscentia*, bk 2 c11 n23.
[8] Mk. 11, 9; Mt. 21, 9.
[9] Gregory, *In Ezechielem*, bk 2 hom. 5 n2.
[10] At the end of n1.

Chapter 2 (87)

1. ON THE FAITH OF THE SIMPLE. What, then, will be said of those simple persons, to whom the mystery of the incarnation was not revealed, who piously believed what was presented to them?

2. It may be said that no one would have been just or saved to whom a revelation was not made, whether manifest or veiled, openly or under a mystery: manifest, as to Abraham and Moses and the other ancestors, who had knowledge of the articles of faith in a distinct form; veiled, as to the simple, to whom it was revealed that they should believe the same things as those elders believed and taught, but who did not have knowledge in the same manifest form. In the Church also there are some who are less able, and so cannot distinguish and explain the articles of faith, but who nevertheless believe all that is contained in the Creed; these believe what they do not know, having a faith veiled under a mystery. In the same way, in that earlier time, too, those who were less able, on the strength of a revelation made to them, adhered in faith to the elders, to whom they, as it were, entrusted their faith.—Hence Job: *The oxen were ploughing, and the she-asses were grazing next to them.*[1] The simple and lesser ones are the she-asses grazing next to the oxen because, by adhering in humility to the elders, they believed under a mystery what the others also taught under a mystery. Such a one perhaps was the widow of Sarephta.[2]

Chapter 3 (88)

1. BEFORE THE MEDIATOR'S COMING, WHAT WAS IT NECESSARY TO KNOW CONCERNING HIM. But it is asked: since salvation would not have been available to the ancients, as it is not to the moderns, without faith in the mediator, would it have been necessary for them to believe concerning the mediator all the things that we now believe?

2. To some, it seems that it would have been sufficient for them to believe only four things, namely [Christ's] birth, death, resurrection, and coming in judgement; they gather this from the words of Augustine above, where he set out these four things.[1]

3. To others, it seems that, if they had faith in the Trinity, then it would have been sufficient, concerning faith in the mystery of the incarnation, if they believed that the Son of God would be born of woman and would come in judgement. These use John the Baptist as evidence for their view; according to Gregory's exposition,[2] in the Gospel, John seems to have had

[1]Job 1, 14.
[2]Cf. 3 Kings 17, 10-16.

[1]Above, c1 n1.
[2]Gregory, *In Ezechiel*em, bk 1 hom. 1 n5; *In Evangelia*, hom. 6 n1.

doubts concerning Christ's death and descent into hell, when he asked through the disciples: *Are you the one who is to come, or are we to await another?*[3] As if to say: are you yourself going to descend into hell, or will you send another for these mysteries?—But some say that he did not doubt from ignorance, but from piety, that is, he showed himself to doubt not because he did not know, but because he was seized with pious devotion toward Christ, and so, with wonder, he indicated his humility.

Chapter 4 (89)

1. ON THE FAITH OF CORNELIUS. It is also usual to ask concerning Cornelius, whether he had faith in the incarnation, since he was told by the angel: *Your alms have been accepted, and your prayers have been granted.*[1] For if he did not then have faith in the incarnation, then he had justice without this faith, because of him it is written that he was *just and God-fearing.*[2] But if he had faith in the incarnation, to what end then was Peter sent to him?

2. It may well be said that, just as he already had faith in God's unity by revelation, so he also had faith in the incarnation, but that he did not know that the Son of God had already become incarnate, and so Peter was sent to him in order to announce to him that the Son of God was already born and to confer on him the sacrament of regeneration. And so he had faith in the incarnation, but he did not know whether it had already occurred or was yet to come.—GREGORY. And so "by faith, he came to works, and by works he was made more firm in faith." For as Gregory says, "it is through faith that one comes to works. Cornelius also came to works through faith: for he believed in the one God, but did not know that his Son had become incarnate. Through faith, his works were pleasing to God, for *without faith, it is impossible to please God.*"[3,4]

3. But Augustine says that "the angel said to Cornelius: *Your alms have been accepted, and your prayers have been granted,*[5] before he believed in Christ; and yet he did not give alms or pray without some faith. For how did he call on him in whom he did not believe?[6] But if salvation had been possible without faith in Christ, Peter, the Church's architect, would not have been sent to him."[7]—Note carefully how he says that

[3]Mt. 11, 3; Lk. 7, 19.

[1]Act. 10, 4.
[2]Act. 10, 22.
[3]Hebr. 11, 6.
[4]Gregory, *In Ezechielem*, bk 2 hom. 7 n9.
[5]Act. 10, 4.
[6]Cf. Rom. 10, 14.
[7]Augustine, *De praedestinatione sanctorum*, c7 n12.

there cannot be salvation without faith in Christ, and yet Cornelius' prayers were heard before he believed in Christ. This may be understood in this sense: namely, before he knew that Christ, in whom he believed under a mystery, had become incarnate.

Chapter 5 (90)

1. ON THE EQUALITY OF FAITH, HOPE, CHARITY, AND WORK, WHICH ARE EQUAL IN SOME RESPECT. Nor is it also to be omitted that faith, hope, charrity, and work are equal in some respect in our present state.—GREGORY, *ON EZECHIEL*. Hence Gregory: "For so long as we are in this life, we find that in us faith, hope, charity, and work are equal to each other because we love as much as we believe, and insofar as we love wc are certain of our hope. For each of the faithful believes as much as he hopes and loves, and works as much as he believes, loves, and hopes. And yet charity is said to be greater than hope and faith because, when we come before God's face, hope and faith pass away, but charity remains,"[1] and because (AMBROSE) "charity is the mother of all the virtues."[2] And so it is not placed after faith and hope because it arises from them,[3] but because it will remain and increase after they pass away, since *charity shall never fail.*[4] Therefore the aforesaid equality is to be properly considered according to the intention of interior acts.

2. But what has been said here and earlier,[5] namely that charity is not from faith and hope, but that the converse is true, seems to be contradicted by the Apostle's statement: *The end of the commandment is charity from a pure heart, and a good conscience, and a faith unfeigned.*[6]—AUGUSTINE. Expounding this, Augustine takes *heart* for intellect, and *conscience* for hope; he says: "Which charity is *the end of the commandment*? The one proceeding *from a pure heart*, that is, from a pure intellect, so that nothing is loved but God; *and a good conscience*, that is, hope; *and a faith unfeigned*, that is, not simulated."[7] And so it is not charity that precedes faith or hope, but faith and hope seem to precede charity.—But understand this to be taught in this sense: not that faith and hope precede charity, which is the mother of all the virtues, in cause or time, but because without them charity cannot exist in anyone. But they can exist without charity, although there is no pious faith or hope without charity. And

[1]Gregory, *In Ezechielem*, bk 2 hom. 10 n17.
[2]Cf. Ambrosiaster, on Rom. 14, 5.
[3]Cf. above dist. 23 c9 n2.
[4]1 Cor. 13, 8.
[5]Dist. 23 c8 n3 and c9.
[6]1 Tim. 1, 5.
[7]Augustine, *De doctrina christiana*, bk 1 c40 n44.

so charity is said to proceed from faith and hope because it cannot come to anyone without them.

Distinction XXVI

Chapter 1 (91)

1. On hope; what it is. Hope is the virtue by which spiritual and eternal goods are hoped for, that is, they are awaited with trust. For there is a sure expectation of future blessedness, coming from God's grace and from merits which precede either the hope itself, which charity by nature precedes, or the thing hoped for, that is, eternal blessedness. Indeed, to hope for something in the absence of merits may be called presumption rather than hope.

Chapter 2 (92)

With what hope is concerned.—Augustine, in the *Enchiridion*. Just like faith, so hope too concerns invisible things. Hence Augustine: "We speak of faith with regard to those things which are not seen. Concerning hope too, it is said: *Hope that is seen is not hope; for who hopes for what he sees?*[1] That we do not see the things we believe, or those we hope for, is common to faith and hope."[2]

Chapter 3 (93)

In what hope and faith differ. "And yet faith is distinguished from hope not only because they are different terms, but also by a reasonable distinction. ... For faith concerns both evil and good things, because both are believed, and this by a good faith, and not an evil one. Faith is also concerned with past, present, and future things. And so we believe in Christ's death, which has already occurred; we believe that he is enthroned, which occurs now; we believe that he will come to judge, which is future. Moreover, faith concerns both one's own affairs and those of others. Each person, for example, believes that his existence had a beginning, and that he was not eternal; in religious matters, we also believe many, many things not only concerning other men, but also regarding angels. But hope concerns only good things, and only future things, and only things pertaining to the person who entertains the hope of them."[1]

[1]Rom. 8, 24.
[2]Augustine, *Enchiridion*, c8.

[1]Augustine, *Enchiridion*, c8.

Chapter 4 (94)

HE RETURNS TO THE QUESTION POSED EARLIER, NAMELY WHETHER FAITH AND HOPE WERE IN CHRIST. After these matters, it remains to investigate whether faith and hope were in Christ, which is where this treatise had its beginning.[1]—To some, not unlearnedly, it seems that the virtue of faith and hope would not have been in him, as they are not in the saints who are already blessed, or in angels. And yet the saints believe and hope that the resurrection is to come, and angels believe the same; but the virtue of faith or hope is not in them, because they already enjoy the contemplation of God face to face, and in God's Word they already perceive most clearly, and not *darkly through a mirror*,[2] the resurrection and the judgement to come. If it is true that they have faith merely because they believe that the resurrection is to come, then they will in like manner be said to have faith after the resurrection has come, after the judgement, because they will believe it has happened. Indeed, they will then believe, and yet not have the faith which makes the faithful such, because they will not believe without a direct knowledge free of all darkness. In the same way, they believe even now and hope for the resurrection [which is to come], and yet do not have faith, because by believing they know. For they now have *that which is perfect*, and *that which is imperfect* has passed away.[3] They now have knowledge, and faith has become unnecessary; they see face to face, and hope has passed away.—In the same way, Christ, in whom were the goods of the fatherland, believed and hoped that his resurrection would occur on the third day, and he prayed to the Father for it.[4] But he did not have the virtue of faith or hope, because he did not have a darkened and ambiguous knowledge of his resurrection, but the clearest, because he did not know it more perfectly once it had happened than he had understood it when it was still future. And yet Christ hoped, as he says in the Psalm: *In you, o Lord, I placed my hope*;[5] but he did not have the virtue of faith or hope, because he saw face to face the things which he believed.

Chapter 5 (95)

WHETHER THE JUST WHO WERE HELD IN HELL HAD FAITH AND HOPE. But as to the Fathers of old, who were held in hell until Christ's passion, it can be said not incongruously that they had the virtue of faith and hope, because they believed and hoped that they would see God's face in a way in which they could not then do. The direct knowledge of God did not

[1]Beginning of dist. 23.
[2]1 Cor. 13, 12.
[3]Cf. 1 Cor. 13, 10.
[4]Cf. Jn. 17, 1.
[5]Ps. 30, 2.

become available to them before Christ's passion; after its consummation, they passed from faith to gaze.

DISTINCTION XXVII

Chapter 1 (96)

1. ON THE CHARITY BY WHICH GOD AND NEIGHBOUR ARE LOVED, WHICH IS IN CHRIST AND IN US. Although Christ did not have faith and hope, yet as a man he had such love than which there can be no greater; it was due to his most excellent charity that he gave his life for his friends and for his enemies.[1] He also had in his heart that charity which he showed to us by deed, so that by the form of his showing he might instruct us in love.

2. Here something is to be said of charity, and of the manner and order of loving God and neighbour.

Chapter 2 (97)

1. WHAT IS CHARITY. Charity is the love by which God is loved for his own sake, and our neighbour is loved for the sake of God or in God.

2. ON THE TWO COMMANDMENTS OF CHARITY. Charity has two commandments: one pertains to the love of God, and it is the greatest commandment of the Law;[1] the other pertains to the love of neighbour, and it is like the first. The first is: *You shall love God with all your heart, all your mind, and all your soul*, which is written in Deuteronomy.[2] The second is: *You shall love your neighbour as yourself. On these two commandments hang the whole Law and the Prophets.*[3]—AUGUSTINE, *ON CHRISTIAN DOCTRINE*, IN BOOK 1: "For the end of the commandment is love, and a twofold one, that is, of God and neighbour."[4]

Chapter 3 (98)

WHETHER GOD AND NEIGHBOUR ARE LOVED BY THE SAME CHARITY. Here it is asked whether God is loved by the same love as our neighbour, or whether the love of God is one thing, that of our neighbour another.—The love by which God and our neighbour are loved is certainly the

[1]Jn. 15, 13.

[1]Cf. Mt. 22, 36-40.
[2]Deut. 6, 5.
[3]Mt. 22.39-40.
[4]*De doctrina christiana*, bk 1 c26 n27.

same, and it is the Holy Spirit, as was said above,[1] because *God is love.*[2] —AUGUSTINE, *ON THE TRINITY*, IN BOOK 8. Hence Augustine: "John says: *He who does not love his brother, whom he sees, cannot love God, whom he does not see.*[3] But if he loved with spiritual charity the one whom he sees with human sight, he would see God, who is charity itself, with the inner sight by which he can be seen. And so, how can he who does not love his brother, whom he sees, love God, who is the very love which he lacks by not loving his brother? Therefore we love God and our neighbour by one and the same charity; but we love God for the sake of God, and ourselves and our neighbours for the sake of God."[4]

Chapter 4 (99)

1. WHY CHARITY IS CALLED TWOFOLD. But if the love of God and neighbour is one and the same, why is it called 'twofold'?[1]—For the two who are loved, that is, God and neighbour. For although the charity is one, yet two diverse objects are loved, namely God and man or an angel.

2. FOR THIS SAME REASON, IT HAS TWO COMMANDMENTS. For the same reason, there are two commandments, because even though the same charity is commended by both, yet diverse objects are commanded to be loved. —AUGUSTINE, IN A SERMON ON THE ASCENSION. Hence Augustine: "And so I judge that the Holy Spirit was given twice,[2] once on earth and then again from heaven, so that the two commandments of love should be commended to us, namely one of God and the other of neighbour. The charity is one, but the commandments are two; there is one Spirit, but two gifts given. It is not another charity that loves our neighbour, but only the same one which loves God. And so we love our neighbour by the same charity with which we love God. But because God is one thing and our neighbour another, even though they are loved by the same charity,"[3] that is perhaps the reason why the commandments are said to be two, and one is called greater and the other lesser. Or perhaps because of the two movements which are felt in the mind when God and neighbour are loved; for the mind is moved to love God, and it is moved to love our neighbour, and much more toward God than toward neighbour.

[1]Dist. 23 c9 n2.
[2]1 Jn. 4, 8 and 16.
[3]1 Jn. 4, 20.
[4]Augustine, *De Trinitate*, bk 8 c8 n12.

[1]See Augustine's words, above, at the end of c2.
[2]Cf. Jn. 20, 22; Act. 2, 4.
[3]Augustine, *Sermo 265*, c8 n9.

Chapter 5 (100)

1. ON THE MANNER OF LOVING. We must next turn to the manner of each love.—AUGUSTINE, IN HIS BOOK *ON CHRISTIAN DOCTRINE*. As Augustine says: "This rule of love was divinely instituted,"[1] that you love God for his own sake *with your whole heart*, and your neighbour *as yourself*,[2] that is, to the same end and for the same reason for which you must love yourself. For it is in goodness and for the sake of God that you must love yourself.—AUGUSTINE: "And so our neighbour is to be loved in goodness, and not in evil,"[3] and for the sake of God.—AUGUSTINE, ON PSALM 11: "And we are to understand every man to be our neighbour, because there is no one with whom evil is to be worked."[4]—AUGUSTINE, *ON THE TRINITY*, BOOK 8: "And so he who loves men, must love them either because they are just, or in order that they may become just, that is, in God or for the sake of God. For it is also in this way that he must love himself, namely in God and for the sake of God, that is, either because he is just, or so that he may become just. For he who loves himself otherwise loves himself unjustly, because he loves himself to the end that he may be unjust, and so to the end that he may be evil. And so he does not love himself at all, since *he who loves iniquity hates his own soul*."[5,6]

2. AUGUSTINE, *ON THE TRINITY*, IN BOOK 14: "The human mind, then, is made in such a way that at no time does it not remember, understand, and love itself. But because he who hates someone looks for ways to harm him, not undeservedly is the mind of man also said to hate itself when it harms itself. For it unwittingly wills ill to itself, when it does not consider that what it wills is harmful to itself; and yet it does will ill to itself, when it wills what would be harmful to it, according to that text: *He who loves iniquity hates his own soul*.[7] And so he who knows how to love himself loves God. But he who does not love God, even if he does love himself, as is implanted in him by nature, is nevertheless not unsuitably said to hate himself, since he does what is against himself, and assails himself as if he were his own enemy."[8]

3. AUGUSTINE, IN THE BOOK *ON CHRISTIAN DOCTRINE*: "And so the manner of loving is to be taught to man, that is, how he may love himself so as to be good to himself. For it is insane to doubt that he does love him-

[1]Augustine, *De doctrina christiana*, bk 1 c22 n21.
[2]Mt. 22, 37-39; Rom. 13, 9.
[3]Augustine, *De Trinitate*, bk 8 c6 n9.
[4]Augustine, *Enarrationes in Psalmos*, on Ps. 11, 3.
[5]Ps. 10, 6.
[6]Augustine, *De Trinitate*, bk 8 c6 n9.
[7]Ps. 10, 6.
[8]Augustine, *De Trinitate*, bk 14 c14 n18.

self, and does want to be good to himself."[9] The manner is commanded by the words: *as yourself*,[10] so that you love your neighbour to the same end as yourself.—IN THE SAME PLACE: "Therefore, if you ought not to love yourself for your own sake, but for him in whom your love finds its most righteous object, no other man has a right to be angry if you also love him for God's sake."[11]—AUGUSTINE, *ON JOHN*. Truth indicates the manner of this love, saying: *I give you a new mandate, that you love each other as I have loved you*,[12] that is, for the same end for which I have loved you, namely so that you become children [of God] and have life.[13]

4. ON THE MANNER OF LOVING GOD. The manner of loving God is indicated by the words: *with your whole heart*, that is, with your whole intellect; *with your whole soul*, that is, your will; *with your whole mind*, that is, your memory,[14] "so that you bring all your thoughts, your whole life and your whole intelligence to him from whom you have all that you bring." In saying these things, "he leaves aside no part of our life that may be left uninvolved; whatever may come into our soul is to be brought to the same place toward which the current of our love flows."[15]—The manner of loving God is 'for his own sake' and, as it pleases some to hold, these are the two ways of loving God.

Chapter 6 (101)

1. ON THE FULFILLMENT OF THAT COMMANDMENT. And that precept is not wholly fulfilled by man in this mortal life, but only in part; not entirely, because we only love in part, just as *we know in part*;[1] but in future it shall be wholly fulfilled.—AUGUSTINE, *ON THE PERFECTION OF HUMAN JUSTICE*. Hence Augustine: "While there still remains some concupiscence of the flesh, God is not wholly loved *with all your soul*. Yet the flesh is not said to lust, unless because the soul lusts carnally.[2] *But when that which is perfect will come*, in order to destroy *what is only in part*,[3] that is, that it may no longer be in part, but wholly, then charity shall not be taken away, but it shall be increased and fulfilled. In such plenitude, that commandment of charity shall be fulfilled: *You shall love the Lord*

[9] Augustine, *De doctrina christiana*, bk 1 c25 n26.
[10] Mt. 22, 39; Rom. 13, 9.
[11] Augustine, *De doctrina christiana*, bk 1 c22 n21.
[12] Jn. 13, 34.
[13] Cf. Augustine, *In Ioannem*, tr. 65 nn1-2.
[14] Cf. Mt. 22, 37, and the interlinear gloss.
[15] Augustine, *De doctrina christiana*, bk 1 c22 n21.

[1] Cf. 1 Cor. 13, 9.
[2] Cf. Gal. 5, 17.
[3] 1 Cor. 13, 10.

your God with your whole heart, etc.[4] Then the just man shall be without sin, because there will be no law warring against his mind;[5] then you shall wholly love God, *with your whole heart, with your whole soul, with your whole mind*, which is the highest commandment."[6]

2. QUESTION REGARDING THE REASON FOR THE COMMANDMENT.—AUGUSTINE, IN THE SAME PLACE: "But why is such perfection commanded to man, since none attains it in this life?—Because one does not run rightly without knowing the goal of the race. But how would it be known, if it were not indicated by precepts?"[7]—Here you have why that precept is given, which cannot be wholly fulfilled here; and yet it is fulfilled in part, namely according to the perfection of [our earthly] way. The perfection of the runner is one thing, that of the one who completes the race another; one who loves God before all and more than all carries out this mandate in the manner of a runner, and yet does not wholly fulfil it.

Chapter 7 (102)

THAT THE ONE MANDATE IS CONTAINED IN THE OTHER.—AUGUSTINE, IN THE BOOK *ON THE TRINITY*: "Because there are two precepts of charity, the one is often posed for the other. Nor is this done unworthily, for God cannot be loved without neighbour, nor neighbour without God."[1] Hence the Apostle says that every mandate of the Law is *renewed*, that is, contained and fulfilled, *in this word: Love your neighbour as yourself*.[2] And Christ recalls more especially love of neighbour, saying: *I give you a new commandment, that you love one another as I have loved you*;[3] (AUGUSTINE, *ON JOHN*:) "where that greater commandment on the love of God appears to have been omitted. But those who well understand find both commandments in each of them. For he who loves God cannot despise him whom God commands him to love; and what does he who loves his neighbour love in him, except God? That is the love, distinct from all worldly love, which the Lord distinguished, saying: *As I have loved you*. For what, except God, did he love in us? Not that we had God, but so that we might have him. In the same way, the physician loves the sick; and what does he love in them, except the health which he means to restore, and not their sickness, which he comes to remove? Let us too so love one another that,

[4] Mt. 22, 37; Deut. 6, 5.
[5] Cf. Rom. 7, 23.
[6] Augustine, *De perfectione iustitiae hominis*, c8 n19.
[7] Ibid.

[1] Augustine, *De Trinitate*, bk 8 c7 n10.
[2] Rom. 13, 9.
[3] Jn. 13, 34.

insofar as we are able, we may by our love draw one another to have God in us."[4]

Chapter 8 (103)

WHAT THINGS ARE TO BE LOVED IN CHARITY. But let us now inquire what things are to be loved by this love.—AUGUSTINE, IN THE BOOK *ON CHRISTIAN DOCTRINE*. For as Augustine says: "Not all things which we use are to be loved, but only those which are joined with us in some manner in relation to God, such as a man or an angel, or those which are related to us and need God's favour through us, such as the body,"[1] which is "commanded to be so loved that it be cared for with right order and prudence."[2]

DISTINCTION XXVIII

Chapter 1 (104)

1. WHETHER BY THAT COMMANDMENT WE ARE COMMANDED TO LOVE ALL OF OUR NEIGHBOUR AND OUR WHOLE SELVES. Here it can be asked whether by that commandment of love of neighbour we are commanded to love our whole neighbour, that is, soul and body, and our whole selves.

2. AUGUSTINE, IN THE BOOK *ON CHRISTIAN DOCTRINE*. To which we say that all manner of loveable things are contained in those two commandments. "For," as Augustine says, "there are four kinds of things that are to be loved: first, that which is above us, namely God; second, ourselves; third, that which is near us, namely our neighbour; fourth, that which is below us, namely the body. No precepts need to be given concerning the second and fourth of these,"[1] namely that we love ourselves or our body. It is commanded that we love God and neighbour, "but there is no need to command that each love himself."[2] "However much a man may fall away from truth, there remain in him love of himself and love of his own body,"[3] because *no one has ever hated his own flesh*.[4] Indeed, those righteous men who torture their body, "do not hate their body, but its corruptions and burdensomeness."[5]

[4]Augustine, *In Ioannem*, tr. 65 n2.

[1]Augustine, *De doctrina christiana*, bk 1 c23 n22.
[2]Ibid., bk 1 c25 n26.

[1]Augustine, *De doctrina christiana*, bk 1 c23 n22.
[2]Ibid., bk 1 c26 n27.
[3]Ibid., bk 1 c23 n22.
[4]Eph. 5, 29.
[5]Augustine, *De doctrina christiana*, bk 1 c24 n24.

3. Here Augustine seems to teach that we are not bound by precept to love ourselves or our body. If this is the case, then not all manner of loveable things is contained in those two precepts, since we must also love ourselves and our body, for which [another] precept is necessary, since it is written: *He who loves iniquity hates his own soul.*[6]

4. But it was not necessary to give a special precept concerning this, nor was there need to command by a special commandment that one love himself or his own body, since that is contained in the precept: *You shall love your neighbour as yourself.*[7] Hence Augustine in the same place: "If you take yourself as a whole, that is, soul and body, and your neighbour as a whole, that is, soul and body (since a man is constituted of soul and body), then no manner of things that are to be loved is omitted in these two commandments. For although the love of God comes first, and the manner of our love for him is prescribed, and love of neighbour comes next, nothing seems to be said concerning your love of self. But when it is said: *You shall love your neighbour as yourself,*[8] then your love for yourself has not been omitted."[9] See, here he plainly states that in that precept is contained not only love of neighbour, but also of myself, and of my whole neighbour and my whole self.

5. From which it is apparent that the above statement, 'No precepts need to be given concerning the second and fourth of these, namely concerning the love of ourselves and our body,'[10] is to be understood as regarding special and distinct precepts, because all is contained in that one commandment, and "because that which we are and that which is below us, and yet pertains to us, we love by the law of nature, which is present even in beasts."[11] And so "we received distinct precepts concerning that which is above us and that which is near us,"[12] in the second of which is contained the love of that which we are and of that which is below us.

Chapter 2 (105)

WHETHER THE LOVE OF ANGELS IS CONTAINED IN THAT PRECEPT.—AUGUSTINE, IN THE BOOK *ON CHRISTIAN DOCTRINE*: "The question arises here concerning angels, whether the love of angels also pertains to that commandment of love of neighbour."[1]

[6]Ps. 10, 6.
[7]Mt. 19, 19; 22, 39.
[8]Ibid.
[9]Augustine, *De doctrina christiana*, bk 1 c26 n27.
[10]Above, n2.
[11]Augustine, *De doctrina christiana*, bk 1 c26 n27.
[12]Ibid.

[1]Augustine, *De doctrina christiana*, bk 1 c30 n31.

Chapter 3 (106)

1. WHO IS OUR NEIGHBOUR.—AUGUSTINE, IN THE BOOK *ON CHRISTIAN DOCTRINE*: "That he who commanded love of neighbour excepted no man is shown by the Lord in the parable of *the man left half-dead,*[1] where he calls the one who was merciful to him *neighbour.*[2] Then he adds: *Go and do you likewise,*[3] so that we understand him to be our neighbour to whom we are bound to show mercy, if he needs it, or would be bound to show it, if he needed it. But who does not see that no one is excepted from our duty to show mercy, since it extends even to our enemies? For the Lord says: *Love your enemies; do good to those who hate you.*"[4,5] "And so it is clear that every man is to be considered our neighbour."[6]

2. THAT THE TERM NEIGHBOUR IS RELATIVE.—THAT THE ANGELS ARE CONTAINED IN THAT PRECEPT: "The term neighbour is a relative one, nor can anyone be a neighbour, except to a neighbour."[7] And so it follows "that the one to whom, and the one by whom, mercy is to be shown is rightly called a neighbour. Hence it is clear that the holy angels are also contained in the precept to love our neighbour, since they show us mercy in so many ways."[8]

3. THAT CHRIST IS ALSO OUR NEIGHBOUR: ACCORDING TO HIS HUMANITY, BUT NOT ACCORDING TO HIS DIVINITY, HE TOO IS COMMANDED BY THAT COMMANDMENT TO BE LOVED AND TO LOVE. "As to this, even the Lord willed to be called our neighbour, as he indicates in the parable of the Samaritan[9] and in the Prophet: *I bore myself as if he had been my neighbour or brother.*[10] But because the divine substance is more excellent than, and above, our nature, the command to love God is distinct from that of love of neighbour."[11] And so, even though God confers all benefits on us, yet he, whom we are to love not as ourselves, but more than ourselves, *with our whole heart and soul,*[12] is not included in the term 'neighbour' in that precept. But we are to love Christ as ourselves, insofar as he is man; love of him according to his humanity is contained in that precept. Even insofar as he is man, we are to love him more than

[1]Cf. Lk. 10, 30-37.
[2]Mt. 5, 44; Lk. 10, 37.
[3]Lk. 10, 37.
[4]Mt. 5, 44; Lk. 6, 27.
[5]Augustine, *De doctrina christiana*, bk 1 c30 n31
[6]Ibid., bk 1 c30 n32.
[7]Ibid., bk 1 c30 n31.
[8]Ibid., bk 1 c30 n33.
[9]Cf. Lk. 10, 36-37.
[10]Ps. 34, 14.
[11]Augustine, *De doctrina christiana*, bk 1 c30 n33.
[12]See above, dist. 27 c5 n4.

ourselves, but not as much as we love God because, insofar as he is man, he is less than God.

Chapter 4 (107)

IN WHAT WAYS THE TERM NEIGHBOUR IS USED. Here is to be noted that the term neighbour is used in different ways, namely by the condition of first birth, by hope of conversion, by nearness of relationship, by reason of the conferral of a benefit.

DISTINCTION XXIX

Chapter 1 (108)

1. ON THE ORDER OF LOVING: WHAT [COMES] BEFORE, WHAT AFTER. After the above matters, we must discuss the order of charity, because the bride says: *He brought me into the wine cellar and he set in order charity within me.*[1]—AMBROSE: "And so let us examine the order, what is to be before and what after. For he sins, who acts in a disorderly manner; indeed, to know what you are to do, but not to know the order in which to do it, does not pertain to perfect knowledge. Ignorance of right order upsets the form of merits."[2]

2. AUGUSTINE, IN BOOK 1, *ON CHRISTIAN DOCTRINE*. Augustine indicates the order of loving, saying: "He has an ordered love who does not love what is not to be loved, nor fails to love what is to be loved, nor loves equally what ought to be loved either less or more, nor loves less or more what ought to be loved equally. Any sinner, insofar as he is a sinner, is not to be loved; and any man, insofar as he is man, is to be loved for God's sake, but God for his own sake. And God is to be loved for his own sake more than any man, and anyone ought to love God more than himself. Moreover, another man is to be loved more than our own body, because all things are to be loved for the sake of God, and another man can enjoy God with us, whereas our body cannot, since the body only lives through the very soul by which we enjoy God."[3]

3. You have now heard some things regarding the order of charity; it has been made clear that we are to love God more than all men and ourselves, and another man's soul more than our own body. In the enumeration outlined above[4] of the four things to be loved, first is placed that

[1]Canticle 2, 4.
[2]Ambrose, *Expositio de Psalmo 118, 27*, sermon 4 n12.
[3]Augustine, *De doctrina christiana*, bk 1 c27 n28.
[4]Dist. 28 c1 n1.

which is above us, second that which we are, third that which is near us, fourth that which is below us; the order of loving is manifested by the arrangement of the enumeration itself.—But it has not been revealed whether we must love all men equally, and whether as much as ourselves or less.

Chapter 2 (109)

1. WHETHER ALL MEN ARE TO BE LOVED EQUALLY. And so, as to this, too, a question is frequently raised, which the various views expressed by the saints make perplexing.

2. HE SETS OUT SOME AUTHORITIES WHICH APPEAR TO SAY THAT ALL ARE TO BE LOVED EQUALLY, BUT THAT THERE IS SOME DIFFERENCE IN THE DOING OF IT. For some seem to teach that all are to be loved with equal affection; but a distinction is to be preserved in the doing of it, that is, in the manifestation of respect.—AUGUSTINE, IN BOOK 1, *ON CHRISTIAN DOCTRINE*. Hence Augustine: "All men are to be loved equally. But since you cannot be useful to all, you are to be particularly attentive to those who, by occasion of places, or times, or any other circumstances, are joined more closely to you, as if by some destiny. For that is to be considered destiny by which someone is more closely connected to you for the time being, and by reason of which you read that you are to give more to him."[1] —THE SAME [AUGUSTINE], *ON THE EPISTLE TO THE GALATIANS*: "*Let us work good to all men, but especially to those who are of the household of the faith*,[2] that is, to Christians. For eternal life is to be wished for everyone with equal love, even though the services of love cannot be shown to everyone."[3] These are to be shown especially to the brethren, "because they are *members of one another*,"[4,5] "since they have the same Father."[6] —These are the authorities by which they, who say that all men are to be equally loved by the affection of charity, but that there is a difference in the performance of works, support their view.

3. WHAT [AUTHORITIES] SEEM TO BE IN OPPOSITION TO THESE. But in opposition to these stands the commandment of the Law concerning the love of parents: *Honour your father and your mother, so that you may have long life upon the earth.*[7] For what reason would this be especially commanded concerning parents, if not because they are to be loved with a greater love?—But they say that this is to be referred to the provision of

[1]Augustine, *De doctrina christiana*, bk 1 c28 n29.
[2]Gal. 6, 10.
[3]Augustine, *Epistolae ad Galatas expositio*, 6, 10, n61.
[4]Eph. 4, 25.
[5]Ambrosiaster, *In Epistolas s. Pauli*, Gal. 6, 10.
[6]Jerome, *In quattuor Epistolas Paulinas*, Gal. 6, 10.
[7]Ex. 20, 12; Deut. 5, 16.

external goods, in which parents are to be placed first; that is why it says *honour*, and not *love*.

4. JEROME. In opposition to these stands also what Jerome says, in *On Ezechiel*, namely "that by the order of charity, as it is written: He set charity in order within me,[8] after God the father of all, our father according to the flesh is also to be loved, and our mother, our son and daughter, our brother and sister."[9]

5. AMBROSE. Ambrose too, describing the order of charity, when commenting on that text of the Canticle: *He set charity in order within me*,[10] in the second chapter, says: "The charity of many is disordered: what ought to be in the first place, they place in the third or fourth. God is to be loved first, parents second, then children, then the members of the household; if these last are good, they are to be placed ahead of wicked children. In accordance with this, the Gospel expresses what is proper to the love of each: *You shall love the Lord your God with your whole heart and with all your strength*, and *your neighbour as yourself*,[11] and *your enemies*:[12] not *with all your power*, nor *as yourself*, but simply. For it suffices that we love them, and not hold them in hate."[13]

6. HERE IS SHOWN THE ORDER OF LOVING. See, by the foregoing the distinction which is to be kept in the feeling of charity is clearly indicated, so that we love men with a different feeling, and not an equal one, and that we love God before all, ourselves second, parents third, then children and siblings, then members of our household, and finally enemies.—But they say that the things said above about the order of love are to be referred to the performance of works, which are to be extended differently to our neighbours: to our parents first, then to our children, afterwards to the members of our household, and finally to our enemies; but God is to be loved before all in both feeling and the manifestation of respect.

7. THAT SOME OF THE SAME PEOPLE TEACH THAT WE OUGHT TO LOVE OUR NEIGHBOUR AS MUCH AS OURSELVES. A few of them also teach that, by the feeling of charity, we are to love our neighbours as much as we love ourselves.—AUGUSTINE, IN BOOK 8, *ON THE TRINITY*. They confirm this by the authority of Augustine, who says: "And do not let that other question be troublesome as to how much charity we ought to show our brother, and how much to God: incomparably more to God than to ourselves, to our brother as much as to ourselves; and the more we love God,

[8]Canticle 2, 4.

[9]Jerome, *In Ezechielem* 44, 25; ordinary gloss, on the same text.

[10]Canticle 2, 4.

[11]Lk. 10, 27; cf. Mt. 22, 37-39, Mk. 12, 30-31.

[12]Mt. 5, 44; Lk. 6, 27.

[13]Ordinary gloss, on Canticle 2, 4; not from Ambrose, but from Origen, *Homiliae in Cantica*, hom. 2 n8.

so much more do we love ourselves."[14]—From this and the above testimonies of Augustine, they assert that all men are to be loved equally by us, and as much as we love ourselves; but God more than ourselves, and our own body less than ourselves or our neighbours. They also say that an order of loving is not set out in the above enumeration of the four things to be loved,[15] but only the things to be loved.

8. ACCORDING TO OTHERS, ALL ARE NOT TO BE LOVED WITH EQUAL FEELING. But because the above words of Ambrose, to those who examine them with diligence, seem to set out the order of loving according to feeling more than according to doing, others say not unlearnedly that not only in the performance of works, but also in the feeling of charity, a different order is set out: so that before all things we love God, ourselves second, parents third, children or siblings and suchlike fourth, afterwards members of our household, and finally our enemies.

9. DETERMINATION OF THE AUTHORITIES WHICH SEEM TO CONTRADICT EACH OTHER. But what Augustine says, that all are to be loved equally and that, with equal love, life is to be desired for everyone, can be taken in this sense: that the parity be referred not to the feeling, but to the good which is desired for them, because we must desire by charity that all deserve equal goods, as the Apostle says: *I wish all men to be like me.*[16] Indeed, the perfection of their betters is to be wished for those who are less good, so that they too become perfect and so deserve an equal blessedness. Or 'with equal love,' that is, all are to be loved by the same love.—Also, his statement, that we love our brothers as much as ourselves, can be taken in this sense: that is, let us love our brothers for the sake of as much good as for ourselves, so that we desire as much good for them in eternity as for ourselves, even though with not as much feeling. But there 'as much' denotes likeness, not quantity.

10. QUESTION REGARDING EVIL PARENTS AND OTHERS WHO ARE GOOD. It is also usual to ask: if our parents are evil, or our children, or our siblings, whether they are to be loved more or less than other people who are good, but not joined to us by such a bond.—It seems that good people who are not linked to us by the flesh are to be loved more than others who are so linked to us, because the former are joined to us at heart by the bond of charity; for the joining of hearts is holier than the one of bodies.—BEDE. Hence Bede says of those words of the Lord, *These are my mother and my brothers, who fulfil God's word*:[17] "He does not wrongfully neglect his mother, nor is the mother denied, who is acknowledged even

[14]Augustine, *De Trinitate*, bk 8 c8 n12.
[15]Above, c1 n1.
[16]1 Cor. 7, 7.
[17]Lk. 8, 21.

from the cross,[18] but the joinings of minds are shown to be holier than those of bodies."[19]—But this is a complicated question, nor can it be fully resolved by us as we move to other matters.

11. For we are troubled by those words above: "He commands that you love your enemies not with all your power, nor as yourself, but simply: for it suffices that we love them, and not hold them in hate."[20]—This is not to be understood as if it sufficed to love your enemies, and not *as yourself*, because you must love all, both friends and enemies, as yourself. But in order to show the degrees of loving God, our neighbour, and our enemy, who nonetheless is our neighbour, 'the Lord sets out what is proper to each,' saying: *Love God with all your power*, and *your neighbour as yourself*:[21] he does not say [of the latter] *with all your power*, in order to show that our neighbour is to be loved less than God. And so he says: *Love your enemies*,[22] without adding *with all your power*, nor *as yourself*, 'but simply: for it suffices that we love them, and not hold them in hate': that is, it suffices to say that we love them and do not have them in hate; not that we must not love them as ourselves, because they are our neighbours; but it suffices if we love them less than our other neighbours: which the manner of expression indicates.

12. QUESTION.—AUGUSTINE, IN THE BOOK OF *RETRACTATIONS*. It is also usual to ask "why the Lord would command that we love our enemies,[23] where elsewhere he commands that we hold in hate our parents and children."[24,25]—To which it must be said that two things are to be loved in a man: nature and virtue; but vice and sin are to be hated. And so parents, insofar as they are evil, are to be hated; and enemies are to be loved, insofar as they are human beings. "And so let us love our enemies who gain God's kingdom, and let us hate our relatives, if they keep us from God's kingdom";[26] and in everyone in common let us love the nature which God made.

Chapter 3 (110)

1. ON THE DEGREES OF CHARITY. It is to be noted that there are different degrees of charity: for there is a beginning charity, a progressing one, a perfect one, and a most perfect one.—AUGUSTINE, *ON THE EPISTLE OF*

[18]Cf. Jn. 19, 26.
[19]Ordinary gloss, on Lk. 8, 20.
[20]Above, n5.
[21]Mk. 12, 30-31.
[22]Mt. 5, 44; Lk. 6, 27.
[23]Mt. 5, 44.
[24]Lk. 14, 26.
[25]Augustine, *Retractationes*, bk 1 c19 n5.
[26]Ibid.

JOHN. Hence Augustine: "This is perfect charity: that one is prepared even to die for his brothers. But is it already entirely perfect, as soon as it is born? No. It is born so that it may be made perfect; when born, it is nourished; when nourished, it is strengthened; when strengthened, it is perfected; when it has come to perfection, it says: *I desire to be dissolved*,"[1] etc.[2] Here the progress and perfection of charity is clearly indicated.

2. Truth too commends this perfection of charity, saying: *No greater love has any man than to lay down his life for his friends*.[3] And this is said with reference to the work of love, because there is no greater act of love than to lay down one's life for others. Do not let it trouble you that he says *for his friends*, for he who lays down his life for his friends lays it down for his enemies too, so that they too may become friends.

DISTINCTION XXX

Chapter 1 (111)

1. WHETHER IT IS BETTER TO LOVE FRIENDS THAN ENEMIES, AND VICE VERSA. Here it is usual to ask what is better and of greater merit, to love friends or to love enemies.—But this comparison is tangled. For if the love 'of friends only' is compared to the love 'of friends, and also of enemies,' the answer is very clear. But if it is asked which of these loves is greater in one particular man, who loves both a friend and an enemy, then the answer is obscure. What is at issue here is a movement of the mind, as to which it is not easy for us to form a judgement whether one and the same movement is toward the friend and the enemy, but is more intense toward the friend; or whether there are two: one, which is called more difficult, toward the enemy; the other toward the friend, and this seems more fervent. Nor is it unsuitable to regard as better the one which is more fervent. But if it is one and the same, then it is not inappropriate to esteem it as better when it is more ardent.

2. AUGUSTINE, IN THE *ENCHIRIDION*. But Augustine appears to feel that it is a greater thing to love an enemy than a friend. He says that it pertains to those who are perfect to love one's enemies and to do them good, nor is this achieved by as many people as have their prayer heard when they say in the Lord's prayer: *Forgive us our debts, as we forgive our debtors*.[1] For he says that that promise is fulfilled by many who do not love their enemies. He speaks as follows: "It is a great thing to wish well and to do

[1]Phil. 1, 23.
[2]Augustine, *In I Ioannis* 3, 9, tr. 5 n4.
[3]Jn. 15, 13.

[1]Mt. 6, 12.

good to one who has done no evil to you. It is a much greater thing, and it pertains to the most magnificent goodness, to love your enemy also, and always to wish well to and, if possible, to do good to one who wishes you ill and, if he can, does you harm. In this, you hear Jesus saying: *Love your enemies*, and *do good to them who hate you, and pray for those who persecute and calumniate you.*[2] But this only pertains to the perfect children of God, and although every believer ought to strive for it and, by prayer to the Lord and earnest struggle with himself, bring the human soul to this feeling, yet such a great good is not for such a multitude as we believe are heard when they say in prayer: *Forgive us our debts, as we forgive our debtors.*[3] Without doubt, the words of this promise are fulfilled, if a man who has not yet made progress to the point of loving his enemy, when asked for forgiveness by one who has sinned against him, does forgive him from his heart. He also desires forgiveness for himself, when he prays: *as we forgive our debtors.*"[4]—"But he who asks forgiveness of the man against whom he has sinned, if he is moved by his sin to ask forgiveness, is not to be regarded as an enemy, in the sense of its being as difficult to love him now as it was when he was actively inimical. And he who does not forgive another who repents of his sin and asks forgiveness ought not to suppose that his own sins are forgiven by God, for the Truth cannot lie. When he taught us this prayer, he also commended this sentence contained in it, saying: *If you forgive men their sins, your Father will also forgive you yours; but if you do not forgive, neither will your Father forgive you your sins.*"[5,6]

3. See, here it seems that what we said earlier is true, namely that it is a greater virtue to love and do good to one's enemy than to one who has done us no evil, or who is a friend.—Someone may not be willing to simply grant this, saying: a friend is loved more intensely than an enemy, and so the one is loved better than the other; if so, let him determine these things in accordance with the understanding set out earlier,[7] repeating the comparison made there between the love by which a friend only is loved, and one by which a friend and an enemy are loved.

4. But what follows troubles us more, namely that he says that 'to love one's enemies is not for such a multitude as are heard when they say in prayer: *Forgive us our debts*,' etc., where he gives it to be understood that someone who does not love his enemy has his sins forgiven by God, so long as he forgives the brother who has sinned against him and has asked

[2]Mt. 5, 44; cf. Lk. 6, 27.
[3]Mt. 6, 12.
[4]Augustine, *Enchiridion*, c73.
[5]Mt. 6, 14-15.
[6]Augustine, *Enchiridion*, c74.
[7]Above, n2.

for forgiveness.—But since sins are not forgiven to any adult, unless he have charity, it follows that one who does not love his enemy nonetheless has charity. But how, then, is every man understood by the term 'neighbour' in that commandment: *Love your neighbour as yourself?*[8] For if every man is a 'neighbour,' then so is an enemy; and so we are commanded to love our enemies. And because that precept is a general one, it is commanded to all that they love all, even their enemies.

5. Some, who wish to hold simply what is said here, interpret that precept and say that to love all men, even an enemy, is given as a commandment to those who are perfect, but as a counsel to those who are less so; but it is a precept [for all] to love those who have done them no evil, and not to hate their enemies.—But it is better to understand that it is commanded to all by that commandment to love all, even their enemies; this is the sense supported by the authorities set out above and by many others.[9]

6. But that text of Augustine set out immediately above[10] is understood to speak of perfect charity, which pertains only to the perfect, who not only perfectly love and do good to their friends, but also to their enemies. This perfection of love 'is not for such a multitude as are heard when they say the Lord's prayer.' And this is indeed a great thing and of a most excellent goodness, namely to love one's enemy perfectly. And so, when he says that 'the words of that promise are fulfilled by a man who has not yet made progress to the point of loving his enemy,' it is to be taken in regard to perfect love.

DISTINCTION XXXI

Chapter 1 (112)

1. WHETHER CHARITY, ONCE HAD, MAY BE LOST. Nor is it to be passed over that some assert that charity, once it is had by someone, cannot fall away, and that no one who is to be damned ever has it. And they defend this view with authorities.

2. The Apostle says: *Charity shall never fall away.*[1]—AUGUSTINE, TO COUNT JULIAN. Augustine too says: "Charity which can fail was never true."[2]—ON PSALM 103. Also: "Charity is the fountain entirely reserved for the good, and the stranger has no share in it. Strangers are all those

[8]Mt. 22, 39; Mk. 12, 31.
[9]In dist. 27-28.
[10]Above, n2.

[1]1 Cor. 13, 8.
[2]Rather, Paulinus of Aquileia, *Liber exhortationis de salutaribus documentis*, c7.

who will hear: *I do not know you.*"[3,4] Of this fountain, Scripture says: *The fountain of living water is to be yours alone, and no stranger is to share it with you.*[5] But if strangers are those who will hear those words, it follows that those who are to be damned do not share in this fountain.

3. AUGUSTINE. Also Augustine, in *On the Epistle of John*: "Is charity rooted there? Rest assured: nothing evil can come of that."[6]—GREGORY. Also Gregory, in his *Moralia*: "*Love is as strong as death.*[7] For love is compared to the power of death, in that in the mind which it has once taken hold of, it wholly kills to the love of the world."[8]—AUGUSTINE. Also Augustine, in *On the Epistle of John*: "Charity is the invisible *unction* which, in whomsoever it may be, shall be as a root to him; even in the burning sun, it cannot wither. It is nourished by the sun's warmth, not withered."[9]

4. BEDE. Also Bede, in *On John*: "We must also investigate how it was a special sign for recognizing the Son of God that the Spirit descended and remained over him. Why is it a great thing for the Son of God that the Spirit is understood to remain in him? It must also be noted that the Spirit remained always in the Lord; but in the saints, for so long as they bear a mortal body, the Spirit in part is always in them, but in part leaves them only to come back again. For he remains with them in order that they may strive after good works; but he also recedes from them for a time, so that they do not always have the power of curing the sick, raising the dead, casting out demons, and prophesying. And so he always remains so that they may always be able to have the virtues by which to live wonderfully; he also comes for a time in such a way that, by the signs of miracles, the saints may appear to others as radiant as they are inwardly."[10]

5. GREGORY, *ON EZECHIEL*. Also Gregory: "The Spirit remains ever in the hearts of the saints, according to some virtues; according to some other virtues, he comes for a time and withdraws for a time. With regard to those virtues without which it is impossible to attain to life, he remains always in the hearts of his elect; but with regard to those by which the power of holiness is made manifest, as in the working of miracles, he is at times present, and at times he withdraws."[11]—AMBROSE. Also Ambrose: "It is a fictitious charity that departs in adversity."[12]

[3]Mt. 7, 23.
[4]Augustine, *Sermo 1*, n9.
[5]Cf. Prov. 5, 17-18.
[6]Augustine, *In I Ioannis* 4, 12-16, tr. 8 n9.
[7]Canticle 8, 6.
[8]Gregory, *Moralia*, bk 10 c21 n39.
[9]Augustine, *In I Ioannis* 2, 27, tr. 3 n12.
[10]Pseudo-Bede, *In Ioannem* 1, 33.
[11]Gregory, *In Ezechielem*, bk 1 hom. 5 n11.
[12]More accurately, ordinary gloss, on 2 Cor. 6, 6; cf. Ambrosiaster, on the same place.

6. These statements appear to indicate that charity, once had, is not lost. But some leapt to the aforementioned rash conclusion, saying that charity is not had by those who are to be damned, and that it cannot be lost by anyone who ever had it.

7. Both reason and authority defeat these people. For some are good for a time, who afterwards become evil, and vice versa. And so Christ says that the names of some *were written*[13] in the book of life, who nonetheless afterwards *went back*;[14] but he calls them *written* not according to foreknowledge, but according to the present justice which they served, because at that time they were worthy of that good which those who are written according to foreknowledge are going to have.—AMBROSE, *ON THE EPISTLE TO THE ROMANS*. Hence Ambrose: "To some, grace is given in use, as to Saul, Judas, and those disciples to whom the Lord said: *See, your names are written in the heavens*,[15] and afterwards *they went back*.[16] But he said this because of the justice which they were serving, because they were good. Frequently, there are some who are at first evil, who afterwards will become good; and at times some are at first good, who afterwards will become and remain evil,"[17] according to which they are said to be written in the book of life, and then to be expunged from it.

8. DETERMINATION OF THE AFORESAID AUTHORITIES. But the fact that the Apostle says: *Charity shall never fall away*, does not at all support their view. It is to show the dignity of charity that he says that it does not fall away, because it shall exist here and in the future; but faith and hope shall be made void, as will knowledge.[18]—Also, when it is said that 'charity which can fail was never true,' it does not refer to the essence of charity, but to its efficacy, because a charity which fails does not make a man truly blessed and does not lead to the true good.—'But strangers, that is, those to be damned, have no share in this fountain': that is, in the end, because they do not persevere.

9. But this and the other things which have been said of charity can be understood about perfect charity, which only the perfect have. Once that is had, it is not lost; but the beginnings of charity at times grow, at times fail. For there are beginnings, progress, and perfection of this virtue. These degrees will be clear to one who understands that parable: *Such is the kingdom of God, as if a man should cast seed into the earth, and should sleep, and rise*, and the seed *should spring, and grow*, etc.[19] And

[13]Cf. Lk. 10, 20.
[14]Jn. 6, 67.
[15]Lk. 10, 20.
[16]Jn. 6, 67.
[17]Ambrosiaster, *In Epistolas s. Pauli*, Rom. 9, 11-13.
[18]Cf. 1 Cor. 13, 8-10; see below, c2.
[19]Mk. 4, 26-27.

so, although perfect charity is so rooted that it cannot be lost, yet beginning or progressing charity can be, and often is, lost.

10. But while it is had, it does not allow the one who has it to sin criminally. Augustine shows this, saying: "Because *cupidity is the root of all evils,*[20] and charity is the root of all goods, both cannot exist at the same time: unless the one is entirely uprooted, the other cannot be planted. It is pointless for one to attempt to cut away the branches, if he does not make a strenuous effort to dig up the root."[21]

Chapter 2 (113)

1. WHY FAITH, HOPE, AND KNOWLEDGE ARE SAID TO BE MADE VOID, AND NOT CHARITY, EVEN THOUGH IT TOO IS ONLY IN PART. It is to be noted too how faith, hope, and knowledge are said to be made void, because they are *in part,*[1] and not charity, even though it too is in part. For it is in part, that is, imperfectly, that we love, just as in part that we know, as says Hesychius, in *On Leviticus*.[2] But since all that *is in part* is made void, why is charity excepted, which is said *never* to fail?[3]

2. Charity too is in part, as the saints frequently teach, because we now love in part; and so it too will be made void insofar as it is in part, because imperfection will be taken away and perfection will be added, but charity itself will remain, but increased, both its acts, and the manner of loving, so that you may love God for his own sake and with your whole heart and your neighbour as yourself, but the mode of imperfection shall be eliminated. But faith and hope shall be made entirely void. As for knowledge, it shall be taken away in regard to its present act and mode, but not in regard to its essence: for the virtue itself of knowledge will remain, but it will have another use and mode.

Chapter 3 (114)

1. WHETHER CHRIST HAD THE ORDER OF CHARITY SET OUT EARLIER. Now it remains to investigate whether Christ, according to his humanity, preserved the order of loving which was set out earlier.[1] If this is the case, then he loved every man like himself; and so he desired life for all, and

[20] 1 Tim. 6, 10.
[21] Rather, Caesarius of Arles, *Sermo 182*, n1.

[1] Cf. 1 Cor. 13, 8-10.
[2] Ordinary gloss, on Lev. 2, 2.
[3] 1 Cor. 13, 8.

[1] Cf. dist. 27 c5 and dist. 29 cc1-2.

he willed that all should be saved. But not all are saved, and so that which he desired did not happen.

2. But it should not be forgotten that in him there was charity according to the manner of the fatherland, not of the way; and he fulfilled the order of loving which is observed in the fatherland, and not on the way. For those who are in the fatherland, that is, who are already blessed, are so attached to God's justice that nothing pleases them, except what pleases God; because of this, they will only the salvation of those whom God wills to be saved, and these alone do they love like themselves. And so Christ loved the elect alone like himself and desired their salvation.

DISTINCTION XXXII

Chapter 1 (115)

1. ON GOD'S CHARITY. To the above we must add [something] concerning the love of God, by which he loves us; which is nothing else than the love by which we love him. For God's love is the divine *usia*, and it is by the same love that Father, Son, and Holy Spirit love each other and us, as we discussed above.[1]

2. THAT GOD LOVES SOME THINGS MORE, SOME LESS.—AUGUSTINE, *ON JOHN*. And although his love is immutable and eternal, yet he loves someone more, and another less. Hence Augustine: "The love is incomprehensible and immutable by which God loves in each of us what he has done, just as he hates what we have done. And so, in a wonderful and divine manner, even when he hates, he loves us; and this can be understood in everything. Who, then, can worthily describe how much he loves the members of his only-begotten, and how much more he loves the only-begotten himself? Of him, it is also said: *You have hated none of the things which you have made*."[2,3]—From this, we perceive that God loves all his creatures, because it is written: *You have hated none of the things which you have made*,[4] and also: *God saw all the things that he had made, and they were very good*.[5] If all the things which he made are good, and if he loves all that is good, then he loves all the things that he has made. And among them, he loves rational creatures more; and of these, he loves more those which are members of his only-begotten, and much more the only-begotten himself.

[1]Bk 1 dist. 10 and 17.
[2]Wis. 11, 25.
[3]Augustine, *In Ioannem* 17, 21-23, tr. 110 n6.
[4]Wis. 11, 25.
[5]Gen. 1, 31.

Chapter 2 (116)

1. ACCORDING TO WHAT MEANING IS HE SAID TO LOVE MORE OR LESS THESE OR THOSE THINGS. But since God's love is immutable, and so it does not expand or decrease, one may ask what is the sense of the statement that God is said to love this thing more or less than that one, or that he loves all things. We say that God's love, like his peace,[1] surpasses all human understanding, which can hardly aspire to the understanding of such sublimity.

2. IN WHAT SENSE GOD IS SAID TO LOVE ALL THE THINGS WHICH HE HAS MADE. And yet it may certainly be understood that the reason for saying 'God loves all the things which he has made' is that they all please him and he approves of all of them, insofar as they are his works. Nor did they please him earlier or more when they were made, but even before they were made, nay rather they all pleased him from all eternity no less than after they had come into existence.

3. HOW HE IS SAID TO LOVE SOME PEOPLE MORE AND SOME LESS. And the fact that, among rational creatures, that is, men and angels, he is said to love some of them more and some less, does not indicate any mutability in his charity, but that he loved some of them for greater goods and others for lesser goods, some for better uses and others for less good ones. For all our goods come to us from his love. And so, from all eternity and even now, he loved and loves some of the elect more and others less, because out of his love he prepared greater goods for the first and lesser ones for the second, just as in time he confers greater goods on some and lesser ones on others, and as a result of this he is said to love these more and those less.

Chapter 3 (117)

1. THAT GOD'S LOVE IS TO BE REGARDED IN TWO WAYS. For God's love is considered in two ways: according to essence and according to efficacy. It does not admit of more or less according to its essence, but only according to its efficacy, so that they are said to be more loved for whom, in love and from all eternity, God prepared a greater good and conferred it in time; those on whom not as much [was conferred are called] less loved.

2. So it is also that some, when they are converted and justified, are then said to begin to be loved by God: not that God can love someone by a new love, since he loved those whom he now loves with an eternal love, *from before the foundation of the world*;[1] but they are then said to begin

[1]Cf. Phil. 4, 7.

[1]Eph. 1, 4.

to be loved by him, when they begin to receive the effect of God's eternal love, namely grace or glory.—AUGUSTINE, BOOK 5, IN *ON THE TRINITY*. Hence Augustine: "Far be it from us to say that God loves someone in time, as if with a new love, which was not in him earlier, before whom past things have not passed away, and future things have already happened. And so he loved all his saints *before the foundation of the world*, as he predestined them. But when they are converted and find him, then they are said to begin to be loved by him, in order that what is said may be expressed in a way in which it can be grasped by human feeling. In the same way, when he is said to be angry with the unrighteous, and gentle toward the good, they are changed, not he. Just as the light is harsh to weak eyes, pleasant to those that are strong, namely because of change in them, not in it," so also, when someone by justification "begins to be a friend of God, he himself is changed,"[2] not God.

Chapter 4 (118)

WHETHER ONE IS LOVED BY GOD MORE OR LESS AT ONE TIME THAN AT ANOTHER. But if it is asked concerning someone whether he is loved more by God at one time than at another, we must distinguish the meaning of the statement: if it refers to the working of love, it may be granted; but if to the essence of love, then it is to be denied.

Chapter 5 (119)

WHETHER GOD LOVED THE REPROBATE FROM ALL ETERNITY. As for the reprobate, who are prepared not for life, but for death, if it is asked whether it ought to be granted that God may have loved them from all eternity, we say that this is to be granted simply only with regard to the elect, that God loved from all eternity them whom he prepared for justice and the crown. Concerning those who are not of the elect, it is to be granted simply that he held them in hate, that is, he reprobated them, as we read: *I loved Jacob; I held Esau in hate.*[1] Yet it is not to be simply said that he loved them, lest they be understood to be predestined, but with this qualification: he loved them insofar as they were to be his work, that is, he loved what and of what kind he was going to make them.

[2]Augustine, *De Trinitate*, bk 5 c16 n17.

[1]Rom. 9, 13; cf. Mal. 1, 2-3.

Distinction XXXIII

Chapter 1 (120)

1. On the four principal virtues. After the above matters, we must treat the four virtues which are called principal or cardinal; they are justice, fortitude, prudence, temperance.

2. On their uses here.—In book 14, *On the Trinity*. Concerning these, Augustine says: "Justice consists in helping the wretched, prudence in guarding against treacheries, fortitude in bearing troubles, temperance in controlling evil pleasures."[1]

3. Of these, it is said in the book of Wisdom: *He teaches sobriety and prudence, justice, and truth.*[2] This text calls temperance *sobriety*, and fortitude *truth*. These virtues are called 'cardinal,' as Jerome says;[3] "by them, it is possible to live well in this mortal life,"[4] and afterwards to come to eternal life.

Chapter 2 (121)

That these virtues were in Christ. They were and are most fully in Christ, *of whose fullness we have received*;[1] in him, they had the same uses which they have in the fatherland, and even some of those which they have on the way.

Chapter 3 (122)

1. On their uses.—Augustine, in book 14, *On the Trinity*. But "there is a little question as to whether these virtues, since they begin to be in the mind (which was a mind even when it existed before without them), cease to be when they have brought us to things eternal. To some, it has seemed that they will cease, and in the case of three [of them], namely prudence, fortitude, and temperance, such an assertion seems not to be entirely empty."[1]

2. On the use of justice in the future. "*For justice is immortal,*[2] and will then be made more perfect in us rather than cease to be, when we may blessedly live in contemplation of the divine nature, which created

[1]Augustine, *De Trinitate*, bk 14 c9 n12.
[2]Wis. 8, 7.
[3]Cf. Jerome, *Epistola 66* (*ad Pammachium*), n3.
[4]Augustine, *De Trinitate*, bk 14 c9 n12.

[1]Jn. 1, 16.

[1]Augustine, *De Trinitate*, bk 14 c9 n12.
[2]Wis. 1, 15.

and established all other natures, and than which nothing is better and more loveable. It pertains to justice to be subject to the rule of this nature, and so justice is wholly immortal; nor will it cease to exist in that [state of] blessedness, but it will be such and so great that it cannot be more perfect or greater."[3]

3. ON THE USES OF THE OTHER THREE IN THE FUTURE. "Perhaps, the other three virtues (prudence, but now without any risk of error, and fortitude without the trouble of bearing evils, and temperance without the thwarting of lust) will also exist in that [state of] felicity: there it will pertain to prudence to prefer or equate no other good to God; and to fortitude to adhere to him with the greatest steadfastness; and to temperance to take pleasure in no harmful defect."[4]

4. "But that which justice now does in assisting the wretched, and prudence in guarding against treacheries, and fortitude in bearing troubles, and temperance in controlling evil pleasures, will not at all exist there, where there will be no evil. And so these works of the virtues, which are necessary to this mortal life, like the faith to which they are to be referred, will be reckoned among things past."[5] See, Augustine plainly states here that the aforesaid virtues will exist in the future, but they will then have other uses than they have now.

5. BEDE. And Bede agrees with him, speaking as follows, on Exodus: "The columns before which hangs the veil are the heavenly powers, shining brightly with the four most excellent virtues, namely fortitude, prudence, temperance, justice; these are kept otherwise in heaven by the angels and the holy souls than they are here by the faithful."[6] Bede then distinguishes the uses of those virtues according to the present state and the future one, imitating Augustine in the distinctions placed above.

DISTINCTION XXXIV

Chapter 1 (123)

ON THE SEVEN GIFTS OF THE HOLY SPIRIT. Now we must treat the seven gifts of the Holy Spirit, where first we must consider whether these gifts are virtues; second, whether in the future they will cease, and [if so] whether all or any of them; finally, whether all these gifts were in Christ.

[3]Augustine, *De Trinitate*, bk 14 c9 n12.
[4]Ibid.
[5]Ibid.
[6]Ordinary gloss, on Ex. 26, 32; from Bede, *De tabernaculo*, bk 2 c8.

Chapter 2 (124)

1. THAT THE SEVEN GIFTS ARE IN THE ANGELS AND THAT THEY ARE VIRTUES.—AMBROSE, IN BOOK 1, *ON THE HOLY SPIRIT*. Ambrose shows that these gifts are virtues and will not cease in the future; he says that these seven are virtues and that they exist most abundantly in the angels: "The city of God, that heavenly Jerusalem, is not watered by the flow of any earthly river; the Holy Spirit, proceeding from the fount of life, a small swallow of which satiates us, seems to flow more abundantly among those celestial spirits, carried briskly by a full flow of the seven spiritual virtues. For if a river overflows when it rises above its banks, how much more does the Spirit—rising above every creature, when he grazes the hidden depths, as it were, of our minds—make glad that heavenly nature of the angels with the more abundant fertility of his sanctifications!"[1]

2. AMBROSE. Afterwards, expounding these sanctifications, he adds: "By these sanctifications is signified the fullness of the seven spiritual virtues, which Isaias enumerates by saying: *The spirit of wisdom and understanding, of counsel and fortitude, of knowledge and piety and fear of God.*[2] One, then, is the river, but many the channels of the spiritual gifts."[3] "Therefore, although *the spirits* are called many, as in *spirit of wisdom and understanding*, etc., yet God's Spirit is but one,"[4] the arbiter of his own liberty, by the authority of his own will *sharing out everything to each one*.[5]—Here it is expressly taught that the seven gifts are virtues and sanctifications of the minds of the faithful, and that they shall not cease in the future, since they exist also in the angels.

Chapter 3 (125)

1. THAT THOSE SEVEN GIFTS WERE IN CHRIST. That these same gifts were also in Christ is shown by Isaias who says: *There shall come forth a rod out of the root of Jesse, and a flower shall rise up out of his root. And the spirit of the Lord shall rest upon him: the spirit of wisdom and understanding, the spirit of counsel and fortitude, the spirit of knowledge and piety, and the spirit of the fear of the Lord shall fill him.*[1]

2. SOMETHING THAT SEEMS TO CONTRADICT THE ABOVE.—BEDE. But this seems to be contradicted by what Bede says about fear of the Lord in *On the Parables*, namely that all fear shall cease in the future. For he says

[1]Ambrose, *De Spiritu sancto*, bk 1 c16 n158.
[2]Is. 11, 2-3.
[3]Ambrose, *De Spiritu sancto*, bk 1 c16 n159.
[4]Ibid., bk 1 c4 n60.
[5]Cf. 1 Cor. 12, 11.

[1]Is. 11, 1-3.

on that text: *The fear of the Lord is the beginning of wisdom*: "There are two fears of the Lord: one is that of a servant, and it is the beginning of wisdom; the other is that of a friend, and it is joined with the perfection of wisdom. The servile one is the beginning of wisdom because one who, after erring, begins to know, is first corrected by divine fear, lest he be punished; but *perfect charity casts out*[2] this fear. To this fear succeeds *the holy fear of the Lord, which perdures forever and ever,*[3] and which charity does not cast out, but rather increases; by this fear, the son fears lest he offend even in the least way the eyes of a most loving father. Each of these will cease in the future. But *charity shall never fall away.*"[4,5]

3. AUGUSTINE. Augustine too, on that place in the Psalm: *I shall worship in fear of you at your holy temple*, says that fear shall have an end: "Fear of the Lord is a great defence to those who are progressing toward salvation, but it is removed from those who have arrived. For they do not fear him who has become their friend, namely once they have been brought to that which was promised."[6]—From these authorities, it is signified that there shall not be fear in the future. But if fear shall not exist in the future, then neither shall the seven gifts, nor are they now in the angels or in the holy souls.

4. SOLUTION. To which we say, resolving the apparent contradiction among the authorities above, that those seven gifts are now in the angels and in the holy souls which live in blessedness, and they shall be in us in the future; but they will not have all the same uses and functions which they have now. For example, filial fear now makes us fear lest we offend the one whom we love and lest we become separated from him; it also makes us revere him; but in the future it will cause us to revere without fear of separation or offence. And so the fear of separation or offence is not now in the angels or in the holy souls, nor will it be in us in the future, but only the reverence, which is love mixed with submission. This was also in Christ, as the Apostle says in the Epistle to the Hebrews, speaking of Christ, *who was heard because of his reverence.*[7]—But some contend that fear is in Christ and the angels only according to effect.

Chapter 4 (126)

1. FULL DISTINCTION OF THE FEARS. And because we have been given an occasion to treat fear, it ought to be known that there are four fears,

[2] 1 Jn. 4, 18.
[3] Ps. 18, 10.
[4] 1 Cor. 13, 8.
[5] Bede, *Commentarium in Parabolas Salomonis*, bk 1 c1.
[6] Augustine, *Enarrationes in Psalmos*, on Ps. 5, 8, n9.
[7] Hebr. 5, 7.

namely worldly or human, servile, initial, chaste or filial or friendly.—CASSIODORUS. As Cassiodorus says, human fear is when "we fear the dangers of the flesh or the loss of worldly goods,"[1] and because of it we sin. This fear is an evil one, which "in the first degree, is abandoned with the world"; the Lord forbids it in the Gospel, saying: *Do not fear those who kill the body*, etc.[2]—AUGUSTINE. As Augustine says, servile fear is "when a man abstains from sin because of the fear of hell ... by which he fears the presence and penalties of the judge; and it is by fear that he does whatever good he does: not by fear of losing the eternal good, which he does not love, but by fear of suffering the evil which he fears. He does not fear to lose the embrace of the fairest spouse, but fears lest he be sent to hell. This fear is good and useful," even though it is not sufficient, and through it "little by little, the habit of justice is achieved."[3]—And initial fear succeeds it, when "what used to be hard begins to be loved," and so "servile fear" begins to be cast out "by charity."[4]—And afterwards comes chaste or friendly fear, "by which we fear lest the bridegroom be late, lest he go away, lest we offend him, lest we be left without him. This fear comes from love. That servile one is useful, but it does not *perdure forever and ever*[5] like this one."[6] "Divine fear is our companion through all the various degrees."[7]

2. COMPARISON OF THE ABOVE. And note that here four fears are distinguished, although Bede said above that there are two.[8] But Bede omitted human fear, and under the term 'servile' he combined two of the ones which we have distinguished here, namely servile and initial; he calls the friendly fear 'chaste.'

3. Augustine also plainly distinguishes servile and chaste fear in expounding that text of the Epistle to the Romans: *For you have not received the spirit of bondage again in fear; but you have received the spirit of adoption as sons of God*;[9] he says: "Two fears are indicated here: one which is in perfect charity, namely the chaste fear; the other which is not in charity, that is, the servile one, in which, although one believes God, one does not believe in God; and although good is done, yet it is

[1]Cassiodorus, *In Psalmum 127*, prol.
[2]Mt. 10, 28.
[3]Augustine, *Enarrationes in Psalmos*, on Ps. 127, 1, nn7-8.
[4]Ibid.
[5]Cf. Ps. 18, 10.
[6]Augustine, *Enarrationes in Psalmos*, on Ps. 127, 1, nn7-8.
[7]Cassiodorus, *In Psalmum 127*, prol.
[8]In c3 n2.
[9]Rom. 8, 15.

not done well. ... No one does good unwillingly, even if he does that which is good."[10]

Chapter 5 (127)

1. HE TREATS MORE FULLY CHASTE AND SERVILE FEAR, TOUCHING ALSO ON INITIAL FEAR.—AUGUSTINE, IN HOMILY 9, *ON THE EPISTLE OF JOHN*. He discusses these same fears more broadly, saying: "Someone begins to believe in the day of judgement. If he begins to believe, he also begins to fear. But one who still fears does not yet have *confidence in the day of judgement*, and *perfect charity* is not yet in him."[1,2] "If perfect charity were in him, he would not fear. For perfect charity would make perfect justice, and he would have no reason to fear, but would rather have reason to desire that iniquity pass away and God's kingdom come. (HERE HE TOUCHES ON INITIAL FEAR.) And so, *there is no fear in charity*.[3] But in what charity? Not in initial charity. In which one, then? In the perfect one, as he says: *Perfect charity casts out fear*.[4] And so let fear begin, because *the fear of the Lord is the beginning of wisdom*.[5] It is as if fear prepares a place for charity, but once charity has begun to dwell, the fear which prepared the place for it is expelled. For in proportion as charity increases, fear decreases, and as charity comes to be within, fear is cast out. Greater charity, less fear; less charity, greater fear."[6]

2. AN ANALOGY OF SERVILE FEAR IS PRESENTED. "But if there is no fear, there is no way for charity to enter. Just as we see when something is sewn, the thread is introduced through a bristle; the bristle enters first, but if it does not come out, the thread does not enter. In the same way, fear first occupies the mind, but the fear does not remain there, because it entered in order to introduce charity."[7]

3. AN APPARENT CONTRADICTION WITH WHAT HAS BEEN SAID. "But there is another sentence, which seems contrary to this one, if it does not find a pious interpreter. For it is said in the Psalm: *The fear of the Lord is chaste, perduring forever and ever*.[8] This shows us an eternal fear, but a

[10]Ordinary gloss, on Rom. 8, 15, in part from Augustine, *De spiritu et littera*, c32 n56, and *Confessiones*, bk 1 c12 n19. The text is actually taken from Prosper of Aquitaine, *Sententiae*, n172 (173).

[1]Cf. 1 Jn. 4, 17.
[2]Augustine, *In I Ioannis* 4, 17, tr. 9 n2.
[3]1 Jn. 4, 18.
[4]Ibid.
[5]Ps. 110, 10; Eccli. 1, 16; Prov. 1, 7.
[6]Augustine, *In I Ioannis* 4, 18, tr. 9 n4.
[7]Ibid.
[8]Ps. 18, 10.

chaste one. But if there it shows us an eternal fear, does the Epistle contradict it, when it says: *There is no fear in charity, but perfect charity casts out fear*?[9] No, because the latter is said by John, the former is said by David. But do not believe that there is more than one Spirit. If one breath fills two pipes, cannot one Spirit fill two hearts and move two tongues? If the two pipes filled by the one spirit, that is, by the one breath, sound in unison, can two tongues filled with the Spirit of God be discordant? And so there is some consonance here and some concord, but it requires an attentive listener, and not a lazy one [to hear it].—See, this Spirit of God has moved two tongues, and we have heard from the one: *There is no fear in charity*; we have heard from the other: *The fear of the Lord is chaste, perduring forever and ever.* How is this? Are they in discord? No! Open your ears, hear the melody. It is not without cause that here he added *chaste*, there he did not, because there is one fear which is called chaste, and there is another fear which is not called chaste. Let us distinguish these two fears, and understand the harmony of the pipes. How are we to distinguish?—Let your charity attend. There are men who fear God lest they be cast into hell, lest perhaps they burn with the devil in the eternal fire. This is the fear which introduces charity, but it comes so that it may depart. For if you fear God because of punishments, you do not yet love him whom you so fear. You do not desire the good things, but are afraid of the evil things. But because you are afraid of evil things, you correct yourself and begin to desire the good things. When you have begun to desire the good, the chaste fear shall be in you. What is the chaste fear? To fear losing the good things themselves, to fear that God depart from you. But when you fear God lest his presence abandon you, you embrace him and you long to enjoy him."[10]

Chapter 6 (128)

1. HE SHOWS HOW THE TWO FEARS DIFFER BY THE ANALOGY OF TWO WOMEN.—AUGUSTINE: "You cannot better explain the difference between these two fears than by positing the case of two married women, one of whom, say, is willing to commit adultery, but fears being condemned by her husband. She fears her husband because she still loves wickedness. To this woman, the presence of her husband is not welcome, but burdensome; and if perhaps she lives evilly, she fears that her husband might come. Such are they who fear the day of judgement.—Posit that the other woman loves her husband, that she owes him chaste embraces, that she has no desire to stain herself with the uncleanness of adultery: this one desires the presence of her husband. The one woman fears, the other also

[9] 1 Jn. 4, 18.
[10] Augustine, *In I Ioannis*, 4, 18, tr. 9 n5.

fears. Let them be questioned as to why they fear. The one will say: I fear that my husband might come; the other will say: I fear that my husband might leave. The one will say: I fear lest my husband condemn me; the other will say: I fear lest my husband abandon me. Ponder these things in your mind, and you find the fear which *charity casts out*, and the other *chaste* fear which will *perdure forever and ever*."[1] Perfect charity casts out that fear "because fear contains torment: the awareness of sins torments [the heart] and justification has not yet occurred. There is in it that which titillates, which pricks, which goads. That fear does goad, but charity enters in, and she heals the wound that fear inflicts."[2] A chaste fear "makes for assurance in the soul."[3]

2. "We have heard two pipes, John and David, sounding in harmony. The one speaks of the fear of God by which the soul fears being damned, the other speaks of the fear by which the soul fears being forsaken. The first is the fear which charity casts out, the second is the fear that shall perdure forever and ever."[4] See, in the above words Augustine plainly shows which is the chaste fear and which the servile one, and how they differ.

3. And he also indicated the initial fear, which is neither entirely servile, nor entirely chaste, but a sort of middle one. It has something from servile fear and something from the chaste one. For it leads one to serve in part by fear of punishment, in part by love of justice; through it, we fear to be punished, and we fear to offend. This fear exists in an initial, but not yet perfect, charity, and as charity increases, so this fear decreases, both as to the fear of punishment, that is, as to that which makes for the fear of punishment, and as to the torment of conscience; indeed, as much as we love, so much less do we fear.—This fear is signified in those words of Augustine where he does not deny that there is fear in an initial charity, but not in the perfect one. This could not be said of servile fear because, as he himself said above,[5] servile fear does not remain, once charity has come; nor does charity enter, unless that fear has first gone out; nor does anyone in that fear believe in God, even though he believes God; nor does he act well, even if he does that which is good.[6] And so that fear does not exist in charity, even the initial one, because anyone who has charity, even if it is not perfect, both believes in God and does good things well. And so that fear is not servile which he granted exists in charity begun, and which he said decreases as charity increases; that

[1]Augustine, *In I Ioannis* 4, 18, tr. 9 n6.
[2]Ibid., n4.
[3]Ibid.
[4]Ibid., n8.
[5]In c5 n2.
[6]Above, c4 n3.

is the initial fear, which he does not deny exists in charity, unless the charity be perfect.

Chapter 7 (129)

1. THAT SERVILE AND INITIAL FEAR ARE CALLED THE BEGINNING OF WISDOM, BUT DIFFERENTLY. Yet it ought to be known that each of these fears, namely the servile or the initial, in several places in Scripture is called *the beginning of wisdom*;[1] and you will ascertain this to be the case, if you diligently note the places in Scripture in which mention is made of fear of the Lord.

2. And yet servile fear is called the beginning of wisdom for one reason and a different cause, and initial fear for another. For the servile one is called the beginning of wisdom because it prepares a place for wisdom and leads to wisdom; but it does not remain with it, but goes out [at its coming].[2] But the initial one is called the beginning of wisdom because it exists in initial wisdom, and as one begins to have this fear, he begins to have wisdom and charity. And so it is that each of these fears is called initial, which you will be able to find in several places in Scripture. Each of these fears is also at times called servile,[3] because even the initial one, which exists in charity begun, has something of the servile, namely the anguish of punishment; it also has something of the chaste one, namely that it fears to offend and be separated.

Chapter 8 (130)

1. ON AUGUSTINE'S ASSERTION THAT CHASTE FEAR IS ETERNAL. It should also be diligently noted that Augustine, in what was quoted earlier,[1] says that chaste fear is eternal. This is confirmation of the earlier statement,[2] namely that the spirit of fear will exist in the future, just like the other gifts of the Holy Spirit, but it will not have every use which it has now, for then it will make us revere God, but not fear to be separated from or to lack him.

2. And so that fear was also in Christ,[3] but according to the use which it will have in the future in the saints. For Christ did not fear to be separated from, or to offend, God, but he revered him before all things.[4]

[1]Cf. Ps. 110, 10; Eccli. 1, 16; Prov. 9, 10.
[2]See the words of Bede, above, c3 n2.
[3]See above, c4 n2, c6 n3.

[1]In c5 n3.
[2]Above, cc2 and 3.
[3]As to which, see above, c3 n4.
[4]Cf. Hebr. 5, 7.

Chapter 9 (131)

1. WHETHER THE FEAR OF PAIN, WHICH WAS IN CHRIST, WAS SERVILE, INITIAL, OR SOME OTHER KIND. But since there was in Christ fear of pain,[1] it is asked whether this fear was worldly, or servile, or initial.—To which we say that none of these was in Christ, because worldly fear is evil, as was said earlier, and "in the first degree, it is abandoned with the world";[2] but servile or initial fear does not exist in perfect charity, and so none of these fears was in Christ.

2. Which, then, was that fear by which he feared pain? That fear may be called natural or human, which exists in all men, by which death makes one shiver and pain engenders fear. And this fear is not called natural because it was part of man from nature as it was first instituted, since this fear was not made part of man, nor is it one of the natural goods; [it is so called] because it came to everyone from a nature corrupted by sin, upon which corruption grew as if it had been natural. And this fear is the effect of sin, as has been said earlier.[3]

DISTINCTION XXXV

Chapter 1 (132)

1. HOW WISDOM AND KNOWLEDGE DIFFER. After the above matters, it is to be diligently considered in what wisdom differs from knowledge.

2. AUGUSTINE, IN BOOK 14, *ON THE TRINITY*.—DEFINITION OF WISDOM ACCORDING TO THE PHILOSOPHERS. Concerning this, Augustine says: "In disputing about wisdom, the philosophers have defined it in these words: Wisdom is the knowledge of things human and divine. I too do not deny that the knowledge of both of these, that is, divine and human things, may be called both wisdom and knowledge."[1]

3. DISTINCTION BETWEEN WISDOM AND KNOWLEDGE ACCORDING TO THE THEOLOGIANS. "But this definition is to be divided according to the distinction of the Apostle, in which he said: *To one is given the word of wisdom, to another the word of knowledge*,[2] so that the knowledge of things divine may properly be called wisdom, and the cognition of things human may properly obtain the name of knowledge. But I do not attribute everything that can be known by man as to things human to this science,

[1]As to which, see above, dist. 15 c2.
[2]See above, c4 n1, from Cassiodorus.
[3]Dist. 16 c1 n2.

[1]Augustine, *De Trinitate*, bk 14 c1 n3.
[2]1 Cor. 12, 8.

in which there is very much empty vanity and harmful curiosity, but only that by which that most wholesome faith, which leads to true blessedness, is generated, nourished, defended, fortified. In this knowledge not many of the faithful are strong, even if they are very strong in the faith itself. For it is one thing to know only what man ought to believe in order to obtain a blessed life; it is another thing to know in what way this knowledge may both help the pious, and be defended against the impious: this is called knowledge by its proper name."[3]

4. AUGUSTINE. Concerning these same two virtues, the same Augustine, setting out their distinction while commenting on the Psalm, says: "As holy Job attests, there is a difference between wisdom and knowledge; as if defining each of them, he says: *Wisdom is piety, but knowledge is abstention from evils.*"[4,5] "But he uses piety here in the sense of worship of God, which in Greek is called *theosebeia*,"[6] "which consists in the knowledge and love of that which always is and remains unchangeably, which is God. But to abstain from evils is to walk cautiously *in the middle of an evil nation.*"[7,8]

5. AUGUSTINE, IN BOOK 12, *ON THE TRINITY*. The same, plainly distinguishing between these two, says: "Action, by which we use temporal things well, differs from contemplation of eternal things, and the latter is ascribed to wisdom, the former to knowledge. But that which is wisdom can also be called knowledge, as the Apostle does, where he says, *Now I know in part*,[9] when surely he wished his words to be understood of the knowledge of the contemplation of God. And so the difference lies in this: that wisdom pertains to contemplation, but knowledge pertains to action."[10]—See, it has been plainly demonstrated in what the spirit of wisdom differs from the spirit of knowledge, namely "that wisdom is attributed to divine things, knowledge to human ones."[11]

6. AUGUSTINE, IN BOOK 13, *ON THE TRINITY*. And, as Augustine teaches, "we know each of these in Christ," namely the divine thing and the human one, and so from him we have both wisdom and knowledge. "For when we read: *The Word was made flesh*,[12] in *the Word* is understood the true Son of God, in *flesh* is acknowledged the true son of man." Also, when

[3]Augustine, *De Trinitate*, bk 14 c1 n3.
[4]Job 28, 28, according to Augustine's version.
[5]Augustine, *Enarrationes in Psalmos*, on Ps.135, 9, n8.
[6]Augustine, *De Trinitate*, bk 12 c14 n22.
[7]Cf. Phil. 2, 15.
[8]Augustine, *Enarrationes in Psalmos*, on Ps. 135, 9, n8.
[9]1 Cor. 13, 12.
[10]Augustine, *De Trinitate*, bk 12 c14 n22.
[11]Ibid., bk 13 c19 n24.
[12]Jn. 1, 14; see above, dist. 6 c2 n2.

we say: "*We saw him filled with grace and truth*,[13] let us refer *grace* to knowledge and *truth* to wisdom,"[14] because knowledge and wisdom were fully in Christ,[15] and we have knowledge and wisdom from him, who is God and man.

Chapter 2 (133)

1. IN WHAT WISDOM DIFFERS FROM UNDERSTANDING. After showing the difference between knowledge and wisdom, let us see what distinguishes wisdom from understanding.—These two differ in this: that wisdom properly is of eternal things because it extends to contemplating eternal truth; understanding, on the other hand, is not only of eternal things, but also of invisible and spiritual things which have arisen in time. For through it is considered the highest nature (that is, the divine nature), which made all other natures, and those spiritual and invisible natures, which are after the highest one (such as angels and all the favourable dispositions of a good soul), are perceived. In this then lies the difference: that by wisdom the Creator alone is contemplated, but by understanding both the Creator and some creature. Also, by the understanding we grasp only intelligible things, but by wisdom we not only grasp the higher things, but also find pleasure in what is known.

2. HOW KNOWLEDGE, UNDERSTANDING, AND WISDOM DIFFER. And so a distinction can be made in this way among those three, namely knowledge, understanding, and wisdom: knowledge is effective for the right administration of temporal things and for good relations among the wicked; understanding for enquiry about the Creator and invisible creatures; but wisdom for the contemplation of, and delectation in, the eternal truth alone.

Chapter 3 (134)

1. THAT THE UNDERSTANDING AND KNOWLEDGE OF WHICH WE SPEAK HERE ARE NOT THE ONES WHICH MAN HAS NATURALLY. And it is to be noted that the understanding and knowledge which are called gifts of the Holy Spirit are other than the understanding and knowledge which are naturally in man's soul. For the former are virtues which are infused through grace in the souls of the faithful so that they may live righteously by them; but man has the latter naturally by the benefit of creation, and yet from God. Through those virtues which are called gifts of the Holy Spirit, those natural ones are reformed and assisted, just as, for example,

[13]Jn. 1, 14.
[14]Augustine, *De Trinitate*, bk 13 c19 n24.
[15]See above, dist. 14 c1 nn3-5.

natural understanding, darkened by sin, is reformed and assisted in understanding by some virtue and grace which is called *the spirit of understanding*. In the same way, by that virtue which is called *the spirit of wisdom*, the mind's reason is helped and raised up to contemplation of, and delectation in, the eternal truth.

2. THAT THIS WISDOM IS GOD'S, BUT IT IS NOT THE ONE WHICH IS GOD. —AUGUSTINE, IN BOOK 14, *ON THE TRINITY*. It is also to be known that, as Augustine says, the wisdom of which we now speak is not "that wisdom of God which is God, but the wisdom of man; yet it is a true wisdom, which is according to God, and is his true and principal worship."[1] And so, if "man's mind worships God, of which it is capable because it was made by him and can be partaker of him, then it becomes wise. And it becomes wise not by its own light, but by participation in that highest light. For this wisdom of man is also of God; yet it is not God's in such a way as that by which God is wise, for he is not wise by participation in himself, as the mind is wise by participation in God. In the same way, not only that by which he himself is just, but also that which he gives to man when he justifies the impious, is called *God's justice*."[2,3]

DISTINCTION XXXVI

Chapter 1 (135)

1. ON THE CONNECTION OF THE VIRTUES WHICH ARE NOT SEPARATED. It is also usual to ask whether the virtues are so conjoined that they cannot be possessed separately by anyone: one who has one of them has all of them. —JEROME, *ON ISAIAS*. Concerning this, Jerome says: "All the virtues are joined to each other, so that he who lacks one of them lacks all of them";[1] and so one who has one of them has all of them.

2. And this indeed seems probable. For since charity is the mother of all the virtues,[2] it is rightly believed that in whomever is the mother herself, namely charity, in him also are all her children, that is, the virtues.—AUGUSTINE, *ON JOHN*. Hence Augustine: "Where there is charity, what can possibly be wanting? But where there is none, what is there that can possibly be profitable?"[3]—AUGUSTINE, *TO JEROME*: "Why, then, do we not say that, whoever has this virtue has all of them, since charity is the

[1]Augustine, *De Trinitate*, bk 14 c1 n1.
[2]Cf. Rom. 10, 3.
[3]Augustine, *De Trinitate*, bk 14 c12 n15.

[1]Interlinear gloss, on Is. 56, 1; see also Jerome, *In Isaiam* 16, 11.
[2]See above, dist. 23 c3 n2.
[3]Augustine, *In Ioannem* 15, 12, tr. 83 n3.

fullness of the Law?[4] And the more it is in a man, the more he is endowed with virtue; the less, the less is there virtue in him; and the less virtue is in him, the more is there vice."[5]

Chapter 2 (136)

1. WHETHER ALL THE VIRTUES ARE EQUALLY PRESENT IN ANYONE IN WHOM THEY ARE. But it is a question whether one who possesses all the virtues has them in equal measure, or whether some flourish more and some less in someone.

2. For it has seemed to some that some of them are had more and some less by someone, as patience was eminent in Job, humility in David, meekness in Moses. These also grant that one may merit more by one virtue than by another, just as he has the one more fully than the other. And yet they say that one cannot merit more by any other virtue than by charity, nor can any other be had more fully by anyone than charity. And so they say that the other virtues can be more or less in someone, but none more fully than charity, which generates the others. And they say that these are the many faces which the Apostle mentions, saying: *From the persons of many faces*, etc.[1]

3. Others say more truly that all virtues are joined and equal in anyone in whom they are, so whoever is equal to another in one of the virtues, is also equal to him in all the others.—AUGUSTINE, IN BOOK 6, *ON THE TRINITY*. Hence Augustine: "The virtues which are in the human mind, although each is understood in its own distinct way, are yet in no way separable from each other, so that, for instance, those who are equal in fortitude are also equal in prudence, and in justice, and in temperance. For if you were to say that these men are equal in fortitude, but that one of them is greater in prudence, it follows that the fortitude of the other is less prudent, and so they are not equal in fortitude, since the fortitude of the former is more prudent. And so you will find it to be with the other virtues, if you consider them in the same way."[2]

4. From these words, it is clear that all the virtues are not only connected, but also equal in a man's spirit. And so, when someone is said to be pre-eminent in some virtue, as Abraham in faith, Job in patience, this is to be taken according to external uses, or by comparison to other men. Either such a man especially displays the habit of humility, or he particularly performs the work of faith, or of another of the virtues, so that

[4]Cf. Rom. 13, 10.
[5]Augustine, *Epistola 167*, c3 n11.

[1]Cf. 2 Cor. 1, 11.
[2]Augustine, *De Trinitate*, bk 6 c4 n6.

he is said to be stronger in it than others, or to excel singularly in it among other men.

5. AUGUSTINE, *TO JEROME*. According to this manner, namely according to the reasons for external acts, Augustine says elsewhere that in someone one virtue is more and another less, or that one virtue is in him and another not. For he speaks as follows: "From that most famous dissertation of yours, it is sufficiently clear that it has not seemed good to our authors, or rather to truth itself, that all sins are equal, even if this is true of the virtues."[3] "For even though it is true that he who has one virtue has all of them, and that he who lacks one virtue has none of them, all sins are not equal in the same way. For where there is no virtue, there is nothing right, and yet it does not follow that worse cannot become even worse, or what is distorted become even more so. But if, as I believe to be more true and more congruent with the sacred Letters, the dispositions of the soul are like the members of the body (not that they appear in [higher or lower] places, but that they are perceived by the affections), then one is illuminated more fully, another less so, and a third entirely lacks light. If this is the case, then just as each person is affected by the light of pious charity, and more in one action, less in another, or not at all in a third, so he may be said to have one virtue and to lack another one, or to have one virtue more and another less. For insofar as it pertains to that charity which is piety, we may rightly say that 'charity is greater in this man than in that one,' and 'there is some of it in this man, none in that one.' Also, as to an individual, [we may say] that he has greater chastity than patience, and that he has it in a higher degree today than he had yesterday, if he is making progress; or that he still lacks continence, but possesses not a small measure of mercy. To summarize generally and briefly the view which I have of virtue: Virtue is the charity with which that which ought to be loved is loved. This is greater in some people, in others less, and in others not at all; but in its greatest fullness, which admits of no increase, it exists in no man while in this life."[4]

6. Here it seems to be indicated that one may be said to have one virtue more than another by reason that, through charity, he applies himself more to the act of one virtue than of another; and because of the difference in acts, he may be said to have the virtues themselves more or less, or not to have one of them, even though he has all of them equally and conjointly as to the habit of mind or the essence of each. But in act he has the one more, the other less; he may also lack one of them, as a just man, who makes use of marriage, does not have continence in act, which he nevertheless has in habit.

[3]Augustine, *Epistola 167*, c2 n4.
[4]Ibid., c4 nn14-15.

7. AUGUSTINE. "Why then may not all sins be called equal? Perhaps because one who sins more gravely transgresses more against charity than one who sins less gravely. For no one sins, except by going against charity, which is *the fullness of the Law*.[5] And so it is rightly said: *Whoever offends against one* [*of the commandments*], *becomes guilty of all of them*, that is, he acts against charity, from which hang all the commandments."[6]

Chapter 3 (137)

1. HE RETURNS TO CHARITY, IN ORDER TO ADD HOW THE WHOLE LAW HANGS FROM IT. Since there are two commandments of charity, from which, as has been set out earlier,[1] *hangs the whole Law and the Prophets*,[2] we must address how this may be, since in the Law and the Prophets there were many ceremonial precepts which, if they had pertained to the sanctification of charity, it would seem ought never to have ceased. But because they were not established for the sake of justification, which charity brings about, but as a prefiguring of what was to come, and they were imposed as a burden,[3] once truth came shining out, they ceased as if a shadow.[4] And yet even the ceremonial precepts, according to the spiritual understanding which they contain, and all the moral ones are referred to charity. For they all pertain to the ten commandments written on the tablets,[5] where a summation of all of them is briefly related, and from these ten emanate all the others; in the same way, in the Lord's sermon on the mount eight virtues are set forth,[6] and all the rest are referred to these. And just as all the rest of the commandments are referred to the ten of the Decalogue, so these same ten are referred to the two commandments of charity.[7] And so all the commandments pertain to the two of charity, because they are fulfilled through charity, and they must be referred to charity as to their end.[8]

2. AUGUSTINE, IN THE BOOK *ON CHRISTIAN DOCTRINE*. Hence Augustine: "Charity, by which we love God and our neighbour and which is the root of all goods, possesses the whole greatness and breadth of God's utterances. And so Truth says: *On these two commandments hangs the whole*

[5]Rom. 13, 10.
[6]Augustine, *Epistola 167*, c5 nn16-17.

[1]In c1 and in dist. 27 c2.
[2]Mt. 22, 40.
[3]Cf. Hebr. 10, 1; Act. 15, 28.
[4]Cf. Col. 2, 16-17.
[5]The commandments are treated in the next distinction.
[6]Mt. 5, 3-12.
[7]See above, dist. 27 c2.
[8]Cf. Rom. 13, 10; 1 Tim. 1, 5.

Law and the Prophets.[9] And so, if there is no time to examine all the holy Pages and to unroll all the rolls of sermons, keep charity, from which they all depend,"[10] because it is the perfection and end of them all.—AUGUSTINE, IN THE *ENCHIRIDION*: "For it is then that precepts and counsels are rightly done, when they are referred to loving God, and our neighbour for the sake of God. Whatever is done out of fear of punishment or some other carnal intention, so that it is not referred to charity, is not at all done as it ought to be, even though it seems to be so done."[11]—AUGUSTINE, TO ANASTASIUS: "For he is an enemy of justice who does not sin because of fear of punishment; but he is a friend [of justice] who does not sin because of love of it."[12]—AUGUSTINE, IN THE BOOK *ON CHRISTIAN DOCTRINE*: "And so this is the summation of all [that we have been saying], that love of God and neighbour be understood as the fullness of the Law and of all divine Scripture."[13]

DISTINCTION XXXVII

Chapter 1 (138)

1. ON THE TEN COMMANDMENTS: HOW THEY ARE CONTAINED IN THE TWO COMMANDMENTS OF CHARITY. But we must now consider the division of the Decalogue, which is fulfilled in the two mandates.—AUGUSTINE, ON THE TEN CHORDS: "For the Decalogue has ten precepts, which form a ten-chorded lute.[1] They are arranged in such a way that the three which are on the first tablet pertain to God, namely to the knowledge and love of the Trinity; the seven which are on the second tablet pertain to the love of neighbour."[2]

2. ON THE FIRST PRECEPT. The first on the first tablet is: *You shall not have strange gods; you shall not make for yourself a graven thing, nor any likeness*, etc.[3] Origen says that these are two commandments,[4] but Augustine [says there is] only one. For he explains that which said, *You shall not have strange gods*, more completely with the prohibition against worshipping an image, namely an idol or a likeness of any thing.—ORIGEN. Origen says that the distinction between these is that an *idol* is

[9]Mt. 22, 40.
[10]Augustine, more accurately, *Sermo 350*, n2.
[11]Augustine, *Enchiridion*, c121.
[12]Augustine, *Epistola 145*, n4 .
[13]Augustine, *De doctrina christiana*, bk 1 c35 n39.

[1]Cf. Ps. 143, 9.
[2]Augustine, *Sermo 9*, cc5-6.
[3]Ex. 20, 3-4; Deut. 5, 7-8.
[4]Origen, *In Exodum*, hom. 8 n2.

that which has nothing like itself; but a *likeness* has the semblance of some thing, so that, for example, "if someone makes in gold, or wood, or some other material, the semblance of a snake, or a bird, or some other thing, and sets it up for adoration, he did not make an idol, but a likeness. On the other hand, one who makes a form which the eye has not seen, but the spirit fashions it for itself, as if someone shapes the head of a dog or a ram upon human limbs, or places two faces upon a human figure, he makes not a likeness, but an idol, because he makes something which does not have something else of which it is a likeness."[5]

Chapter 2 (139)

1. HOW AN IDOL IS SAID TO BE NOTHING IN THE WORLD. "It is for that reason that the Apostle says: *that an idol is nothing in the world.*[1] For it does not take its appearance from any existing thing, but is what an idle and exceedingly curious mind has devised. A likeness, however, occurs when one shapes something *from the things that are* either *in the sky*, or *on earth*, or *in the waters*."[2,3]—AUGUSTINE [SAYS] OTHERWISE.— AUGUSTINE, *ON JOHN*. But Augustine expounds that text as follows: "*An idol is nothing in the world*, that is, the form of the idol does not exist among the creatures of the world. For God made the material, but the foolishness of man gave the form. All things that are made naturally are made through the Word; but the form of man in an idol is not made through the Word. Similarly, sin is not made through the Word, but is nothing; and men become nothing when they sin."[4]

2. QUESTION. ON THE EXPOSITION OF THESE WORDS: ALL THINGS ARE MADE THROUGH HIM. But it is asked how it can be said here that the form of the idol is not made through the Word, since elsewhere we read: "Each form, each structure, each harmony of parts is made through the Word."[5] —This is resolved differently by different people. For some say that every form, and everything that is, is from God insofar as it is; and the form of the idol, insofar as it is or insofar as it is a form, is from God, but not insofar as it is an idol's, that is, set up for adoration. For in this case it is not a creature, but the perversion of a creature. Similarly, that which is sin, insofar as it is sin, "is nothing; and men become nothing when they sin,"[6] because they separate themselves from him who truly is.—JEROME,

[5]Augustine, *Quaestiones in Heptateuchum*, q71.

[1]1 Cor. 8, 4.
[2]Cf. Ex. 20, 4; Deut. 5, 8.
[3]Origen, *In Exodum*, hom. 8 n2.
[4]Augustine, *In Ioannem* 1, 3, tr. 1 n13.
[5]Ibid.
[6]Augustine, as above, at end of n1.

ON EZECHIEL. Hence Jerome: "Whatever is not from God, who alone truly is, is said not to be";[7] and so sin, which leads us away from true being, is said to be nothing or not to be.—But others say that each form, namely any form which naturally is, and all that naturally is, is from God; but the form of an idol does not exist naturally, because it does not serve the nature of justice. For that is said to exist naturally which serves, and does not rebound against, the simple nature of justice, which is God, and does not deform a created nature.

3. ON THE SECOND PRECEPT. The second precept is: *You shall not take the name of your God in vain.*[8] This is to say, according to the letter: You shall not swear God's name for nothing.[9]—ISIDORE. But what is commanded allegorically is that "you do not hold Christ, the Son of God, to be a creature (because every creature *is subject to vanity*),[10] but to be equal to the Father."[11]

4. ON THE THIRD. And the third is: *Remember to make holy the Sabbath day.* According to the letter, observing the Sabbath is being commanded; allegorically, that you hope for rest—here from vices and in the future in contemplation of God—from the Holy Spirit, that is, from God's charity and gift; not that the Holy Spirit works this without the Father and the Son.

Chapter 3 (140)

1. WHY REMISSION IS PROPERLY SAID TO BE DONE IN THE HOLY SPIRIT. —AUGUSTINE, *ON THE BLASPHEMY AGAINST THE HOLY SPIRIT*: "The Church without fail receives this gift so that remission of sin be done in the Holy Spirit. Although the Trinity works this remission, yet it is properly said to pertain to the Holy Spirit, because he is *the Spirit of our adoption as children*";[1,2] he is the love and connection or fellowship of Father and Son,[3] and for that reason our justification and rest is more often attributed to him.[4]

2. These are the three commandments of the first tablet and they pertain to God. And the first, which is about the worship of the one God,

[7]Jerome, *In Ezechielem* 26, 19.
[8]Ex. 20, 7; Deut. 5, 11.
[9]Interlinear gloss, on Ex. 20, 7.
[10]Cf. Rom. 8, 20.
[11]Ordinary gloss, on Ex. 20, 2 and Deut. 5, 11; from Isidore, *Quaestiones de veteri et novo Testamento, In Exodum,* c29 n3.

[1]Cf. Rom. 8, 15.
[2]Augustine, *Sermo 71*, c17 n28.
[3]See Bk 1 dist. 10 c2 nn4-5 and dist. 31 c6.
[4]Interlinear gloss, on Ex. 20, 8.

pertains to the Father, in whom is unity or authority; the second to the Son, in whom is equality; the third to the Holy Spirit, in whom is the fellowship of both.[5]

Chapter 4 (141)

1. ON THE COMMANDMENTS OF THE SECOND TABLET. On the second tablet were the seven commandments pertaining to the love of neighbour.

2. ON THE FIRST OF THE SECOND TABLET. The first of these is referred to the father according to the flesh, just as the first of the first tablet refers to the heavenly Father, and it is: *Honour your father and your mother, so that you may have long life upon the earth*, namely [*the land*] *of the living*.[1] And parents are to be honoured in such a way that due reverence is shown them and necessities are provided for them.

3. ON THE SECOND. The second is: *You shall not kill*.[2] According to the letter, the act of homicide is forbidden here, but according to the spirit even the will to kill. And so an addition to this commandment, read according to the letter, is made in the Gospel,[3] because the letter of the Gospel expresses what the letter of the Law did not.

4. ON THE SPIRITUAL SENSE AND THE CARNAL ONE. The letter of the Gospel expresses the spiritual understanding, that is, the one which spiritual people have, and according to which one lives spiritually; the letter of the Law expresses the carnal sense, that is, the one which carnal people have, and according to which one lives carnally, and it was this one to which an addition was made.

5. ON THE THIRD.—ISIDORE. The third is: *You shall not commit adultery*,[4] "that is, you shall not have intercourse with anyone, except under the pact of marriage. For the whole is understood from the part."[5]—AUGUSTINE, ON EXODUS: "And so by the term adultery is to be understood every illicit union and every illegitimate and forbidden use of those members."[6]

[5]Cf. ordinary gloss, on Deut. 5, 11.

[1]Ex. 20, 12; Deut. 5, 16; cf. Ps. 26, 13.
[2]Ex. 20, 13; Deut. 5, 17.
[3]Cf. Mt. 5, 21-22.
[4]Ex. 20, 14; Deut. 5, 18.
[5]Interlinear gloss, on Ex. 20, 14; from Isidore, *Quaestiones de veteri et novo Testamento, In Exodum,* c29 n11.
[6]Ordinary gloss, on Ex. 20, 14; from Augustine, *Quaestiones in Heptateuchum*, bk 2 q71.

Chapter 5 (142)

1. ON THE FOURTH. The fourth is: *You shall not commit theft.*[1] Here is forbidden sacrilege and every form of theft with violence.—AUGUSTINE, ON EXODUS: "For he did not allow theft with violence, who forbade theft, but by the term theft he surely willed to be understood any illicit usurpation of another's thing."[2]

2. Sacrilege is committed in three ways: namely when a sacred thing is taken from a sacred place, or a non-sacred thing from a sacred place, or a sacred thing from a non-sacred place. Any thing designated for divine worship, such as a church, or a thing of a church, is called sacred.

3. JEROME, IN A CERTAIN LETTER. Here usury is also forbidden, since it is contained under theft with violence. Hence Jerome: "It is not at all different to seek usuries, or to defraud, or to steal. Lend to your brother, receive what you gave, and seek nothing above it, because such excess constitutes usury."[3]—AUGUSTINE, ON THE PSALM. For usury, as Augustine says, is "when one exacts more, in regard to either injury or any other thing, than he may have suffered."[4]—JEROME, *ON EZECHIEL*. Also Jerome: "Some believe that usury consists only in money; but let them understand that usury is called a superabundance, namely if whatever thing it is is more than he may have given, as if we give ten measures in winter, and take fifteen measures at harvest-time."[5]

4. WHETHER THE CHILDREN OF ISRAEL COMMITTED THEFT WHEN THEY DESPOILED THE EGYPTIANS. The children of Israel, at God's command, took away from the Egyptians gold and silver vessels and costly clothes; if it is asked whether they committed theft, we say that they who did this in obedience to God's command did not commit theft, nor sinned in any way.—AUGUSTINE, ON EXODUS. Hence Augustine: "The Israelites did not commit theft, but offered service to God at his command. For God who gave the Law commanded this. Just as the judge's servant without sin kills him whom the law commands, but is a murderer if he does it of his own accord, even if he kills someone whom he knows is about to be condemned to death by the judge."[6]—AUGUSTINE, ON THE PSALM: "As for those weak ones who deceived the Egyptians out of greed, it is more

[1]Ex. 20, 15; Deut. 5, 19.

[2]Ordinary gloss, on Ex. 20, 14; from Augustine, *Quaestiones in Heptateuchum*, bk 2, q71.

[3]Not in Jerome, but found with the same attribution in *Summa sententiarum*, bk 4 c4.

[4]Ordinary gloss, on Ps. 54, 12; from Augustine, *Enarrationes in Psalmos*, on Ps. 54, 12, n14.

[5]Ordinary gloss, on Ez. 18, 8; from Jerome, *In Ezechielem* 18, 8.

[6]Ordinary gloss, on Ex. 11, 2; from Augustine, *Quaestiones in Heptateuchum*, bk 2 q39.

the case that they were allowed, rather than commanded, to do this to those who suffered it by law."[7]

5. AUGUSTINE, ON THE PSALM. Here the objection is made that even the good sinned in that deed, because they transgressed the natural law, with which the Gospel and the law of moral command agree, which is: *What you do not wish done to yourself, do not do to another.*[8] "Which Truth wrote on the heart of man; and because man did not read it in his heart, he repeated it on the tablets so that, after being admonished by an external voice, man should return *to his heart,*[9] and there find what he could read outside."[10] And so they appear to have breached this in that deed, because they did to others what they did not wish to be done to themselves.—But there 'unjustly' is to be understood, that is, that you do not do unjustly to another what you do not wish to be done to you. Otherwise the judge is also in breach of this, when he punishes a guilty person while not wishing any such thing to be done to himself. And so it is that even that text of the Lord: *Whatever you wish that men do to you,* etc.,[11] is to be understood as concerning good things, which we ought to do for each other.

Chapter 6 (143)

1. ON THE FIFTH. The fifth commandment is: *Do not bear false witness against your neighbour.*[1] Here the crime of lying and perjury is forbidden.

2. AUGUSTINE, ON EXODUS, ON WHETHER ALL LYING IS FORBIDDEN: "It is usual to ask whether all lying is forbidden. Some say that only the one is forbidden which does harm and is of no profit to the one to whom it is told. For such a lie is not *against your neighbour,* and so that seems to be why Scripture added this. But the question regarding lying is a great one, and cannot be explained hurriedly."[2]

[7]Ordinary gloss, on Ps. 104, 37; from Augustine, *Enarrationes in Psalmos*, on Ps. 104, 37, n28.

[8]Cf. Tob. 4, 16; Mt. 7, 12; Lk. 6, 31.

[9]Cf. Is. 46, 8.

[10]Partially in ordinary gloss, on Ps. 57, 1; from Augustine, *Enarrationes in Psalmos*, on Ps. 57, 1, n1.

[11]Mt. 7, 12, and interlinear gloss.

[1]Ex. 20, 16; Deut. 5, 20.

[2]Ordinary gloss, on Ex. 20, 1; from Augustine, *Quaestiones in Heptateuchum*, bk 2 q71.

DISTINCTION XXXVIII

Chapter 1 (144)

1. ON THE THREEFOLD KIND OF LYING.—AUGUSTINE, ON PSALM 5. It is to be known that there are three kinds of lies. "For there are some lies told for the safety or advantage of someone, and not with malice, but with kindness: in this way lied the midwives"[1] and Raab.[2]—"There is another kind of lying, which is done for amusement, and it does not deceive, for the person to whom it is told knows that it is done for the sake of amusement. And these two kinds of lying are not without fault, but it is not a great fault. It is not suitable for the perfect to lie, however, not even for the sake of another's temporal life, lest they kill their own soul for the sake of someone else's body. It is lawful for them to be silent about the truth, but not to speak falsehood, so that if one does not want to betray another to his death, he is to be silent about the truth, but he is not to speak falsehood."[3]—There is a third kind of lying, which springs from malignity and duplicity, and this is to be much guarded against by all.

2. Here it seems to be indicated that those lies which are told for the sake of amusement or for someone's safety are venial sins for the imperfect; but for the perfect, the lie told for another's advantage is damnable. The same may also be held regarding an amusing lie, particularly if it should be repeated.

3. THAT THE LYING OF THE MIDWIVES AND RAAB WAS VENIAL.—AUGUSTINE, ON LEVITICUS. As for the lying of the midwives and Raab, Augustine defines it as venial, saying: "Perhaps the midwives were rewarded not because they lied, but because they freed the children, and because of this mercy [of theirs] their sin was venial, although still a sin; in the same way, Raab was freed because she freed the spies, and on account of this it was a venial sin. But let no one believe that in the case of other sins too, if they are done for the sake of freeing men, the same forgiveness may be granted. For many detestable evils follow from such an error."[4]—AUGUSTINE, IN THE *ENCHIRIDION*. "For we can also assist another by theft, if the poor man to whom we give what is stolen feels the benefit, and the rich man from whom we steal never feels the loss. And we can do the same by adultery, if some woman appears about to die of love, unless we consent to her, while if she lived she might purge herself by penance; yet no one will for this reason deny that such an adultery is a grave sin."[5]

[1]Augustine, *Enarrationes in Psalmos*, on Ps. 5, n7; cf. Ex. 1, 15-21.
[2]Cf. Jos. 2, 3-6.
[3]Augustine, *Enarrationes in Psalmos*, on Ps. 5, n7; cf. Ex. 1, 15-21.
[4]Augustine, *Quaestiones in Heptateuchum*, bk 3 q68.
[5]Augustine, *Enchiridion*, c22.

Chapter 2 (145)

1. ON THE EIGHT KINDS OF LYING. It is also to be known that there are eight kinds of lying, as Augustine explains in his book *On Lying*; these are to be diligently noted, so that it may be clear which lie is venial and which damnable. "The first and to be carefully avoided is that capital lie which is done in the teaching of religion; to this lie one ought not be induced for any reason whatever. The second is such that it profits no one, but hurts someone. The third is that which profits one so as to hurt another. The fourth, that which is done exclusively for the lust of lying and deceiving, which is an astonishing lie. The fifth, that which is done out of a deep desire to please by sweet-talk. All these being avoided, there follows a sixth kind, which hurts no one and helps someone, as when, if someone else's money is about to be unjustly taken from him, one who knows where the money is should lie about this knowledge. The seventh, which hurts no one and profits someone, as when, not wishing to betray a man who is sought in order to be put to death, one should lie. The eighth is that which hurts no one, and helps to preserve someone from bodily uncleanness."[1]

2. "In these, a man sins much less, when he lies, the further he moves away from the first kind. But whoever thinks that there is any sort of lie which is not sin, deceives himself awfully, since he judges a deceiver of other people to be honest."[2]—"And so flee every kind of lie as much as you can,"[3] "because no lie is of God."[4]

Chapter 3 (146)

WHAT IS LYING. Here we must see what lying is and what it is to lie, and then whether every lie is a sin, and why.—AUGUSTINE, IN THE BOOK *AGAINST LYING*. As Augustine says: "A lie is a false signification of speech with the intention of deceiving."[1] And so, in order for there to be a lie, it is necessary that falsehood be spoken and with the intention of deceiving: "for this evil is characteristic of the liar, that he has one thing enclosed in his heart and another ready on his tongue."[2]

[1]Augustine, *De mendacio*, c14 n25.
[2]Ibid., c21 n42.
[3]Isidore, *Synonyma de lamentatione animae peccatricis*, bk 2 n52.
[4]Rufinus of Aquileia, *Historia monachorum, De Iohanne I*, bk 1, c2 n5.

[1]Augustine, *Contra mendacium*, c21 n26.
[2]Augustine, *Enchiridion*, c18.

Chapter 4 (147)

1. WHAT IT IS TO LIE. But to lie is to speak against what one feels in one's soul, whether what one says is true or not. And so anyone who speaks a lie lies, because he speaks against that which he feels in his soul, that is, with the will to deceive; but not anyone who lies tells a lie, because sometimes when lying he says what is true, just as conversely sometimes one reveals the truth while telling a falsehood.—AUGUSTINE, IN THE *ENCHIRIDION*. Hence Augustine: "Certainly, no one is to be deemed a liar who tells a falsehood which he believes to be true, because such a one, insofar as it is in him, does not deceive, but is deceived. And so a man is not to be accused of lying, if incautiously he believes falsehoods and holds them to be true; but, on the other hand, he lies who says what is true, believing it to be false. For insofar as it pertains to his soul, he does not tell the truth, because he does not say what he feels, even though what he says turns out to be true. Nor is that person free of lying who unknowingly speaks the truth, while knowingly he wills to lie."[1]

2. QUESTION REGARDING THE JEW WHO SAYS THAT CHRIST IS GOD. Here it is usual to ask: if a Jew says that Christ is God, even though he does not feel this in his soul, is he telling a lie?—What he says is not a lie because, even though he holds otherwise in his soul, nonetheless what he says is true, and so it is not a lie; and yet he lies by saying what is true.

Chapter 5 (148)

1. THAT EVERY LIE IS A SIN.—AUGUSTINE, IN THE *ENCHIRIDION*. Augustine indicates that every lie is a sin, saying: "It seems to me that every lie is a sin, but it is very relevant with what intention and on what subjects one lies. For the man who lies to help another does not sin in the same way as the man who tells a lie to do harm; neither does the man who by his lying sends a traveller on the wrong road do as much harm as the man who by his lie distorts the way of life."[1]

2. WHY EVERY LIE IS A SIN. "Next, every lie is to be called a sin, because a man must always say what is in his soul, whether it is true, or whether he thinks it to be so and it is not. For words were instituted not so that men might deceive one another through them, but so that they might by words make their thoughts known to others. Therefore, to use words in order to deceive, and not for the end for which they were instituted, is a sin."[2]

3. THAT A LIE DOES NOT CEASE TO BE A SIN IF IT IS OF HELP. "Nor should one suppose that some lie is not a sin, because at times we can be of help

[1]Augustine, *Enchiridion*, c18.

[1]Augustine, *Enchiridion*, c18.
[2]Ibid., c22.

to someone by telling a lie. As we said earlier,[3] it is possible to be of help by stealing and committing adultery."[4]

4. THAT A LIE IS NOT SUCH ONLY WHEN IT DOES HARM.—AUGUSTINE, ON LEVITICUS: "Moreover we cannot call it a lie only when someone is harmed by it; for when a falsehood is knowingly spoken by someone, it is a lie, whether anyone is harmed or not."[5]

5. HERE THE QUESTION POSED EARLIER IS RESOLVED.[6] See, from these authorities, it is clear that every lie is a sin. And yet it is not to every lie that that text is to be applied: *You will destroy all who speak a lie*;[7] nor the other one: *The mouth that lies kills the soul.*[8] Nor does it seem that every lie is forbidden by this precept, nor is the amusing lie included in the above discussion.

Chapter 6 (149)

1. IN WHAT IT IS DANGEROUS TO ERR, IN WHAT NOT.—AUGUSTINE, IN THE *ENCHIRIDION*. It is also to be known that "in some things, it is a great evil to be deceived; in some it is a small evil, and in others none at all."[1] "Some matters are of no relevance to our obtaining the kingdom of God, whether we believe them or not, and whether they are held to be true or false, and whether they are as we hold them to be: to err with regard to these, that is, to believe one of them instead of another is not to be thought to be a sin; or if it is one, then it is a very small and trifling sin."[2] "But there are truths which, although they cannot be seen, must be believed, or it is impossible to come to eternal life."[3]

2. WHAT ERROR IS. And although "error ought to be avoided with the greatest care, not only in greater, but even in smaller things, and even though error is only possible through ignorance, it does not follow that a man who is ignorant of a thing necessarily errs, but a man who thinks he knows what he does not know does err, because he accepts what is false as if it were true, which is characteristic of error. But it is very relevant in regard to what a man errs. For there are some things which it is better not to know than to know. And it has sometimes been advantageous for some to depart from the right way, but in travelling and not in morals."[4]

[3]Above, c1 n3.
[4]Augustine, *Enchiridion*, c22.
[5]Augustine, *Quaestiones in Heptateuchum*, bk 3 q68.
[6]Posed at the end of dist. 37 c6 n2.
[7]Ps. 5, 7.
[8]Wis. 1, 11.

[1]Augustine, *Enchiridion*, c19.
[2]Ibid., c21.
[3]Ibid., c20.
[4]Ibid., c17.

3. CONCERNING JACOB, WHETHER HE LIED. It is usual to ask concerning Jacob whether he lied, when he said that he was Esau, even though he knew otherwise in his soul.[5]—On this, Augustine says: "As for Jacob and that which he did at his mother's bidding so as to deceive his father, if it is considered with diligence, it does not seem to be a lie, but a mystery."[6] For he intended to obey his mother, who had known the mystery through the Spirit. And so, because of the familiar counsel of the Holy Spirit which his mother had received, Jacob is excused from lying.

DISTINCTION XXXIX

Chapter 1 (150)

WHAT IS PERJURY. Now let us consider perjury. Perjury is a lie confirmed by an oath.

Chapter 2 (151)

1. WHETHER SOMETHING WHICH IS NOT A LIE CAN BE A PERJURY.—JEROME, *ON JEREMIAS*. Here it is asked whether there can be perjury, where there is no lie. This seems to be the case to some, on the authority of Jerome, who says: "It is to be noted that the swearing of an oath has three components: truth, judgement, and justice. If these are lacking, there is no oath, but perjury."[1] But where a falsehood is sworn, truth is lacking; and so if a falsehood is sworn, even if there is no intention to deceive, it seems to constitute perjury, because truth is lacking.

2. THE OPINION OF SOME ON THIS MATTER. It pleases some to hold that there is no perjury where there is no lie; and just as at times a falsehood is uttered without lying, so a falsehood is sworn without perjury. Perhaps the Apostle spoke a falsehood when he said that he would be coming to Corinth,[2] and yet, despite charges to the contrary,[3] he did not incur the fault of lying because he said what he felt in his soul. And if he had confirmed that by an oath, he would not have incurred perjury, because he told the truth insofar as it was in him; and if he had added an oath, he would have sworn the truth insofar as it was in him, even if it turned out otherwise than he said. And so, just as one is not a liar, unless he feels in his soul otherwise than he says, whether the matter is so or not, so it

[5]Cf. Gen. 27, 19-24.
[6]Augustine, *Contra mendacium*, c10 n24.

[1]Jerome, *In Ieremiam* 4, 2.
[2]Cf. 1 Cor. 16, 5.
[3]Cf. 2 Cor. 1, 15-23.

seems to some that no one is made a perjurer, unless he feels in his soul otherwise than he says, whether the matter is so or not.

Chapter 3 (152)

1. ON THE TRIPLE MANNER OF PERJURY.—THE TRUER VIEW. But the better view is that he commits perjury who swears what is false with the will to deceive, as well as he who swears what is true while believing it to be false, and he who swears what is false while believing it to be true.—Hence Augustine: "Men swear falsely either when they deceive, or when they are deceived. Either a man believes to be true that which is false, and he swears rashly; or he knows or believes it to be false, and yet swears it to be true, and then he swears criminously. But these two perjuries which I have mentioned are different. Suppose someone swears, who believes that which he swears to be the truth: he believes it to be true, and yet it is false. Such a one does not commit perjury from his soul, but is deceived; he holds as true something which is false, but he does not knowingly utter an oath for a false thing. Posit another who knows it to be false and says it is true, and swears as if it were true, even though he knows it to be false. See how detestable this wild animal is. Posit yet another who believes something to be false, and swears as if it were true, and perhaps it is true. So that you may understand, here is an example: You ask this man: Did it rain in that place? He says that it rained. And then it did rain there, but he believes that it did not: he is a perjurer. How a word proceeds from the soul is relevant; a tongue is not guilty unless a guilty mind makes it so."[1]—Here it is plainly set out that a man commits perjury in three ways, as we said earlier: either when he knowingly swears what is false, or when he swears what is true believing it to be false, or when he swears what is false deeming it to be true.

2. But this last case does not seem to be perjury; or, if it is called perjury because a falsehood has been sworn, the one who so swears does not seem to be guilty of perjury, because his mind is not guilty, and so neither is his tongue.—But his mind is guilty, since he presumes to affirm by oath something which he does not clearly perceive to be true. And so not every perjury is a lie, nor does every perjurer lie; but everyone who lies under oath is a perjurer, and everyone who swears a falsehood, whether or not he lies, commits perjury.

3. QUESTION. But when one swears what is true, believing it to be false, the question arises of where the perjury is in that case. For the very meaning of the words is true, because he unknowingly speaks the truth. And so it is not the meaning itself which is false or a lie, since it is true; and what

[1]Augustine, *Sermo 180*, c2 n2.

is true does not seem to constitute perjury.—SOLUTION. To this, we say that to speak in this way, namely against one's own mind and under the attestation of an oath, is perjury. And so to lie under oath is perjury. Therefore perjury consists either in uttering a falsehood under oath with the intention of deceiving, or in uttering a falsehood under oath without the intention to deceive, or in telling a truth under oath with the intention of deceiving.

4. OBJECTION. Here an objection is made: If anyone who swears a falsehood commits perjury, then one who swears to give something to another by a certain term, which he then will not do, perjured himself at the swearing of his oath, because he swore a falsehood: for it did not turn out as he had sworn.—DETERMINATION. To this, it may be said that not everyone who swears what is false is a perjurer from the moment he swears, and this is the case with the person of whom we speak; it is from the moment that he changes his intention, or fails to meet the deadline, that such an oath becomes perjury.

Chapter 4 (153)

1. WHETHER IT IS AN EVIL TO SWEAR OATHS. But if it is asked whether it is evil to swear, we say that it is sometimes evil, sometimes not. For to swear voluntarily and without necessity, or to swear a falsehood, is a great sin. But to swear from necessity, namely either to assert one's innocence, or to confirm peace treaties, or to persuade one's listeners of something which is useful to them, is not evil because it is necessary.

2. AUGUSTINE, *ON THE LORD'S SERMON ON THE MOUNT*. Hence Augustine: "An oath is to be sworn in regard to necessary things, when men are slow in believing what is good for them. The swearing of oaths is not good; and yet it is not evil, if it is necessary,"[1] that is, it is not to be desired as if it were good, but neither is it to be avoided as if it were evil, when it is necessary.

3. AUGUSTINE, *ON THE EPISTLE TO THE GALATIANS*: "For the swearing of oaths is not against God's precept; the Lord's prohibition against oath-swearing is to be understood in the sense that, insofar as it lies in him, one is not to swear: which many do, having an oath in their mouths as if it were something great and sweet. For the Apostle knew the Lord's precept, and yet he swore.[2] It follows that we are forbidden to swear out of a desire for and pleasure in swearing."[3]

[1]Augustine, *De sermone Domini in monte*, bk 1 c17 n51.
[2]Cf. Rom. 1, 9; 1 Cor. 15, 31; 2 Cor. 11, 31; Gal. 1, 30; Phil. 1, 8.
[3]Augustine, *Epistolae ad Galatas* (1, 20) *expositio*, n9.

4. AUGUSTINE, *ON THE LORD'S SERMON ON THE MOUNT*. And so, when Christ says in the Gospel: *I tell you not to swear at all*,[4] "he is understood to have so commanded, lest any one should desire an oath as a good thing, and by the assiduous use of oaths sink into perjury." And when he added: "*Let your speech be, Yes, yes; No, no*,[5] this is good and desirable. *For whatever is more than this comes from evil*,[6] that is, if you are compelled to swear, understand it to come from the need of the weakness of those whom you are trying to persuade of something. This weakness is certainly an evil, from which we daily pray to be delivered, when we say: *Deliver us from evil*.[7] And so he did not say: *Whatever is more* is evil; for you are not doing what is evil when you make right use of an oath; but *it comes from the evil* of him ... who otherwise does not believe,"[8] that is, from weakness, which at times is punishment, and at times punishment and fault.[9] In this passage, then, the Lord forbade the evil, counselled the good, allowed the necessary.

Chapter 5 (154)

1. ON THE OATH WHICH IS SWORN BY CREATURES. It is also asked whether it is lawful to swear by creatures. It seems not, since it is written in the Law: *You shall render your oaths to the Lord*,[1] and Christ commands in the Gospel *not to swear at all, neither by heaven, nor by earth, nor by Jerusalem, nor by your own head*.[2]

2. JEROME, *ON MATTHEW*: "To Jews, as if to children, it was allowed to swear by the Creator,"[3] and (AUGUSTINE) "it was commanded that, if they should have to swear, they should do so only by the Creator, and not by a creature," because "those who swore by the angels or the elements venerated creatures with honour, and it was better to extend this to God than to creatures."[4] And so he forbade this to the weak; but he did not forbid it to the saints, who in creatures venerated only the Creator. Hence Joseph swore *by the health of Pharaoh*,[5] and so revered God's judgement in the one by whom he had been placed in the depths. But Christ forbade swearing by creatures, lest there should be believed to be something divine in

[4]Mt. 5, 34.
[5]Mt. 5, 37.
[6]Ibid.
[7]Mt. 6, 13.
[8]Ibid.
[9]Cf. Bk 2 dist. 36 c1.

[1]Mt. 5, 33; cf. Deut. 23, 31 and Ps. 49, 14.
[2]Mt. 5, 34-36.
[3]Jerome, *In Matthaeum* 5, 33.
[4]Ibid.
[5]Cf. Gen. 42, 15-16.

them for the sake of which reverence would be owed to them; or perhaps lest, in swearing a falsehood by them, men should believe they were not bound by their oath.[6]

Chapter 6 (155)

WHICH OATH IS MORE BINDING, WHETHER THE ONE DONE BY GOD, OR BY THE GOSPELS, OR BY CREATURES. If it is asked who is more bound, whether one who swears by God, or one who does so by the Gospel or by creatures, we say: the one who swears by God, because these other things were made by him.—JOHN CHRYSOSTOM. Hence Chrysostom: "If this were the case, one who swears by God appears to do little; but the one who swears by the Gospels seems to achieve somewhat more. To whom we ought to say: Fools! The Scriptures are holy because of God, not God because of the Scriptures."[1] In the same way, creatures were made by God.

Chapter 7 (156)

1. WHAT IT MEANS TO SAY: BY GOD. Here it is asked what it means to say: 'I swear by God.' It is to call God as a witness. For the Apostle swore saying: *God is my witness*;[1] as if he had said: By God, it is so.— AUGUSTINE, IN A SERMON ON PERJURY. Hence Augustine: "It is ridiculous to hold this."[2] "You swear, if you say 'by God'; do you not also swear, if you say 'God is my witness'? For what does 'God is my witness' mean, if not 'by God?' What does it mean to swear, if not to render to God his right, when you swear by him? That is, the right of truth, and not of falsehood."[3]

2. IN A SERMON ON PERJURY. Also: "Behold, I say to your charity: Even one who swears a falsehood by a stone is a perjurer," because he does not take as witness the stone, which "cannot hear," but its Creator.[4] And so to swear by any creature is this: namely to produce its Creator as a witness.

3. AUGUSTINE, ON PSALM 7. There is also "a very grave kind of oath, which is done in the form of a curse, as when a man says: If I have done so and so, may I suffer so and so,"[5] or may it happen to my children. In this sense it is also taken sometimes, when someone swears by saying: 'by

[6]Cf. ordinary gloss, on Mt. 5, 34; Augustine, *De sermone Domini in monte*, bk 1 c17 n52.

[1]Pseudo-Chrysostom, *In Matthaeum opus imperfectum*, hom. 44.

[1]Rom. 1, 9; Phil. 1, 8.
[2]Augustine, *De sermone Domini in monte*, bk 1 c17 n51.
[3]Augustine, *Sermo 180*, c6 nn6-7.
[4]Ibid., c12 n13.
[5]Augustine, *Enarrationes in Psalmos*, on Ps. 6, n3.

my health,' or 'by my children,' and suchlike. For in this way he binds these to God.

4. IN A SERMON ON PERJURY. Hence Augustine: "When someone says 'by my health,' he binds his health to God; when he says 'by my children,' he gives his children to God as pledges that whatever comes out of his mouth should fall upon their heads: if truth, truth; if falsehood, falsehood."[6] And just as one who swears by these binds them to God, so one who swears by God calls him as witness. Therefore in every oath either God is taken as witness, or a creature is bound and offered as a pledge to God, and so this is what swearing is, namely to take God as witness, or to give something to God as a pledge.

Chapter 8 (157)

CONCERNING THOSE WHO SWEAR BY FALSE GODS. After these matters, it is asked whether one ought to rely on the promise of one who has sworn by demons or idols.—Concerning this, Augustine writes to Publicola and says: "I wish you to consider first whether, if a man has sworn by false gods and then failed to keep his promise, he does not seem to you to have sinned twice. And indeed he has sinned twice, because he swore by those by whom he should not, and did what he should not have done in violation of the promise which he had sworn. And so anyone who relies on the promise of one who is known to have sworn by false gods, and relies on it not for an evil purpose, but for a good one, does not associate himself with the sin of him who swore by demons, but with the good pact with which he kept his faith. Without any doubt, it is less bad to swear truly by false gods than to swear falsely by the true God. For the holier is that by which we swear, so much more punishable the perjury."[1]

Chapter 9 (158)

1. THAT AN OATH OR VOW WHICH IS CARELESSLY SWORN IS NOT TO BE KEPT, NOR A PROMISE WHICH IS UNJUSTLY MADE. It remains now to see whether every oath is to be fulfilled. For if someone has sworn something against faith and charity, "whose observance might make for a worse outcome,"[1] it is rather to be changed than to be fulfilled.—AMBROSE, IN BOOK 1, *ON OFFICES*. Hence Ambrose: "It is sometimes contrary to duty to fulfil a sworn promise, as Herod did."[2,3]

[6]Augustine, *Sermo 180*, c6 n7.

[1]Augustine, *Epistola 47*, n2.

[1]Bede, *In Evangelia*, bk 2 hom. 23.
[2]Cf. Mt. 14, 7-11.
[3]Ambrose, *De officiis*, c50 n254.

2. ISIDORE, IN THE *SYNONYMS*. Also Isidore: "If you have promised evils, rescind your promise; if you have made a shameful vow, change what you have decreed. If you have made a vow carelessly, do not do it; that promise is impious which is fulfilled by a crime."[4]—ISIDORE, IN THE BOOK OF *SENTENCES*. The same: "That oath is not to be kept by which an evil thing is incautiously promised, as if one should swear to an adulteress a promise to remain with her forever. For it is more tolerable not to fulfil an oath than to remain in defilement."[5]

3. BEDE, IN HOMILY 43. Also Bede: "If it has happened that we have sworn something carelessly, whose observance might make for a worse outcome, we know that we ought freely to change it to a more salubrious counsel; and if necessity presses, we ought rather to perjure ourselves, than to fall into some graver crime for the sake of avoiding perjury. David swore by God to kill Nabal, a foolish man; but at the first intercession of Abigail, a prudent woman, he set aside his threats, put his sword back in its scabbard,[6] nor did he sorrow that he had contracted any guilt by such perjury."[7]

4. AUGUSTINE, IN SOME SERMON. Also Augustine: "It was a greater piety that David did not fulfil his oath by the spilling of blood. David was rash in his swearing, but it was with a greater piety that he did not fulfil his oath."[8]—From these and several other texts, it is shown that some oaths are not to be kept. And one who swears in this way sins gravely; but when he changes, he does well. But one who does not change sins twice: because he swore unjustly, and because he does what he ought not to do.

Chapter 10 (159)

1. WHETHER HE WHO DOES NOT DO WHAT HE HAD INCAUTIOUSLY SWORN IS A PERJURER. But it is usual to ask whether one who changes is to be called a perjurer. Bede, above, called such an oath perjury.[1]—John too, the apocrisary of the Eastern sees, said: "The word of our father Sophronius means that it is better that the swearer should become a perjurer, than to keep the oath to break the holy images."[2]

2. But such an unkept oath is called 'perjury,' and one who does not keep it is called a 'perjurer,' because he swore a falsehood, not because

[4]Isidore, *Synonymorum libri II*, bk 2 n58.
[5]Isidore, *Sententiarum libri III*, bk 2 c31 n9.
[6]Cf. 1 Kings 25, 22-25.
[7]Bede, *In Evangelia*, bk 2 hom. 23.
[8]Augustine, *Sermo 308*, c2 n2.

[1]Above, in c9 n3.
[2]John of Jerusalem, in Session 4 of the Council of Nicaea II (1 Oct. 785).

he is guilty by reason of his failure to keep it, but because he swore something unjust, and so he is as guilty as one who perjures himself.

Chapter 11 (160)

CONCERNING HIM WHO SWEARS WITH VERBAL ARTFULNESS.—ISIDORE, IN BOOK 2 OF THE *SENTENCES*. It is also to be known that, "by whatever artfulness of words one may swear, God, who is the witness of conscience, takes the oath the way it is understood by the one to whom it is made. And the swearer is doubly guilty because he takes God's name in vain, and he entangles his neighbour in fraud."[1]

Chapter 12 (161)

1. CONCERNING HIM WHO COMPELS ANOTHER TO SWEAR. It is also asked whether he sins, who compels another to swear.—AUGUSTINE, IN SOME SERMON. Concerning this, Augustine says: "If one exacts an oath, it is of great relevance whether he does or does not know that the swearer will swear a falsehood. For if he does not know, and so says 'swear to me' in order to establish faith, it is not a sin; yet it is human temptation.[1] But if he knows about the falsehood, and compels him to swear, then he is a murderer."[2]—The same: "Whoever calls another to swear an oath and knows that he is swearing a falsehood, he is worse than a murderer; a murderer will kill the body, but such a one the soul, indeed two souls: that of the one whom he called to swear and his own."[3]

2. FROM THE COUNCIL OF ORLEANS: "The holy synod proclaimed that, except for the making of peace, all the faithful should come fasting to swear oaths."[4]

DISTINCTION XL

Chapter 1 (162)

1. ON THE SIXTH AND SEVENTH COMMANDMENTS. The sixth commandment is: *You shall not desire your neighbour's wife*. The seventh is: *You shall not covet your neighbour's house, nor his slave, nor his handmaid* etc.[1]—But it seems that the commandment about not coveting a neighbour's

[1]Isidore, *Sententiarum libri III*, bk 2 c31 n8.

[1]Cf. 1 Cor. 10, 13.
[2]Augustine, *Sermo 180*, c10 n11.
[3]Ibid., *Sermo 308*, c4 n4 .
[4]Ivo, *Decretum*, bk 12 c70; cf. also Burchard of Worms, *Decretum*, bk 12 c13.

[1]Ex. 20, 17; Deut. 5, 21.

things is the same as the one that says: *You shall not steal*; and the commandment about not desiring another's wife is the same as the one that says: *You shall not commit adultery*.—AUGUSTINE, ON EXODUS: "For the commandment about not stealing could be understood so generally as to include the one about not coveting a neighbour's thing; and in the statement, *You shall not commit adultery*, the other: *You shall not desire your neighbour's wife* could be understood. But in the first two commandments about adultery and stealing, the deeds themselves are singled out and prohibited; in the latter two, it is the desire itself."[2] And so the latter are very different from the former. That is why to the commandment about adultery an addition is made in the Gospel, where all adulterous desire is forbidden.[3]

2. WHY THE LAW IS SAID TO RESTRAIN THE HAND, BUT NOT THE SOUL. But since here the desire of another's wife and another's thing is forbidden, why is the Law said to restrain the hand, but not the soul, while the Gospel restrains both?[4]—SOLUTION. That is said of the Law in regard to the ceremonial mandates, not in regard to the moral ones. Or because in the Law there is not the same general prohibition of all death-dealing desire, as there is in the Gospel.

Chapter 2 (163)

WHAT IS THE LETTER THAT KILLS.—AUGUSTINE, *ON THE BAPTISM OF CHILDREN*. But if it is asked which is the letter which the Apostle describes as killing,[1] "it certainly is the Decalogue. It is not called *the letter that kills* because the Law is evil, but because by forbidding sin it increases concupiscence and aggravates transgression, unless grace frees us,"[2] which grace is not as abundant in the Law as it is in the Gospel. "And so the Law is good, and yet without grace it kills, since it is *the power of sin*,[3] which commands that which cannot be fulfilled without grace."[4] But grace was lacking, and so the letter killed.

[2]Augustine, *Quaestiones in Heptateuchum*, bk 2 q71.
[3]Cf. Mt. 5, 27-28.
[4]Ordinary gloss, on Ps. 18, 8.

[1]Cf. 2 Cor. 3, 6.
[2]Augustine, *De spiritu et littera*, c14 nn24 and 25.
[3]Cf. 1 Cor. 15, 56.
[4]Augustine, *Epistola 145* (*ad Anastasium*), nn 2-3.

Chapter 3 (164)

1. ON THE DIFFERENCE BETWEEN THE LAW AND THE GOSPEL.—AUGUSTINE. But the letter of the Gospel differs from the letter of the Law[1] because different things are promised: earthly ones by the latter, heavenly ones by the former. The sacraments differ too, because the ones of the Law only signified grace, those of the Gospel confer it. The commandments also differ, insofar as the ceremonial ones are concerned; the moral ones are the same, but they are contained more fully in the Gospel.

2. You have heard the ten chords of the lute[2] which have been imposed on both sexes; they are to be plucked with charity, so that the wild beasts of the vices may be killed.

HERE ENDS THE THIRD BOOK

[1]Cf. Augustine, *Enarrationes in Psalmos*, on Ps. 73, 1, n2.
[2]See above, dist. 37 c1 n1; cf. Augustine, *Sermo 9*, c9 n13.

Bibliography

English translations, in print or on-line, of works cited in Book 3.[1]

AMBROSE, SAINT, BISHOP OF MILAN, D. 397.

DE FIDE = "Exposition of the Christian Faith" in *Ambrose: Select Works and Letters*. Nicene and Post-Nicene Fathers: A Select Library of the Christian Church, 2nd ser., v. 10. Edited by Philip Schaff and Henry Wace. New York: Christian Literature Publishing Co., 1890-1898. Rpt. Peabody, MA: Hendrickson Publishers, 1994.
<http://www.ccel.org/ccel/schaff/npnf210.iv.iv.html>
<http://www.newadvent.org/fathers/34041.htm>

DE INCARNATIONIS DOMINICAE SACRAMENTO = "The Sacrament of the Incarnation of Our Lord" in *Saint Ambrose: Theological and Dogmatic Works*. Trans. by Roy J. Deferrari. The Fathers of the Church, v. 44. Washington, DC: Catholic University of America Press, 1963.

DE OFFICIIS. Trans. by Ivor J. Davidson. 2v. The Oxford Early Christian Studies. Oxford; New York: Oxford University Press, 2001.

"Three Books on the Duties of the Clergy" in *Select Works and Letters*. Nicene and Post-Nicene Fathers: A Select Library of the Christian Church, 2nd ser., v. 10. Edited by Philip Schaff and Henry Wace. New York: Christian Literature Publishing Co., 1890-1898. Rpt. Peabody, MA: Hendrickson Publishers, 1994.
<http://www.ccel.org/ccel/schaff/npnf210.iv.i.ii.html>
<http://www.newadvent.org/fathers/3401.htm>

DE SPIRITU SANCTO = "The Holy Spirit" in *Saint Ambrose: Theological and Dogmatic Works*. Trans. Deferrari. The Fathers of the Church, v. 44.

"On the Holy Spirit" in *Ambrose: Select Works and Letters*. Nicene and Post-Nicene Fathers, 2nd ser., v. 10.
<http://www.ccel.org/ccel/schaff/npnf210.iv.ii.html>
<http://www.newadvent.org/fathers/34021.htm>

EXPOSITIO EVANGELII SECUNDUM LUCAM = *Commentary of Saint Ambrose on the Gospel according to Saint Luke*. Trans. by Íde M. Ní Riain. Dublin: Halcyon Press, 2001.

[1]The notes to the translation use the Latin names for the works cited; this bibliography provides a list of available translations arranged alphabetically by author and Latin title so that the text of the authority may be found in any translation which reproduces the accepted divisions of the original texts.

Exposition of the Holy Gospel according to Saint Luke. Trans. by Theodosia Tomkinson. Etna, CA: Center for Traditionalist Orthodox Studies, 1998.

ATHANASIAN CREED

<http://www.ccel.org/creeds/athanasian.creed.html>
<http://www.newadvent.org/cathen/02033b.htm>

AUGUSTINE, SAINT, BISHOP OF HIPPO, 354-430.

CONFESSIONES = *Confessions*. Trans. by F.J. Sheed. 2nd ed. Indianapolis: Hackett Pub. Co., 2006.

Confessions. Trans. by Garry Wills. New York: Penguin Books, 2006.

The Confessions of St. Augustine. Trans. by Rex Warner. New York: Signet Classic, c2001.

The Confessions of Saint Augustine. Trans. by Edward B. Pusey. New York: Modern Library, 1999.
<http://www.ccel.org/ccel/augustine/confess.html>

Confessions. Trans. by Henry Chadwick. Oxford: Oxford University Press, 1998, c1991.

The Confessions. Trans. by Maria Boulding, The Works of Saint Augustine: A Translation for the 21st Century, pt. 1, v. 1. Hyde Park, NY: New City Press, 1997.

The *Confessions* of Augustine: An Electronic Edition. Text and Commentary. 1992. James J. O'Donnell.
<http://www.stoa.org/hippo/>

Confessions. Trans. by R.S. Pine-Coffin. Harmondsworth; New York: Penguin Books, 1986, c1961.

The Confessions of Saint Augustine. Trans. by E.M. Blaiklock. Nashville: T. Nelson, c1983.

Confessions. Trans. by Vernon J. Bourke. The Fathers of the Church, v. 21. Washington, DC: Catholic University of America Press [1966, c1953].

The Confessions of St. Augustine. Trans. by John K. Ryan. Garden City, NY: Image Books [1960].

Confessions and Enchiridion. Trans. by Albert C. Outler. Philadelphia: Westminster Press [1955].
<http://www.ccel.org/ccel/augustine/confessions.i.html>

The Confessions. Nicene and Post-Nicene Fathers, 2nd ser., v. 1.
<http://www.ccel.org/ccel/schaff/npnf101.vi.html>
<http://www.newadvent.org/fathers/1101.htm>

CONTRA ACADEMICOS = *Against the Academicians; The Teacher*. Trans. by Peter King. Indianapolis: Hackett Pub. Co., c1995.

Saint Augustine against the Academicians. Trans. by Mary Patricia Garvey. Mediaeval Philosophical Texts in Translation, v. 2. Milwaukee: Marquette University Press, 1957.

Against the Academics. Trans. by John J. O'Meara. Ancient Christian Writers, v. 12. Westminster, MD: Newman Press, 1950 [1951].

"Answer to Skeptics" in *The Happy Life.* Trans. by Denis J. Kavanagh. The Fathers of the Church, v. 5. New York: CIMA, 1948.

CONTRA MAXIMINUM = "Debate with Maximinus" and "Answer to Maximinus" in *Arianism and Other Heresies.* Trans. by Roland J. Teske. The Works of Saint Augustine: A Translation for the 21st Century, pt. 1, v. 18. Hyde Park, NY: New City Press, 1995.

CONTRA MENDACIUM = "Against Lying." Trans. by H.B. Jaffee. In *Treatises on Various Subjects.* The Fathers of the Church, A New Translation, v. 16. Washington, DC: Catholic University of America Press, 1965, c1952.

"To Consentius, Against Lying" in *On the Holy Trinity; Doctrinal Treatises; Moral Treatises.* Nicene and Post-Nicene Fathers, 1st ser., v. 3. Also in *Seventeen Short Treatises of S. Augustin, Bishop of Hippo.* Oxford: John Henry Parger, 1897.
<http://www.ccel.org/ccel/schaff/npnf103.v.vi.html>
<http://www.newadvent.org/fathers/1313.htm>

DE AGONE CHRISTIANO = "The Christian Combat" in *Christian Instruction; Admonition and Grace; The Christian Combat; Faith, Hope and Charity.* Trans. by Robert P. Russell. 2nd ed. The Fathers of the Church, v. 2. Washington, DC: Catholic University of America Press, 1950, c1947.

DE CIVITATE DEI = *Concerning the City of God against the Pagans.* Trans. by Henry Bettenson. London; New York: Penguin Books, 2003.

The City of God. Trans. by Marcus Dods. New York: Modern Library, 2000.
<http://www.ccel.org/ccel/schaff/npnf102.iv.html>
<http://www.newadvent.org/fathers/1201.htm>

The City of God against the Pagans. Trans. by R.W. Dyson. Cambridge; New York: Cambridge University Press, 1998.

The City of God (De civitate Dei)... [by] Saint Augustine. Trans. by John Healey. 2 vols. London: Dent; New York: Dutton, 1967.

The City of God. Trans. by Demetrius B. Zema and Gerald G. Walsh. The Fathers of the Church, vv. 8, 14, 24. Washington, DC: Catholic University of America Press, 1977, c1950.

DE CONTINENTIA = "Continence." In *Marriage and Virginity.* Trans. by Ray Kearney. The Works of Saint Augustine: A Translation for the 21st Century, pt. I, v. 9. Hyde Park, NY: New City Press, 1999.

"Continence." Trans. by M.F. McDonald. In *Treatises on Various Subjects.* The Fathers of the Church, A New Translation, v. 16.

"On Continence" in *On the Holy Trinity; Doctrinal Treatises; Moral Treatises*. Nicene and Post-Nicene Fathers, 1st ser., v. 3. Also in *Seventeen Short Treatises of S. Augustin, Bishop of Hippo*.
<http://www.ccel.org/ccel/schaff/npnf103.v.i.html>
<http://www.newadvent.org/fathers/1308.htm>

DE CORREPTIONE ET GRATIA = "Rebuke and Grace" in *Answer to the Pelagians, IV*. Trans. by Roland J. Teske. The Works of Saint Augustine: A Translation for the 21st Century, pt. 1, v. 26. Hyde Park, NY: New City Press, 1999.

"Admonition and Grace" in *Christian Instruction; Admonition and Grace; The Christian Combat; Faith, Hope and Charity*. Trans. by John Courtney Murray. The Fathers of the Church, v. 2.

"A Treatise on Rebuke and Grace" in *Anti-Pelagian Writings*. Nicene and Post-Nicene Fathers, 1st ser., v. 5.
<http://www.ccel.org/ccel/schaff/npnf105.xx.i.html>
<http://www.newadvent.org/fathers/1511.htm>

DE DIVERSIS QUESTIONIBUS 83 = "Miscellany of Eighty-Three Questions" in *Responses to Miscellaneous Questions*. Trans. by Boniface Ramsey. The Works of Saint Augustine: A Translation for the 21st Century, pt. 1, v. 13. Hyde Park, NY: New City Press, 2008.

Eighty-three Different Questions. Trans. by David L. Mosher. The Fathers of the Church, v. 70. Washington, DC: Catholic University of America Press, c1982.

DE DOCTRINA CHRISTIANA = *On Christian Teaching*. Trans. by R.P.H. Green. Oxford; New York: Oxford University Press, 1997.

Teaching Christianity. Trans. by Edmund Hill. The Works of Saint Augustine: A Translation for the 21st Century, pt. 1, v. 11. Hyde Park, NY: New City Press, 1996.

On Christian Doctrine. Trans. by D.W. Robertson. New York: Macmillan, 1987.

"Christian Instruction" in *Christian Instruction; Admonition and Grace; The Christian Combat; Faith, Hope and Charity*. Trans. by John Gavigan. The Fathers of the Church, v. 2.

"Christian Doctrine" in *City of God, Christian Doctrine*. Nicene and Post-Nicene Fathers, 1st ser., v. 2.
<http://www.ccel.org/ccel/augustine/doctrine.iv.html>
<http://www.newadvent.org/fathers/1202.htm>

DE DONO PERSEVERANTIAE = "The Gift of Perseverance" in *Answer to the Pelagians, IV*. Trans. Teske. The Works of Saint Augustine: A Translation for the 21st Century, pt. 1, v. 26.

"The Gift of Perseverance" in *Four Anti-Pelagian Writings*. Trans. by John A. Mourant. The Fathers of the Church, v. 86. Washington, DC: Catholic University of America Press, c1992.

De dono perseverantiae. Trans. by Mary A. Lesousky. Patristic Studies, v. 91. Washington, DC: Catholic University of America Press, 1956.

"A Treatise on the Gift of Perseverance" in *Anti-Pelagian Writings.* Nicene and Post-Nicene Fathers, 1st ser. v. 5. <http://www.ccel.org/ccel/schaff/npnf105.xxi.iii.html> <http://www.newadvent.org/fathers/15122.htm>

DE FIDE ET OPERIBUS = "Faith and Works" in *On Christian Belief.* Trans. by Ray Kearney. The Works of Saint Augustine: A Translation for the 21st Century, pt. 1, v. 8. Hyde Park, NY: New City Press, 2005.

"On Faith and Works" in *Treatises on Marriage and Other Subjects.* Trans. by Marie Ligouri. The Fathers of the Church, v. 27. Washington, DC: Catholic University of America Press, 1985, c1955.

"On Faith and Works" in *Earlier Writings.* Trans. by Gregory J. Lombardo. Ancient Christian Writers, v. 48. New York: Newman Press, 1988.

DE GENESI AD LITTERAM = *On Genesis: A Refutation of the Manichees. Unfinished Literal Commentary on Genesis. The Literal Meaning of Genesis.* Trans. by Edmund Hill. The Works of Saint Augustine: A Translation for the 21st Century, pt. 1, v. 13. Hyde Park: New City Press, 2002.

On Genesis: Two Books on Genesis against the Manichees; and, On the Literal Interpretation of Genesis, an Unfinished Book. Trans. by Roland J. Teske. The Fathers of the Church, v. 84. Washington, DC: Catholic University of America Press, 1991.

The Literal Meaning of Genesis. Trans. by John Hammond Taylor. Ancient Christian Writers, vv. 41-42. New York: Newman Press, c1982.

DE LIBERO ARBITRIO = *On Free Choice of the Will.* Trans. by Thomas Williams. Indianapolis: Hackett Pub. Co., c1993.

"The Free Choice of the Will" in *The Teacher. The Free Choice of the Will. Grace and Free Will.* Trans. by Robert P. Russell. The Fathers of the Church, v. 59.

On Free Choice of the Will. Trans. by Anna S. Benjamin and L.H. Hackstaff. Indianapolis: The Bobbs-Merrill Co., 1961.

The Problem of Free Choice. Trans. by Mark Pontifex. Ancient Christian Writers, v. 22. Westminster, MD: Newman Press, 1955.

De libero arbitrio: The Free Choice of the Will. Trans. Francis E. Tourscher. Philadelphia: The Peter Reilly Company, 1937.

DE MENDACIO = "Lying." Trans. by Mary Sarah Muldowney in *Treatises on Various Subjects.* The Fathers of the Church, A New Translation, v. 16. Washington, DC: Catholic University of America Press [1965, c1952].

"On Lying" in *On the Holy Trinity; Doctrinal Treatises; Moral Treatises.* Nicene and Post-Nicene Fathers, 1st ser., v. 3. Also in *Seventeen Short Treatises of S. Augustin, Bishop of Hippo.*

< http://www.ccel.org/ccel/schaff/npnf103.v.v.html>
<http://www.newadvent.org/fathers/1312.htm>

DE NATURA ET GRATIA = "Nature and Grace" in *Answer to the Pelagians*. Trans. by Roland J. Teske. The Works of Saint Augustine: A Translation for the 21st Century, pt. 1, v. 23. Hyde Park, NY: New City Press, 1997.

"On Nature and Grace" in *Four Anti-Pelagian Writings*. Trans. Mourant. The Fathers of the Church, v. 86.

"A Treatise on Nature and Grace" in *Anti-Pelagian Writings*. Nicene and Post-Nicene Fathers, 1st ser., v. 5
<http://www.ccel.org/ccel/schaff/npnf105.xii.html>
<http://www.newadvent.org/fathers/1503.htm>

DE NUPTIIS ET CONCUPISCENTIA = "Marriage and Desire" in *Answer to the Pelagians, II*. Trans. by Roland J. Teske. The Works of Saint Augustine: A Translation for the 21st Century, pt. 1, v. 24. Hyde Park: New City Press, 2003.

"On Marriage and Concupiscence" in *Anti-Pelagian Writings*. Nicene and Post-Nicene Fathers, 1st ser., v. 5.
<http://www.ccel.org/ccel/schaff/npnf105.xvi.i.html>
<http://www.newadvent.org/fathers/1507.htm>

DE PECCATORUM MERITIS ET REMISSIONE ET DE BAPTISMO PARVULORUM = "The Punishment and Forgiveness of Sins and the Baptism of Little Ones" in *Answer to the Pelagians*. Trans. Teske. The Works of Saint Augustine: A Translation for the 21st Century, pt. 1, v. 23.

"A Treatise on Merit and the Forgiveness of Sins, and the Baptism of Infants" in *Anti-Pelagian Writings*. Nicene and Post- Nicene Fathers, 1st ser., v. 5.
<http://www.ccel.org/ccel/schaff/npnf105.x.i.html>
<http://www.newadvent.org/fathers/1501.htm>

DE PERFECTIONE IUSTITIAE HOMINIS = "The Perfection of Human Righteousness" in *Answer to the Pelagians*. Trans. Teske. The Works of Saint Augustine: A Translation for the 21st Century, pt. 1, v. 23.

"A Treatise concerning Man's Perfection in Righteousness" in *Anti-Pelagian Writings*. Nicene and Post-Nicene Fathers, 1st ser., v. 5.
<http://www.ccel.org/ccel/schaff/npnf105.xiii.i.html>
<http://www.newadvent.org/fathers/1504.htm>

DE PRAEDESTINATIONE SANCTORUM = "The Predestination of the Saints" in *Answer to the Pelagians, IV*. Trans. Teske. The Works of Saint Augustine: A Translation for the 21st Century, pt. 1, v. 26.

"On the Predestination of the Saints" in *Four Anti-Pelagian Writings*. Trans. Mourant. The Fathers of the Church, v. 86.

"A Treatise on the Predestination of the Saints" in *Anti-Pelagian Writings*. Nicene and Post-Nicene Fathers, 1st ser., v. 5.

<http://www.ccel.org/ccel/schaff/npnf105.xxi.html>
<http://www.newadvent.org/fathers/15121.htm>

De Sermone Domini in Monte = *Commentary on the Lord's Sermon on the Mount: with Seventeen Related Sermons*. Trans. by Denis J. Kavanagh. The Fathers of the Church: A New Translation, v. 11. Washington, DC: Catholic University of America Press / Consortium Books, 1977, c1951.

The Lord's Sermon on the Mount. Translated by John J. Jepson. Ancient Christian Writers, v. 5. Westminster, MD: Newman Press, 1948.

"Our Lord's Sermon on the Mount" in *Sermon on the Mount; Harmony of the Gospels; Homilies on the Gospels*. Nicene and Post-Nicene Fathers, 1st ser., v. 6.
<http://www.ccel.org/ccel/schaff/npnf106.v.html>
<http://www.newadvent.org/fathers/1601.htm>

De Spiritu et Littera = "The Spirit and the Letter" in *Answer to the Pelagians*. Trans. Teske. The Works of Saint Augustine: A Translation for the 21st Century, pt. 1, v. 23.

"The Spirit and the Letter" in *Later Works*. Trans. by John Burnaby. Library of Christian Classics, v. 8. Philadelphia: Westminister Press, 1955.

"A Treatise on the Spirit and the Letter" in *Anti-Pelagian Writings*. Nicene and Post-Nicene Fathers, 1st ser., v. 5.
<http://www.ccel.org/ccel/schaff/npnf105.xi.html>
<http://www.newadvent.org/fathers/1502.htm>

De Trinitate = *The Trinity*. Trans. by Edmund Hill. The Works of Saint Augustine: A Translation for the 21st Century, pt.1, v. 5. Hyde Park, NY: New City Press, 1991.

The Trinity. Trans. by Stephen McKenna. The Fathers of the Church, v. 45. Washington, DC: Catholic University of America Press, 1970, c1963.

"The Trinity" in *Later Works*. Trans. Burnaby. Library of Christian Classics, v. 8.

"On the Trinity" in *On the Holy Trinity, Doctrinal Treatises, Moral Treatises*. Nicene and Post-Nicene Fathers, 1st ser., v. 3.
<http://www.ccel.org/ccel/schaff/npnf103.iv.i.html>
<http://www.newadvent.org/fathers/1301.htm>

Enarrationes in Psalmos = *Expositions of the Psalms*. Trans. Maria Boulding. The Works of Saint Augustine: A Translation for the 21st Century, pt. 3, vv. 15-20. Hyde Park, NY: New City Press, 2000-2004.

St. Augustine on the Psalms. Trans. by Scholastica Hebgin and Felicitas Corrigan. Ancient Christian Writers, vv. 29-39. Westminster, MD: Newman Press, 1960–.

Expositions on the Book of Psalms. Nicene and Post-Nicene Fathers, 1st ser., v. 8.
<http://www.ccel.org/ccel/schaff/npnf108.ii.html>
<http://www.newadvent.org/fathers/1801.htm>

Expositions on the Book of Psalms. Trans. by J.H. Parker. The Fathers of the Holy Catholic Church, vv.8-13. Oxford: 1847-1857.

ENCHIRIDION = *The Augustine Catechism: The Enchiridion on Faith, Hope, and Love.* Augustine Series, v. 1. Hyde Park, NY: New City Press, 1999.

"Enchiridion" in *On Christian Belief.* Trans. by Bruce Harbert. The Works of Saint Augustine: A Translation for the 21st Century, pt. 1, v. 8.

The Enchiridion on Faith, Hope, and Love. Washington, DC: Regnery Gateway, 1996, c1961.

Confessions and Enchiridion. Trans. by Albert C. Outler. Library of Christian Classics, v. 7. Philadelphia: Westminster Press, 1955. <http://www.ccel.org/ccel/augustine/enchiridion.i.html>

Enchiridion, or, Manual to Laurentius concerning Faith, Hope, and Charity. Trans. by Ernest Evans. London, S.P.C.K., 1953.

"Faith, Hope and Charity" in *Christian Instruction; Admonition and Grace; The Christian Combat; Faith, Hope and Charity.* Trans. by Bernard M. Peebles. The Fathers of the Church, v. 2.

"The Enchiridion" in *Basic Writings of Saint Augustine*, v. 1. Trans. by J. Shaw. New York: Random House, 1948. <http://www.newadvent.org/fathers/1302.htm>

Faith, Hope and Charity. Trans. by Louis A. Arand. Ancient Christian Writers, v. 3. Westminster, MD: Newman Bookshop, 1947.

EPISTOLAE = *Letters*. Trans. by Roland Teske. The Works of Saint Augustine: A Translation for the 21st Century, pt. 2, vv. 1-4. Hyde Park, NY: New City Press, 2001-2005.

Letters 1–29**. Trans. by Robert B. Eno. The Fathers of the Church, v. 81. Washington, DC: Catholic University of America Press, 1989.

Letters. Trans. by Sister Wilfrid Parsons. The Fathers of the Church, vv. 12, 18, 20, 30, 32. Washington, DC: Catholic University of America Press, c1951-c1964. <http://www.newadvent.org/fathers/1102.htm>

IN EPISTOLAM AD ROMANOS INCHOATA EXPOSITIO = "Unfinished Commentary on the Epistle to the Romans" in *Augustine on Romans*. Trans. by Paula Fredriksen Landes. Early Christian Literature Series, v. 6. Chico, CA: Scholars Press, c1982.

IN EPISTOLAM AD GALATAS = *Augustine's Commentary on Galatians*. Trans. by Eric Plumer. Oxford; New York: Oxford University Press, 2003.

IN I IOANNIS = *Homilies on the First Epistle of John*. Trans. by Boniface Ramsey. The Works of Saint Augustine: A Translation for the 21st Century, pt. 1, v. 14. Hyde Park, NY: New City Press, 2008.

"Tractates on the First Epistle of John" in *Tractates on the Gospel of John*, v. 5. Trans. by John W. Rettig. The Fathers of the Church, v. 92. Washington, DC: Catholic University of America Press, 1995.

"Ten Homilies on the First Epistle General of St. John" in *Later Writings*. Trans. Burnaby. Library of Christian Classics, v. 8.

"Homilies on the First Epistle of John" in *Homilies on the Gospel of John, Homilies on the First Epistle of John, Soliloquies.* Nicene and Post-Nicene Fathers, 1st ser., v. 7.
<http://www.ccel.org/ccel/schaff/npnf107.iv.xii.html>
<http://www.newadvent.org/fathers/170209.htm>

IN IOANNEM = *Tractates on the Gospel of John.* Trans. by John W. Rettig. The Fathers of the Church, vv. 78, 79, 85, 88, 90, 92. Washington, DC: Catholic University of America Press, c1988-1995.

"Tractates (Lectures) / Homilies on the Gospel of John" in *Homilies on the Gospel of John, Homilies on the First Epistle of John, Soliloquies.* Nicene and Post-Nicene Fathers, 1st ser., v. 7.
<http://www.ccel.org/ccel/schaff/npnf107.iii.html>
<http://www.newadvent.org/fathers/1701.htm>

RETRACTATIONES = *The Retractations*. Trans. by Mary Inez Bogan. The Fathers of the Church, v. 60. Washington, DC: Catholic University of America Press [1968].

SERMONES = *Sermons*. Trans. by Edmund Hill. The Works of Saint Augustine: A Translation for the 21st Century, pt. 3, vv. 1-11. Hyde Park, NY: New City Press, c1990-1997.

Sermons. Trans. by Mary Sarah Muldowney. The Fathers of the Church, v. 81. Washington, DC: Catholic University of America Press, 1959.

Sermons on Selected Lessons of the New Testament. Trans. J.H. Parker. Fathers of the Holy Catholic Church. Oxford: J.H. Parker, 1844-1875.
<http://www.newadvent.org/fathers/1603.htm>

AUGUSTINE, PSEUDO-

SERMO 238 = "A Translation of Chapters XI-XVI of the Pseudo-Augustinian 'Sermon against Jews, Pagans, and Arians, concerning the Creed.'" Trans. by Edward Noble Stone. *University of Washington Publications in Language and Literature*, v. 4, no. 3. Seattle: University of Washington Press, 1928.

BEDE, THE VENERABLE, SAINT, 673-735.

DE TABERNACULO = *Bede, on the Tabernacle.* Trans. by Arthur G. Holder. Translated Texts for Historians, v. 18. Liverpool: Liverpool University Press, c1994.

HOMILIAE EVANGELII = *Homilies on the Gospels*. Trans. by Lawrence T. Martin and David Hurst. Cistercian Studies Series 110-111. Kalamazoo, MI: Cistercian Publications, 1991.

IN EPISTOLAM IACOBI = "On James" in *The Commentary on the Seven Catholic Epistles of Bede the Venerable*. Translated by David Hurst. Cistercian Studies Series, v. 82. Kalamazoo, MI: Cistercian Publications, 1985.

BOETHIUS, d. 524.

Opuscula V: Liber contra Eutychen et Nestorium = "A Treatise against Eutyches and Nestorius" in *The Theological Tractates.* Trans. by H.F. Steward, E.K. Rand and S.J. Tester. Loeb Classical Library, new edition, v. 74. Cambridge, MA: Harvard University Press, 2003, c1973. <http://www.ccel.org/ccel/boethius/tracts.iv.v.html>

CAESARIUS, OF ARLES, SAINT, 470?-542.

SERMO 182 = In *Sermons, Volume II.* Trans. by Mary Magdeleine Mueller. The Fathers of the Church, v. 47. Washington, Catholic University of America Press / Consortium Press, 1981, c1964.

CASSIODORUS, SENATOR, CA. 487–CA. 580.

EXPOSITIO PSALMORUM = *Explanation of the Psalms.* Trans. by P.G. Walsh. Ancient Christian Writers, vv. 51-53. New York: Paulist Press, c1990-c1991.

CREED OF TOLEDO XI.

In *The Christian Faith in the Doctrinal Documents of the Catholic Church.* Ed. by J. Neuner and J. Dupuis. 7th new and enl. ed. New York: Alba House, 2001. <http://www.fordham.edu/halsall/source/toledo.txt>

FULGENTIUS, SAINT, BISHOP OF RUSPA, 468-533.

DE FIDE AD PETRUM = "To Peter on the Faith" in *Selected Works.* Trans. by Robert B. Eno. The Fathers of the Church, v. 95. Washington, DC: Catholic University of America Press, c1997.

EPISTOLA 14 (ad Ferrandum) = "Fulgentius to Ferrandus" in *Selected Works.* Trans. Eno. The Fathers of the Church, v. 95.

GREGORY I, POPE, CA. 540-604.

DIALOGI = *Dialogues.* Trans. by Odo John Zimmerman. The Fathers of the Church, A New Translation, v. 39. New York: Fathers of the Church, Inc., c1959.

EPISTOLAE = *The Letters of Gregory the Great.* Trans. by John R.C. Martyn. Mediaeval Sources in Translation, v. 40. 3 vols. Toronto: Pontifical Institute of Mediaeval Studies, 2004.

HOMILIAE XL IN EVANGELIA = *Forty Gospel Homilies.* Trans. by David Hurst. Cistercian Studies Series, v. 123. Kalamazoo, MI: Cistercian Publications, 1990.

HOMILIAE IN EZECHIELEM = *The Homilies of St. Gregory the Great on the Book of the Prophet Ezekiel.* Trans. by Theodosia Gray. Etna, CA: Center for Traditionalist Orthodox Studies, 1990.

MORALIA SIVE EXPOSITIO IN IOB = *Morals on the Book of Job.* Oxford: J.H. Parker, 1844-1850.

Hilary, Saint, Bishop of Poitiers, d. 367?.

De synodo = "On the Councils" in *Hilary of Poitiers, John of Damascus*. Nicene and Post-Nicene Fathers, 2nd ser., v. 9. <http://www.ccel.org/ccel/schaff/npnf209.ii.iv.html> <http://www.newadvent.org/fathers/3301.htm>

De Trinitate = *The Trinity*. Trans. by Stephen McKenna. The Fathers of the Church, v. 25. New York: Fathers of the Church, 1954.

"On the Trinity" in *Hilary of Poitiers, John of Damascus*. Nicene and Post-Nicene Fathers, 2nd ser., v. 9. <http://www.ccel.org/ccel/schaff/npnf209.ii.v.html> <http://www.newadvent.org/fathers/3302.htm>

Jerome, Saint, d. 419 or 420.

Dialogi contra Pelagianos = "The Dialogue against the Pelagians" in *Dogmatic and Polemical Works*. Trans. by John N. Hritzu. The Fathers of the Church, A New Translation, v. 53. Washington, DC: Catholic University of America, c1965.

Epistola 66 (ad Pammachium) = in *The Letters of St. Jerome*. Trans. by Charles Christopher Mierow. Ancient Christian Writers, v. 33. New York: Newman Press, c1963- .

In *Select Letters of St. Jerome*. Trans. by F.A. Wright. Loeb Classical Library. Cambridge, MA: Harvard University Press, 1991, c1933.

Letter 66 (to Pammachius) in *Letters and Select Works*. Nicene and Post-Nicene Fathers, 1st ser., v. 6. <http://www.ccel.org/ccel/schaff/npnf206.v.XV.html> <http://www.newadvent.org/fathers/3001015.htm>

In epistolam Paulinam ad Ephesios = *The Commentaries of Origen and Jerome on St. Paul's Epistle to the Ephesians*. Trans. by Ronald E. Heine. Oxford Early Christian Studies. Oxford: Oxford University Press, 2002.

John Chrysostom, Saint, d. 407.

Homiliae in epistolam ad Hebraeos = *Homilies on the Gospel of Saint John and the Epistle to the Hebrews*. Nicene and Post-Nicene Fathers, 1st ser., v. 14. <http://www.ccel.org/ccel/schaff/npnf114.v.html> <http://www.newadvent.org/fathers/2402.htm>

The Homilies of S. John Chrysostom, Archbishop of Constantinople, on the Epistle of S. Paul the Apostle to the Hebrews. The Fathers of the Holy Catholic Church, v. 44. Oxford: James Parker, 1877.

John of Damascus, Saint, c. 676–749.

De fide orthodoxa = "An Exact Exposition of the Orthodox Faith" in *The Fount of Knowledge*. Trans. by Frederic H. Chase, Jr. The Fathers of the Church, v. 37. Washington, DC: Catholic University of America Press, 1970, c1958.

"Exposition of the Orthodox Faith" in *Hilary of Poitiers. John of Damascus.* Nicene and Post-Nicene Fathers, 2nd ser., v. 9.
<http://www.ccel.org/ccel/schaff/npnf209.iii.html>
<http://www.newadvent.org/fathers/3304.htm>

LEO I, POPE, D. 461.

EPISTOLA 35 in *Letters*. Trans. by Edmund Hunt. The Fathers of the Church, v. 34. Washington, DC: Catholic University of America Press, 1957.

SERMO 63 in *Sermons and Letters against the Manichaeans: Selected Fragments.* Trans. by Hendrik Gerhard Schipper and Johannes van Oort. Corpus Fontium Manichaeorum. Series Latina, v. 1. Turnhout: Brepols, 2000.

In *Sermons.* Trans. by Jane Patricia Freeland and Agnes Josephine Conway. The Fathers of the Church, v. 93. Washington, DC: Catholic University of America Press, 1996.

ORIGEN, 185–254.

HOMILIAE IN CANTICA = The Song of Songs: Commentary and Homilies. Trans. by R.P. Lawson. Ancient Christian Writers, v. 26. Westminster, MD: Newman Press, 1957.

IN EPISTOLAM AD ROMANOS = Commentary on the Epistle to the Romans. Books 1-5. Trans. by Thomas P. Scheck. The Fathers of the Church, v. 103. Washington, DC: Catholic University of America Press, 2001.

Commentary on the Epistle to the Romans. Books 6-10. Trans. by Thomas P. Scheck. The Fathers of the Church, v. 104. Washington, DC: Catholic University of America Press, 2002.

IN EXODUM = Homilies on Genesis and Exodus. Trans. by Ronald E. Heine. The Fathers of the Church, v. 71. Washington, DC: Catholic University of America Press, c1982.

PELAGIUS, 360 ca.-420 ca.

LIBELLUS FIDEI AD INNOCENTIUM PAPAM. In *The Letters of Pelagius and His Followers*. Trans. B.R. Rees. Woodbridge, Suffolk; Rochester, NY: Boydell Press, 1991.

Four Letters of Pelagius. [Trans. by] Robert F. Evans. New York: Seabury Press [1968].

Index of Scriptural and Patristic Authorities[1]

Acts of the Apostles 2, 4: 99.2; 2, 31: 71.3; 4, 12: 86.3; 5, 27-29: 55.3; 8, 20: 12.3; 10, 4: 89.1; 10, 22; 89.1; 15, 28: 137.1.

Alcuin, *In Hebraeos* 9, 15: 54.3.

Ambrose, *De fide* Bk1 c13: 70.3; c14: 32.2-3, 33.2-3; c16: 33.3; c19: 30.5, 33.1. – Bk2 c5: 41.11, 48.7, 49.1; c6: 48.7; c7: 41.11, 48.7; c8: 41.11.

— *De incarnationis dominicae sacramento* c5: 33.2, 68.10, 69.3, 71.4; c6: 23.12, 71.4; c7: 38.6.

— *De officiis* Bk1 c50: 158.1.

— *De Spiritu sancto* Bk1 c4: 124.2; c16: 124.1-2. – Bk2 c5: 12.5; wrongly cited: 23.12, 38.6.

— *De Trinitate* cf. *De fide.*

— *Expositio evangelii secundum Lucam* 23, 46: 68.3; wrongly cited: 40.2.

— *Expositio de Psalmo 118* s4: 108.1; s10: 85.3;

Ambrosiaster, *In Epistolas S. Pauli*, in Rom. 5; 14; 54.2; 8, 3: 7.1, 10.1; 9, 11-13: 112.7; 14, 5: 76.2.

— In 2 Cor. 6, 6: 112.5.

— In Gal. 6, 10: 109.2.

— In Eph. 4, 4: 79.2.

— In Phil. 2,9: 50.3, 52.4.

— *Quaestiones veteris et novi Testamenti* q44: 13.1.

Amos 2, 1: 73.3.

Apocalypse 2, 12: 50.2; 5, 5: 54.2.

Athanasian Creed see *Symbolum Athanasium*

Augustinus, *Confessiones* Bk1 c12: 126.1. – Bk10 cc42-43: 61.1.

— *Contra Academicos* Bk 2 cc10-11: 40.3.

— *Contra Maximinum* Bk1 c5: 52.2. – Bk2 c2: 52.2; c10: 23.13; c20: 73.2; wrongly cited: 22.6.

— *Contra mendacium* c10: 149.3; c12: 146.

— *De agone christiano* c2: 55.4; c18: 5.3.

— *De baptismo parvulorum* wrongly cited: 163.

— *De civilate Dei* Bk19 c4: 48.2.

— *De continentia* c8: 48.2.

— *De correptione et gratia* c7: 86.4.

— *De diversis quaestionibus 83* q11: 37; q66: 10.1; q67: 32.3; q73: 22.1.

[1]This index is keyed to the continuous series of chapters and paragraphs within each distinction.

— *De doctrina christiana* Bk1 c22: 100.1, 3-4; c23: 103, 104.2; c24: 104.2; c25: 100.3, 103; c26: 97.2, 104.2, 4-5; c27: 108.2; c28: 109.2; c30: 105, 106.1; c35: 137.2; c38: 90.1; c39: 90.1; c40: 90.2. – Bk3 c31: 36.4; wrongly cited: 137.2.
— *De dono perseverantiae* c24: 23.11.
— *De fide et operibus* c16: 76.3.
— *De Genesi ad litteram* Bk10 c12: 48.2; c19: 9.2; c20: 9.2. – Bk12 c24: 41.2.
— *De libero arbitrio* Bk3 c18: 41.5.
— *De mendacio* c14: 145.1; c21: 145.2.
— *De natura et gratia* c33: 39.2; c36: 8.
— *De nuptiis et concupiscentiis* Bk2 c11: 86.4.
— *De peccatorum meritis et remissione seu de baptismo parvulorum* Bk2 c24: 7.1; c30: 55.4; c31: 55.5.
— *De perfectione iustitiae hominis* c8: 101.1-2.
— *De praedestinatione sanctorum* c7: 89.3; c15: 18.6, 24.2.
— *De sermone Domini in monte* Bk1 c17: 153.2, 4, 154, 156.1.
— *De spiritu et littera* c14 nn24-25: 163; c32 n56: 126.3.
— *De Trinitate* Bk1 c1: 14.5; c4: 3.2; c6: 28.1, 32.2; c7: 14.6, 23.11, 24.3; c10: 23.8; c13: 23.4, 32.1, 70.3, 72.1, 73.2. – Bk2 c5: prol., 6.2. – Bk4 c5: 10.2; c13: 55.3; c20: 1.3; c21: 22.4. – Bk5 c16: 117.2. – Bk6 c4: 136.3. – Bk8 c4: 85.4-5; c6: 100.1; c7: 102; c8: 98, 109.7. – Bk9 c1: 85.3. – Bk12 c14: 132.4-6. – Bk13 c1: 80.2; c2: 76.1, 79.3, 85.2; c10: 62, 63.1; c11: 3.1, 63.2; c12: 63.2; c13: 63.2, 64.1; c14: 64.1-2; c16: 60.2; c17: 18.7, 19.5; c18: 8, 35.2; c19: 18.2, 35.2, 132.5-6. – Bk14 c1: 132.2, 134.2; c9: 120.2-3; c122.1; c12: 134.2; c14: 100.2; wrongly cited: 6.2, 13.2, 14.8, 19.5.
— *Enarrationes in Psalmos* 5, 7: 144.1; 5, 8: 125.3; 7, 5: 156.3; 11, 3: 100.1; 21, 3: 41.13; 29, 1: 61.2; 32, 1, II n2: 48.6; 48, 15, II n2: 68.2; 54, 12: 142.3; 57, 1: 142.5; 64, 5: 16.3; 67, 32-33: 77.1; 73, 1: 164.1; 80, 10: 34.2; 87, 4: 41.2, 41.8, 41.10; 93, 15: 41.13, 42.4, 48.6; 98, 5: 28.6; 101, 24: 84.2; 103, 3: 82.2, 112.2; 104, 37: 142.4; 118, 73: 85.4; 127, 1: 126.1; 130, 2: 69.2; 135, 9: 132.4.
— *Enchidirion* c2: 28.2; c8: 75.1, 80.3, 81.2, 92; c 9: 75.1; c17: 49.2; c18: 146, 147.1, 148.1; c19: 149.1; c20: 149.1; c21: 149.1; c22: 144.3, 147.1, 148.2-3; c35: 18.3; c36: 18.4; c37: 12.3; c38: 3.1, 11.2, 12.1, 12.4, 18.3; c39: 12.2; c40: 12.3; c41: 12.3; c53: 55.2; c73: 111.2; c74: 111.2; c121: 137.2.
— *Epistolae* ep. 47 ad Publicolam: 157; ep. 140 ad Honoratum: 21, 48.3; ep. 145 ad Anastasium: 137.2, 163; ep. 167 ad Hieronymum: 135.2, 136.5-7; ep. 187 ad Dardanum 38.2; ep. 190 ad Optatum: 86.3.
— *In Epistolam ad Galatas expositio* 1, 20: 153.3; 3, 20: 61.1-2; 6, 10: 109.2, 9.
— *In Epistolam ad Romanos inchoata expositio* n4: 22.4.
— *In I Ioannis* tr3: 112.3; tr5: 110.1; tr7: 66.3; tr8: 112.3; tr9: 127.1-3, 128.1-3; tr10: 76.4, 77.1.
— *In Ioannem* tr1: 139.1-2; tr6: 82.2; tr9: 82.2; tr40: prol., 80.3; tr47: 68.8; tr65: 102; tr69: 23.8; tr74: 30.3; tr78: 18.5, 71.3; tr79: 83.2; tr82: 30.5); tr83: 135.2;

tr104: 50.3; tr105: 34.2; tr106: 34.2; tr110: 60.2, 115.2; tr123: 48.3; wrongly cited: 10.2.
— *Quaestiones Evangeliorum* Bk2 q39: 83.3.
— *Quaestiones in Heptateuchum* Bk1 q61: 28.1. – Bk2 q71: 138.2, 162.1; q94: 28.1. – Bk3 q68: 144.3, 148.4.
— *Retractationes* Bk1 c9: 41.5; c19: 25.1, 109.12.
— *Sermones* s9: 138.1, 164.2; s71 140.1; s130: 55.5; s144: 76.4; s152: 10.1; s180: 152.1, 156.2, 161.1; s233: 69.4; s263: 55.5; s265: 99.2; s293: 61.1; s308: 161.1; s344: 48.3; s350: 137.2.
Augustinus, pseudo-, *De fide ad Petrum*, see Fulgentius.
— *Sermones* s233, de fide: 16.3; s238: 19.5; s246 28.5; s270: 112.10.

Baruch 3, 38: 22.6, 41.8.
Bede, *De tabernaculo* Bk2 c8: 122.5.
— *Homiliae evangelii* Bk1 hom1: 40.2; hom12: 38.5. – Bk2 hom20: 158.1, 3.
— *In epistolam Iacobi* 2, 19: 77.1.
— *In Lucam* 8, 19: 109.10.
— *In Marcum* 14, 35-36: 48.4; 14, 38: 48.5.
— *In Parabolas* 1, 7: 125.2, 126.2.
Bede, pseudo-, *In Ioannem* 1, 33: 112.4.
Berengar, *De sacramento corporis et sanguinis Christi* c10: 19.2.
Boethius, *Liber contra Eutychen et Nestorium* c3: 16.2, 29.2.
Burchard of Worms, *Decretum* Bk12 c13: 161.2

Caesarius of Arles, *Sermo* 182: 12.10
Canticle of Canticles 2, 4: 108.1, 109.4; 8, 6: 1123.
Cassiodorus, *Expositio psalmorum* 21, 3: 48.9; 56, divisio: 23.17; 98, 5: 127, 1: 126.1; 138, 6: 39.2.
Colossians 1,13-14: 54.1; 2,3: 39.5; 2, 9: 12.3, 38.1; 2, 14: 54.2, 55.4; 2, 16-17: 137.1; 2, 18: 38.6; 3.
Councils: Constantinople III (680-681), sess. 18, definition: 48.8.
— Nicaea II (787), fourth session: 159.1.
— Toledo I (400/405), Creed n5: 16.3; n6: 69.4.
— Toledo VI (638) c1: 14.4, 11.
— Toledo VIII, wrongly cited for Toledo VI: 14.4.
— Toledo XI (675): 14.4; 14.11.
1 Corinthians 1, 13: 38.6; 1, 24: 7.3; 2, 8: 73.2; 2, 10-11: 39, 2; 39.4; 2, 12: 39.4; 3, 11: 76.3, 83.2; 5, 7: 7.3; 7, 7: 109.9; 8,4: 139.1; 10, 13: 161.1; 12, 8: 132.3; 12, 11: 124.2; 13, 1: 112.2; 13, 2: 77.2; 13, 3: 81.2; 13, 8: 90.1, 112.2, 113.1, 125.2; 13, 8-10: 90.1, 112.8, 113.1; 13, 9: 101.1; 13, 10: 101.1; 13, 12: 94, 132.5; 13, 13: 81.3, 90.1; 15, 26: 57; 15, 31: 153.3; 16, 5: 151.2.
2 Corinthians 1, 11: 136.2; 1, 15-23: 151.2; 3, 6: 163; 5, 15: 46.2; 5, 19: 60.4; 6, 6: 112.5; 11, 31: 153.3; 13, 4: 38.6, 73.2.

Cyril of Alexandria (cited by John of Damascus) 14.12.

Daniel 4, 6: 49.1.
Deuteronomy 4, 24: 68.4; 5, 7-8: 138.2; 5, 11: 139.3, 140.2; 5, 12: 139.4; 5, 16: 109.3, 141.2; 5, 17: 141.3; 5, 18: 141.5; 5, 19: 142.1; 5, 20: 143.1; 5, 21: 162.1; 6, 5: 97.2, 101.1; 23, 21: 154.1.

Ecclesiasticus 1, 1 127.1; 1, 16: 129.1; 31, 10: 36.4.
Ephesians 1, 4: 117.2; 1, 5: 30.5; 1, 10: 1.2; 1, 22-23: 48.6; 2, 3: 30.2, 63.2; 3, 17: 76.3; 4, 5: 79.1; 4, 10: 38.6; 4, 25: 109.2; 5, 2: 66.2; 5, 29: 104.2.
Eusebius of Vercelli, *De Trinitate* Bk6: 68.5.
Evodius, *De fide contra Manichaeos* c22: 22.6; c26: 22.6.
Exodus 1, 15-21: 144.1; 11, 2: 142.4; 12, 35-36: 142.4; 20, 2: 139.3; 20, 2-3: 138.2; 20, 3-4: 138.2; 20, 3-17: 138.1; 20, 4: 139.1; 20, 7: 139.3; 20, 8: 139.4, 140.1; 20, 12: 109.3, 141.2; 20, 13: 141.3; 20, 14: 141.5; 20, 15: 142.1; 20, 16: 143.1; 20, 17: 161.1; 25, 31: 51.1; 26, 32: 122.3.
Ezechiel 18, 8: 142.3; 44, 25: 109.4.

Fulgentius of Ruspe, *De fide ad Petrum* c2 n10: 22.5, 27; n11: 27, 71.1; n14: 14.5, 26.2, 30.4; n15: 7.4; n17: 7.4, 8, 14.2; n19: 14.6; n23: 3.2, 14.8; c18 n59: 6.2, 14.8.
— *Epistola* 14 n29: 39.5.

Galatians 1, 20: 153.3; 1, 30: 153.3; 2, 20: 66.2; 3, 13: 55.3; 3, 19-20: 59; 3, 20: prol., 61.1; 3, 26: 30.2; 4, 4: 13.1, 33.2; 4, 4-5: prol.; 4, 5: 54.1; 5, 6: 76.2, 76.3, 81.2; 5, 17: 48.2, 101.1.
Genesis 1, 31: 115.2; 3, 6: 54.2; 3, 23: 54.2; 3, 24: 50.2, 54.2; 14, 18-20: 9.1; 17, 19-24: 149.3; 42, 15-16: 154.2.
Gennadius, *De viris inlustribus* c72: 1.4.
— *Liber sive diffinitio ecclesiasticorum dogmatum* c2: 1.4, 25.3.
Gregory I, *Dialogi* Bk4 c80.1.
— *Epistolae* ep. 67: 6.2.
— *Homiliae XL in Evangelia* hom6 n1: 88.3; hom7 n3: 5.2; hom26 n8: 80.1.
— *Homiliae in Ezechielem* Bk1 hom1 n5: 88.3; hom5 n11: 112.5. – Bk2 hom4 n13: 82.3; hom5 n2: 86.5; hom7 n9: 89.2; hom10 n17: 90.1.
— *Moralia sive Expositio in Iob* Bk10 c21: 112.3. – Bk18 c52: 6.2.

Hebrews 2, 9: 54.2, 56.2; 2, 11: 56.2; 5, 7: 125.4, 130.2; 5, 9: 54.1; 7, 9-10: 9.1; 9, 15: 59; 9, 27: 45.2; 9, 27-28: 45.2; 10, 1: 137.1; 10, 1-4: 11, 1: 80.1, 80.4; 11, 6: 86.1, 89.2.
Hesychius, *In Leviticum* 2, 2: 113.1; 16, 10: 68.4.
Hilary of Poitiers, *De synodis* n49: 43.6.
— *De Trinitate* Bk3 n11: 30.5. – Bk5 n37: 30.1. – Bk9 n40: 23.10. – Bk10 n22: 22.7; n23: 43.2; n25: 22.7; nn26-28: 43.3; nn29-30: 49.2; n35: 43.4; n36: 44; n37: 44, 49.2; n38: 49.2; n39: 49.2; n57: 18.8. – Bk12 n6: 14.7.

Isaias 7, 9 (LXX): 85.3; 8, 4: 38.6; 11, 1-3: 125.1; 11, 2: 38.8; 11, 2-3: 124.2; 41, 14: 59; 46, 8: 142.5; 49, 7: 59; 49, 26: 59; 53, 4: 41.10; 56, 1: 135.1; 60. 16: 59; 63, 16: 59.
Isidore, *Quaestiones de Veteri et Novo Testamento, In Exod.* c29 n3: 139.3.
— *Sententiarum libri III* Bk2 c31: 158.2, 160.
— *Synonymorum libri II* Bk2 n53: 145.2; n58: 158.2.
Ivo, *Decretum* Bk 12 c70: 161.4.

James 2, 10: 136.7; 2, 19: 76.4; 2, 23: 77.1.
Jeremias 31, 22: 38.3.
Jerome, *Dialogi contra Pelagianos libri III* Bk1 nn18-19: 136.2.
— *Epistolae* ep. 66 ad Pammachium, n3: 120.3; wrongly cited: 142.3.
— *In Ezechielem* 18, 8: 142.3; 26, 19: 139.2; 44, 25: 109.4.
— *In Ieremiam* 4, 2: 151.1; 31, 22: 38.3.
— *In Isaiam* 16, 11: 135.1.
— *In Marcum* 14, 18: 48.5.
— *In Matthaeum* 5, 28: 41.13; 26, 1: 41.13; 26, 37: 42.3.
— *In quatuor epistolas Paulinas*: ad Galatas 6, 10: 109.2; ad Ephesios 1, 5: 30.5.
Jerome, pseudo-, *Epistolae*, ep. 9: 23.12.
— *Expositio catholicae fidei* n4: 4.1.
Job 1, 14: 87.2; 9, 33: 60.1; 28, 13-14: 71.4; 28, 28: 132.4.
John 1, 1: 14.4, 32.2; 1, 3: 32.2, 139.2; 1, 12: 30.2; 1, 14: 6.2, 11.1, 14.4-5, 15.1, 18.2, 18.7, 22.7, 23.8, 23.10, 32.2, 33.2, 43.6, 69.2, 132.6; 1, 16: 38.2, 121; 1, 17: prol.; 1, 33: 112.4; 2, 19: 10.2; 2, 20: 10.2; 3, 5: 12.2, 3, 13: 73.2; 3, 14-15: 55.3; 3, 31: 46; 3, 34: 36.3, 38.1, 39.4; 5, 40: 100.3; 6, 31-33: 69.2; 6, 38: 48.4; 6, 67: 112.7; 8, 25: 34.2; 8, 34: 56; 8, 36: 54.1; 8, 58: 34.2; 10, 17: 67.1; 10, 17-18: 68.8; 12, 27: 38.6, 41.11; 13, 27: 49.2; 13, 31: 49.2; 13, 34: 100.3, 102; 13, 37: 41.11; 14, 1: 28.5; 14, 29: 83.1; 14, 30: 55.5; 15, 13: 96.1, 110.2; 16, 15: 48.7; 17, 1: 30.5, 94; 18, 4-6: 43.3; 19, 26: 109.10; 20, 22: 99.2; 20, 28: 80.1; 20, 29: 83.2; 21, 18: 48.3.
1 John 1, 8: 8; 2, 27: 112.3; 3, 1: 100.3; 3, 9: 110.1; 4, 8: 98; 4, 12-16: 112.3; 4, 16: 98; 4, 17: 127.1; 4, 18: 125.2, 127.1; 4, 20: 98.
John Chrysostom, *Homiliae in epistolam ad Hebraeos* hom21: 82.3.
John Chrysostom, pseudo-, *In Matthaeum, opus imperfectum* hom44: 155.
John of Damascus, *De fide orthodoxa* Bk3 c2: 7.3, 10.1, 24.4; c3: 4.3, 19.4, 23.9; c4: 4.2, 19.3, 23.4; c6: 4.4, 14.12; c7: 10.5, 19.3, 27, 72.2; c8: 28.4.
Josue 2, 3-6: 144.1; 20, 6: 54.3.

1 Kings 9, 2: 112.7; 25, 22-25: 158.3.
3 Kings 17, 10-16: 87.2.

Leo I, *Epistolae* ep. 35 c3: 6.2.
— *Sermones* s63 c4: 41.4.

Leviticus 2, 2: 113.1; 16, 7-8: 68.4; 16, 8-10: 68.4; 16, 10: 68.4; 16, 22: 68.4; 19, 18: 97.2.

Luke 1, 15: 5.2; 1, 32: 40.2; 1, 35: 7.3; 1, 38: 7.3; 2, 40: 38.3, 38.5; 2, 52: 38.4, 38.6; 3, 22: 3.2; 4, 34: 76.4; 6, 27: 106.1, 109.5, 109.11, 111.2; 6, 31: 142.5; 7, 19: 88.3; 8, 20: 109.10; 8, 21: 109.10; 10, 20: 112.7; 10, 27: 109.5; 10, 30-37: 106.1; 10, 33-34: prol.; 10, 36-37: 106.3; 11, 22: 55.3; 14, 1: 42.4; 14, 26: 109.12; 15, 8: 1.2; 15, 9: 1.2; 19, 41: 41.11; 22, 32: 38.6, 49.2; 22, 42: 48.7, 49.1; 22, 51: 43.3; 22, 56-60: 55.3; 23, 15: 64.1.

Malachias 1, 2-3: 119; 3, 6: 38.6.

Mark 1, 7: 5.2; 3, 11-12: 76.4; 4, 26-27: 112.9; 5, 6-7: 76.4; 11, 9: 86.5; 12, 30-31: 109.5, 109.11; 12, 31: 111.4; 14, 33: 41.10-11; 14, 34: 42.4; 14, 35: 48.4, 48.7; 14, 36-38: 48.4; 14, 36: 49.1; 14, 38: 48.5; 14, 66-72: 55.3; 16, 6: 41.11; 16, 15: 32.3.

Matthew 1, 18: 12.5; 1, 25: 33.2; 3, 15: 54.2; 4, 2: 38.6; 5, 3-12: 137.1; 5, 8: 85.4; 5, 21-22: 141.3; 5, 27-28: 162.1; 5, 34: 153.3-4, 154.2; 5, 34-36: 154.1; 5, 37: 153.4; 5, 44: 106.1, 109.5, 109.11-12, 111.2; 6, 12: 111.2; 6, 13: 153.4; 6, 14-15: 111.2; 7, 12: 142.5; 7, 23: 112.2; 8, 24: 42.4; 9, 12: prol.; 10, 18: 55.3; 10, 28: 126.1; 11, 3: 88.3; 12, 29: 55.3, 55.5; 14, 7-11: 158.1; 16, 23: 43.3; 18, 11: 46; 21, 9: 86.5; 22, 36-40: 97.2; 22, 37: 100.4, 101.1; 22, 37-39: 100.1, 109.5; 22, 39: 100.3, 104.4, 111.4; 22, 40: 137.1-2; 23, 15: 12.4; 26, 25: 66.2; 26, 28: 55.4; 26, 33-35: 44; 26, 37: 42.3; 26, 38: 41.10, 44, 49.2; 26, 39: 41.11, 41.13, 42.4, 47, 48.3, 48.6, 49.2; 26, 41: 44; 26, 42: 49.2; 26, 48: 66.2; 27, 18: 66.2; 27, 35: 41.11; 27, 46: 68.3; 27, 50: 68.9; 28, 18: 52.3; 28.

Numbers 21, 9: 55.3; 23, 19: 38.6; 32, 25: 54.3; 32, 28: 54.3.

Origen, *Homiliae in Cantica* hom2: 109.5.
— *Homiliae in Exodum* hom8: 138.2.
— *In Epistolam ad Romanos* 1, 3: 23.2; 8, 3: 10.1.

Paulinus of Aquileia, *Liber exhortationis de salutaribus documentis* c7: 112.2.
Pelagius, *Libellus fidei ad Innocentiurn papam* n4: 4.1, 12.4; n5: 14.7, 41.12.
1 Peter 1, 18-19: 61.3; 2, 22: 41.13; 2, 24: 58; 4, 1: 69.3.
Philippians 1, 8: 153.3, 156.1; 1, 23: 41.13, 42.4, 48.3, 110.1; 2, 6-7: 14.6, 22.7, 24.3, 50.3; 2, 7: 6.2, 11.1, 14.2, 22.1, 22.7, 73.2; 2, 8: 50.2, 54.1; 2, 9: 50.2, 52.2-3; 2, 15: 132.4; 4, 7: 116.1.
Prosper of Aquitaine, *Sententiae ex Augustino delibatae* n172: 126.3.
Proverbs 1, 7: 125.2, 127.1, 129.1; 5, 17-18: 112.2; 5, 22: 55.5; 9, 10: 129.1.
Psalms 5, 7: 148.5; 7, 14: 49.2; 10, 6: 100.1-2, 104.3; 18, 6: 45.2, 69.5; 18, 8: 162.2; 18, 10: 125.2, 126.1, 127.3; 18, 15: 59; 21, 3: 41.13, 48.9; 26, 13: 141.2; 27, 7: 50.5; 30, 2: 94; 34, 13: 53.2; 34, 14: 106.3; 40, 11: 94; 49, 14: 154.1; 54, 12: 142.2; 57, 1: 142.5; 64, 5: 16.3; 64, 12: prol.; 68, 5: 55.4, 58; 76, 10: 63.2; 77, 35: 59; 80, 10: 34.2; 87, 4: 41.2, 41.10; 87, 6: 68.7; 98, 5:

28.6; 101, 14: prol.; 101, 25: 84.2; 103, 24: 1.2; 104, 37: 142.4; 110, 10: 127.1, 129.1; 118, 73: 85.4; 118, 75: 85.3; 127, 1: 126.1; 143, 9: 138.1; 146, 3: prol.; 148, 5: 33.3.

Romans 1, 3: 12.4, 23.2; 1, 4: 23.1, 24.2, 29.5, 31; 1, 9: 153.3, 156.1; 1, 17: 75.1; 1, 25: 28.5; 3, 22: 55.3; 3, 25: 55.3; 3, 26: 58; 5, 8: 55.2, 62; 5, 9: 55.1, 64.1; 5, 10: 60.2; 5, 12: 9.2; 6, 6: 57; 7, 23: 101.1; 8, 3: 10.1, 22.7, 38.6; 8, 10: 41.8, 45.1; 8, 15: 30.2, 30.5, 126.3, 140.1; 8, 20: 32.3, 139.3; 8, 23: 57; 8, 24: 92; 8, 32: 55.2, 66.2; 9, 13: 119; 9, 23: 112.7; 10, 3: 134.2; 10, 14: 89.3; 10, 17: 85.2, 85.5; 11, 16: 19.3; 11, 33: 38.6; 12,3: 74.2; 13, 9: 102; 13, 10: 135, 136.7.

Syagrius, *Sermo* 238: 13.2.
Symbolum Athanasianum 76.1.
Symbolum Concilii Toletani VI and *XI* 14.4.
Symbolum Constantinopolitanum 41.3.
Symbolum Toletanum I 69.4.

1 Timothy 1, 5: 90.2, 97.2, 137.1; 2, 5: prol., 6.2, 25.1, 34.2, 59, 86.3; 6, 10: 112.10.
2 Timothy 2, 25-26: 55.5; 2, 26: 56.
Tobias 4, 16: 142.5.

Vigilius of Thapse, *Contra Eutychen* Bk5 n15; 61.2.
— *Contra Felicianum Arianum de unitate Trinitatis* c11: 23.8; c12: 23.8; c14: 67.1, 68.9, 72.1; c16: 72.1.

Walter of Mortagne, *Epistola ad Hugonem de S. Victore*: 39.2.
Wisdom 1, 11: 148.5; 1, 15: 122.2; 8, 7: 120.3; 8, 20: 4.1; 11, 25: 115.2.